c

The
THROW-IN

THE GAA AND THE MEN WHO MADE IT

The
THROW-IN

THE GAA AND THE MEN
WHO MADE IT

BRENDAN FULLAM

WOLFHOUND PRESS

First published in 2004 by
Wolfhound Press
An Imprint of Merlin Publishing
16 Upper Pembroke Street
Dublin 2, Ireland
Tel: +353 1 676 4373
Fax: +353 1 676 4368
publishing@merlin.ie

Text Copyright © 2004 Brendan Fullam
Editorial, Design and Layout © 2004 Merlin Publishing

ISBN 0–86327–925–2

*The publishers have made every reasonable effort to contact the copyright holders
of material reproduced in this book. If any involuntary infringement of copyright has
occurred, sincere apologies are offered and the owners of such copyright are
requested to contact the publisher.*

A CIP catalogue record for this book is available from the British Library.

5   4   3   2   1

Typeset by Carrigboy Typesetting Services
Cover Design by Graham Thew Design
Printed and bound in Poland

CONTENTS

FOREWORD

It was about dawn in a January day in the late 1880s. Two men set out with a horse and cart from a farmyard in the County of Cavan. They weren't far on their way when they were ambushed head-on by sleet and snow. It got so bad that the horse at times turned his head as if to say 'we should go back'.

The little expedition took shelter at a place called Lavey Strand until the weather improved. Then they journeyed on with their little cargo. They were carrying four long trimmed pine poles and two lengths of wood. Their destination was a field where the first game of Gaelic Football in the county was to be held.

Time went by and in my mind's eye I am at a game in the town of Tipperary. Kerry and Kildare are playing in the All-Ireland final. Kildare are a few points ahead with a few minutes to go. In a last desperate attack it seems that Kerry have got a goal. Kildare object. The ball had gone over the touch line and been kicked back onto the pitch by a spectator. The Umpires are hesitant. A spectator puts up the green flag. The score is recorded as Kerry 1:4 Kildare 1:3. The Central Council sensibly order a replay. It took place in 'the Fair City' of Cork. It ended in a draw. The counties meet again at the same venue. Kerry win by a point. That saga is credited with greatly increasing the popularity of Gaelic Football. The year was 1905.

The Gaelic Athletic Association is often credited with healing the wounds inflicted by the Civil War. This would have been a miracle. But it helped to lessen the bitterness, in varying degrees in different counties. The conflict had been especially obscene in Kerry; the GAA played a big part there in restoring a degree of sanity. John Joe Sheehy was head of the anti-Treaty forces in West Munster; Con Brosnan was a captain in the National Army – they played together in the great Kerry team of the late 20s and early 30s.

The Irish Press went down the slipway in 1931 and created a quiet revolution. Its first sports editor was a small man from the far north of England; he sometimes wore a deerstalker cap and often sported a turndown pipe. He was intimately acquainted with Rugby League and Rugby Union and with Boxing and Soccer; he had never even heard of Hurling or Gaelic Football. He wasn't long in the new job when the All-Ireland Hurling final loomed. He asked his assistant, Mitchel Cogley, to tell him its importance. Mitchel said, 'It's as big as a Wembley Final'. And Joe Sherwood said, 'We'll give the Preview a full page'. He told Mitchel to do the layout but to allow him a little box in the very middle of the page. Mitchel did his job and adjourned to Mulligan's, chapel of ease to *The Irish Press*. When Mitchel saw the completed page, he suffered a mild shock: in the box was 'Kick-Off 3.30'.

If the story has a moral, it is that *The Irish Press* was the first National daily to give decent coverage to Hurling and Gaelic Football. In a later era *The Evening Press* was the first paper to give ample space to Camogie and Ladies' Football.

Now it is as bitter a day as that on which the two gallant men and their faithful horse took shelter at Lavey Strand. And I and a companion are on the town terrace in Semple Stadium watching Cork and Offaly in the final of the Hurling league. A wild wind is bringing showers of hailstone. Cork have the wind but are only a few points up at half-time. Offaly look certain to win. So strong is the gale that early in the second half we see the sliotar move about a foot away from Pat Delaney as he prepares to take a 70. Amazingly, Cork defy the conditions and quarry out a famous victory.

And we come away from Thurles convinced that we have seen the All-Ireland champions for 1981. Now read on . . . Cork didn't even reach the final and Offaly meet Galway on a showery day in early September. The game is on a razor's edge as play enters the last few minutes. And we are in our usual spot down at the fence in the Canal terrace, halfway between the goal and the corner under the Cusack Stand. And we are almost within touching distance of Johnny Flaherty as that artful dodger palms the ball into Michael Conneely's net. And all Heaven breaks loose in green-and-white-and gold.

And it was another rainy day when television beamed the final of the World Cup into every nook and cranny in this island. This epic between England and West Germany opened windows and let in light. The rule about 'foreign' games lingered on for several years but from the Summer of 1966 it was a dead ban walking. The abolition was the best thing that ever happened to the GAA; they made a multitude of friends.

There was a time when aficionados of the Association used to say, 'a poor thing but our own'; now they can say, 'a rich thing but our own'. However, they should never forget the two men and the horse sheltering at Lavey Strand.

And I haven't forgotten a quiet revolution that is taking place under our eyes. Camogie has come of age: now it is played with teams of fifteen and on a full pitch. And Ladies Football is rapidly becoming a salient part of our culture – the best is yet to be.

CON HOULIHAN
sportswriter, author & journalist, writes for the Sunday World

For Gemma

All-Ireland Colleges Senior 'B' Final Cistercian College (Roscrea)
v St Patrick's (Maghera). Second half – preparing for throw-in 2004.

1
The Infant Years

The picture above depicts a typical eviction scene at the turn of the twentieth century. It was scenes like this which inspired the Land Campaign of the late 1800s and early 1900s.

The Gaelic Athletic Association was founded in 1884. This decade could be said to have been an era when the country was on the march – marching in search of nationhood, identity and self-determination.

Four different groups led this march:

THE IRISH REPUBLICAN BROTHERHOOD (IRB)

The Irish Republican Brotherhood was founded in 1855 in America by John O'Mahoney. The Irish branch of the IRB was founded by James Stephens in 1858 and had branches throughout Ireland and in England. The leaders of this movement wanted the Act of Union of 1801 revoked, leading to political freedom and independence – to be achieved by force of arms if necessary.

THE LAND LEAGUE

The Land League was founded in 1879 and its primary aim was 'the land of Ireland for the people of Ireland'. To the tenant farmers this was freedom – political freedom could wait for another day.

THE GAELIC ATHLETIC ASSOCIATION (GAA)

Founded in 1884, its chief objective was for Ireland to take control of its own affairs in the field of athletics and games – national in outlook but non-political.

THE GAELIC LEAGUE.

This came into being in 1893 and its founders had visions of a Gaelic Ireland where the language would be revived and spoken by all. It was strictly non-political and non-sectarian.

It was against this background that the GAA took root. It suffered many growing pains. There were times when it nearly died. But it survived and grew and grew – grew from a tiny acorn into the mighty oak it is today.

Dreamers, idealists, nationalists and men of patriotic vision kept the flame alive in the darkest days. Among them was Thomas F O'Sullivan a

An early Central Council photograph, (possibly 1888); **Back Row From Left**: J J O'Reilly (Dublin), Dr O'Connor (Clare), Rev J Concannon (Tullamore), John Cullinan (Bansha) and George F Byrne (Navan). Middle Row: Rev C Buckley (Buttevant), Alderman Mangan (Drogheda), W Prendergast, Hon Sec (Clonmel), James O'Connor (Wexford), Rev E Sheehy PP (Limerick), J J Cullen (Dun Laoghaire). **Front Row**: R J Frewan, Treas (Aherlow, Co Tipperary), Maurice Davin, President (Carrick-on-Suir) and T O'Riordan (Cork).

Thomas F O'Sullivan, Kerry

staunch supporter of the GAA and its ideals. He was born on December 19, 1874, in Glin, Co Limerick, and died in 1950. While young, his family moved to Listowel where he received his primary and secondary education.

As a journalist he worked initially for *The Kerryman* and then joined the *Freeman's Journal* in 1907. He was the journal's parliamentary correspondent in London from 1916 to 1924. He went on to work for *The Irish Press* from its foundation in 1931 until 1937.

He held the following positions in the Association: Trustee of the GAA; President of the Munster Council; Honorary Secretary of the Kerry County Board; Vice-President of the Association; Chairman of Debts Committee; Captain and Secretary of Listowel Football Club.

He was also a prominent referee and had charge of the 1902 football final between Dublin and London, played at Cork, on September 11, 1904.

In his book *The Story of the GAA* T F O'Sullivan reflected in October 1916 on the birth of the Association:

'The Gaelic Athletic Association has entered on the 31st year of its existence. From a small beginning it has become the greatest athletic organisation the world has ever seen. It has had a stormy, eventful and chequered career, but it has achieved solid and lasting work for Irish athletics and Irish nationality. It has helped not only to develop Irish bone and muscle, but to foster a spirit of earnest nationality in the hearts of the rising generation and it has been the means of saving thousands of young Irishmen from becoming mere West Britons.'

According to Dr Douglas Hyde, the GAA paved the way for the Language Movement. The Association revived athletics, popularised the ancient game of hurling, and nationalised football. It brought a new spirit into Irish life.

In the earlier stages of its career the Gaelic Athletic Association had to surmount many and serious difficulties. It had to withstand the sneers of anti-Irish Irishmen, the apathy of un-national Irishmen; the hostility of a large section of the press, who failed to recognise that the young organisation contained the germs of one of the most powerful national forces of modern times; and the contempt of that superior section of the public who regarded Irish games as vulgar because they did not bear an English hallmark. It had to contend with opposition from without, and, what was worse, with bungling, incapacity, gross mismanagement and treachery, from within its own ranks.

Jim Young, helping UCC in the Sigerson Cup

Its meetings were the scenes of a serious struggle, which threatened to rend it asunder, between what are called advanced Nationalists – those who seek Irish independence – and a Constitutional party, who are satisfied with a self-governing Ireland within the British Empire.

At times the organisation became bankrupt in finance, in reputation, and in resources. It was subjected to every wave of public vicissitude. At various periods its dissolution appeared inevitable. How it continued to exist through all its trials and tribulations is a miracle. But the GAA not only maintained its existence, but progressed, despite all obstacles, and the explanation is – the basic principal on which it was established was sound and patriotic, and at no stage of its career was it entirely bereft of the services of earnest men who appreciated the tremendous potentialities of the organisation as an athletic body and as a great national asset.

And today the Association, which timidly unfurled its banner thirty years ago, is on a sound financial basis, with grounds of its own, with infinite resources at its command, and full of that splendid spirit of earnest Nationalism which has been the salt of the organisation from the day it first saw the light down to this very moment.'

> *'May our future match our past.*
> *May we always be loyal to the*
> *Gaelic Athletic Association.'*
> (Jim Young)

All-Ireland Colleges Senior 'B' Final Cistercian College (Roscrea) v St. Patrick's (Maghera). Second half – immediately after throw-in 2004.

2
Down the Centuries

MYTH & LEGEND

> *'Long, long ago beyond the misty space*
> *Of twice a thousand years,*
> *In Erin old there dwelt a mighty race,*
> *Taller than Roman spears;*
> *Like oaks and towers they had a giant grace,*
> *Were fleet as deers . . .*
> *Great were their deeds, their passions and their sports.'*
> (The Celts, Thomas D'Arcy McGee, 1825–1868)

The GAA was officially founded on November 1, 1884. However, its greatest game hurling, that according to the GAA annual in 1907/8 'gave to the tumultuous spirit of the Gael a zest surpassed only in the rush of battle', had a history going back thousands of years.

> 'Comments on hurling matches and references to them are common place in early Irish Law, in the Red Branch saga, in the Fianna cycle and in the stories of the Kings.'
> (Brother L P O'Caithnia)

The origin of the game is to be found in the twilight of fable. Reference is found in literature to a game between the Tuatha de Danann and the Firbolgs, around the year 1272 BC, that formed part of the Battle of Moytura.

The Tuatha de Danann and the Firbolgs belonged to the Bronze Age. The Tuatha de Danann belonged to the Spiritual World. They inspired their people to believe in the spiritual side of their nature and worshipped the sun, moon and stars together with the elements, earth, fire, wind and water.

The Firbolgs, on the other hand, believed in the power of physical force. They were an earthy race. Primary for them was the urge to gain supremacy over any and all opposition. They liked to conquer.

We are told that the Firbolgs won the hurling game but that the Tuatha de Danann, using their magic powers, won the battle. But do we really know who won the game? It was the goals and points of the physical world measured against the goals and points of the spiritual world. What common denominator could evaluate the two? The search for an answer to that is an eternal one.

Most famous of the many other stories about hurling is the one about Cú Chulainn from the Red Branch Knights (An Craobh Ruadh). It is recounted in *The Tain* and set in the Iron Age – the age of the Celtic people. It was a time when a code of honour was central to behaviour –

you lived honourably; you played honourably. It was the age of chivalry. Skill with the camán was part of the learning process – it was a preparation for manly skills with arms. The young princes carried camáns with bands of gold or silver, according to rank.

Cú Chulainn demonstrated all that was skilful, daring and dashing in the art of hurling. Legend tells us that he – then known as Setanta – set off from his father's house in Dún Dealgan to visit his uncle King Conor Mac Nessa who resided in Eamhain Macha, about a mile to the west of the present city of Armagh.

As he journeyed with his hurley and sliotar he pucked the ball ahead of himself up into the air and fleet of foot pursued same and met it on the drop to send it upwards and onwards again. And so the process continued until he reached his destination.

Mentally he had shortened the journey, displaying as he travelled all the qualities of a class hurler – speed, skill, stamina, accuracy, precision and first touch perfection.

However, on reaching journey's end, he discovered that his uncle had gone to a celebration at the Dún of his friend Culann – a blacksmith. On to the Dún went Setanta.

There in self-defence he slew the hound that guarded Culann's Dún. By way of restitution he undertook to henceforth guard the Dún. Thus was Setanta re-named Cú Chulainn – the hound of Culann.

Cú Chulainn with his hurley. The exact shape of the early hurley is uncertain, but according to old manuscripts it was seemingly broad bossed, as players are described as carrying the ball upon it.

Then there is the story of King Labhraidh Loinsigh. Labhraidh was born with two afflictions. First of all he had horse's ears and these were such an embarrassment to him that he always kept them covered from his subjects.

He was also dumb and could not speak a word. Dumb, that is, until one day when playing his favourite game of hurling he got a fierce belt on the shin. So great was the pain that it enabled him to shout aloud in agony. To his delight his speech defect was cured. Word quickly spread throughout his kingdom. The game of hurling had a special place of honour bestowed upon it after that.

The epic of Diarmuid and Gráinne also gives clear evidence of the antiquity of hurling. Gráinne fell in love with Diarmuid as she watched him playing hurling – a goal he scored sealed her love.

In the age of Finn MacCumhail and the Fianna, prowess and skill with the camán would have been roundly praised by the Bards of those days. In modern times, Charles Kickham's legendary character 'Matt the Thresher' in Knocknagow and Canon Sheehan's heroic character 'Terence Casey' in Glenanaar are but re-creations of the hurling heroes of Oisín's time.

It is clear that the esteem in which hurling was held in Ancient Ireland is greater than for any game in world literature. For example, in ancient times in Ireland, there were three great annual fairs. One of those was Aonach Tailltin, celebrated in Co Meath on the first day of August (Lá Lughnasa) each year. According to tradition the fair was named after Tailte who was the wife of the last king of the Firbolgs. She was also the celebrated Lewy the long-handed's foster mother who instituted the fair in her honour.

Lughnasa is called after Lewy – meaning Lewy's gathering. At Tailtinn the men of Ireland we are told by Douglas Hyde in the *Constitution and Rules of the GAA 1893* 'came together to indulge in such sports as chariot-racing, horse-racing and hurling'. According to the chronology of the Four Masters this took place about 1800 BC – thus predating the days of the Greek and Roman empires.

Writing on those ancient festivals, Douglas Hyde said:

> 'Both the Firbolgs and Tutha-de-Dananns, with Lewy the long-handed himself, may be almost certainly looked upon as Pagan Gods and demigods, like the Roman Jupiter, Mars, the Titans and the rest.'

Elsewhere, Lugh (Lewy) has been described as the pre-Christian god of light and genius.

> *'In ancient times when Eire reigned*
> *A Nation great and grand,*
> *When Oscar's and Cú Chulainn's fame*
> *Was spread throughout the land;*
> *On Tailteann plain with might and main,*
> *In contests fiercely drawn,*
> *What else could grace the pride of place,*
> *But the well-grained ash camán?'*
> (Sliabh Ruadh)

The Brehon Laws, which preceded feudalism in Ireland, provide further evidence of the existence of hurling in the early centuries AD. For example there are sophisticated provisions in the laws to compensate families of any man killed by a hurley or hurling ball. It is also documented that King Caher the Great of Tailteann left fifty brass hurling balls in his will.

It is believed that the game was played at the time of the raids by the Vikings and also at the time of the Norman Invasion.

In 1366 the Statue of Kilkenny attempted to suppress the game:

> 'It is ordained and established that the Commons (the common people) of the said land of Ireland who are in the different marches (territories) at war, do not henceforth use the plays which men call horlings [the French form for hurling] with great sticks and a ball upon the ground . . . but that they do apply and accustom themselves to use and draw bows and throw lances and other gentleman-like games whereby the Irish enemies may be better checked . . . and if any do practise the contrary they shall be taken and imprisoned and fined at the will of our Lord the King.'
> (As translated from the old manuscripts by Dr R A Walsh of Kilkenny for Raymond Smith's book *Decades of Glory*.)

The Statute of Galway in 1527, while favouring 'football with the *grate ball*' made a further attempt to suppress the game of hurling stating: 'At no time to use the hurling of the little ball with hockey sticks or staves.'

All such efforts failed. It would take more than royal decrees to suppress the ancient game of the Gael. According to Michael Cusack 'it was the training of the hurling field that made the men and boys of the Irish Brigade' – also confirming that the game was played during the 1600s.

> *'In far foreign fields*
> *From Dunkirk to Belgrade*
> *Lie the soldiers and chiefs*
> *Of the Irish Brigade.'*

So ran a four-liner in our junior history in the National School.

Now to the eighteenth century – a century that has been referred to as the Golden Age of hurling. However, one has to wonder in what way such a title could fit the scene when you briefly look at some historical facts.

Following the Treaty of Limerick, 1691 – as Thomas Davis commented 'the Treaty broken ere the ink wherewith 'twas writ could dry' – the plight of the ordinary Irish rapidly deteriorated. A quarter of a million acres were confiscated and given to King William's friends. Emigration was heavy and 20,000 Irish troops, accompanied by Patrick Sarsfield, joined the service of France. Between 1692 and 1793 it is estimated that over 450,000 Irish – the Wild Geese – died in the service of the armies of France, Spain and Austria.

There was a famine in 1741 during which 400,000 people perished of starvation. The Penal Laws, which began in 1692, were augmented up to 1746. In the main the laws dealt with suppression of the Catholic faith, dispossession of property and rights of ownership and denial of legal rights and education. For example, Catholic peers were deprived of their right to sit in parliament and Catholic gentlemen were forbidden to run for election as Members of Parliament.

All Catholics were denied the liberty of voting and excluded from offices of trust and all remunerative employment such as any Government office, the legal profession or a commission in the army and navy.

A key factor in sustaining these exclusions was the requirement to take qualifying oaths that contained statements such as the following:

> 'I do believe, that in the sacrament of the Lord's supper there is not any transubstantiation of the elements of bread and wine into the body and blood of Christ, at or after the consecration thereof by any person whatsoever; and that the invocation, or adoration of the virgin Mary, or any other saint, and the sacrifice of the Mass, as they are now used in the church of Rome, are superstitious and idolatrous . . .'

These were oaths that no Catholic could take.

Eighty per cent of the population was Catholic but only 14 per cent of the land was owned by Catholics and by 1778 this was reduced to 5 per cent.

Social and economic conditions bred secret societies and the first of the coercion acts was passed in 1765. Emigration continued to grow – 48 per cent of those who fought under Washington in the American War of Independence (1775–1783) were Irish.

Writing on that century in *Stair-Sheanchas Éireann*, Mícheál Ó Siochfhradha MA had this to say:

> 'Gael fé chois, fé dhaoirse, fé pheannaid, fé tharcaisne agus fé aincolas gan feidhm gan fuascailt; iad 'a gcéasadh le fóirneart agus péin-dlighthe . . . ní raibh ionnta ach sclábhaithe gan spioraid.'

For many of the peasantry the difficult financial circumstances in which they found themselves meant that even a donkey and cart was a luxury.

In *The Course of Irish History* Maureen Wall refers to the general condition of poverty and wretchedness of the mass of the Catholic peasantry. She quotes Arthur Young who toured Ireland in the 1770s.

'The cottages of the Irish, which are called cabbins, are the most miserable looking hovels that can well be conceived . . . The furniture of the cabbins is as bad as the architecture; in very many consisting only of a pot for boiling their potatoes, a bit of a table, and one or two broken stools; beds are not found universally, the family lying on straw . . . '

In the era in question hurling was certainly played but it was hardly a Golden Age. Yes, the ordinary people were involved, but the game was primarily for the benefit of the landlords who, for their own fulfilment, chose to patronise it. Football, in whatever form it might have existed, did not have the same attraction for the landlords.

The following paragraphs bear testimony to the playing of the game of hurling.

In Wexford, it is told that about 300 years ago King William and his wife were highly impressed by the performance of the team of Sir Caesar Colclough's tenants of Tintern in Lower Wexford as they watched them defeat a team in Cornwall.

On June 26, 1708 the following notice appeared in the *Dublin Flying Post*:

'On St Swithen's Day, about 3 in the afternoon, will be a Hurling Match over the Curragh, between 30 men from each side of the Liffey, for 30 shillings. A barrel of ale, tobacco, and pipes will be given to the hurlers.'

On September 4, 1769, the following notice appeared in the *Cork Evening Post*:

'A bet of 300 guineas, a cold dinner and a Ball at night for the Ladies, to be hurled for on Friday 9th inst., by 21 married men and 21 batchelors, on the Green of Ardfinnan in the County of Tipperary. N.B. None admitted to play but the Gentlemen of the Baronies of Iffa and Offa in the said county.'

In September 1773 a game was played at Banagher between Galway and Tipperary and the Countess of Northumberland was reputed to have wagered a thousand guineas on the game. She was an enthusiastic supporter of hurling and she described a game she saw at the Curragh as, 'the most noble and manly exercise in the world'.

In Leckey's *History of Ireland 1783/1850* a detailed and vivid description of a game of hurling is given with the comment, ' . . . par excellence, the game of the peasantry of Ireland'.

As already stated, the landlords patronised the game. They gambled on the contests which added to their entertainment and even played and captained teams. Their involvement ensured crowd-control, discipline and good behaviour. However, their support ended with the Rebellion of the United Irishmen in 1798 and in the century that followed the game went rapidly into decline.

Dan Breen gets the 1920 All-Ireland Football Final under way between Dublin and Tipperary on the June 11, 1922 at Croke Park.

3
Foundation of the GAA – The Clarion Call

'From its inception it consistently strove to mould the National outlook to its own ideals, to re-awaken a legitimate pride of race and to further the resurgence of the national spirit.'
(Pádraig Puirséal)

'I would love to turn back the calendar and be in at the birth of the Gaelic Athletic Association. It provokes a question: do great movements spring from a collective or from an individual urge?'
(Con Houlihan)

It was a fateful and momentous day for Gaeldom – its athletics and in particular its games – when the first concrete steps to establish the Gaelic Athletic Association were taken. On October 27, 1884, a circular was issued from 4 Gardiner's Place, Dublin, as outlined below:

'Dear Sir,

You are earnestly requested to attend a meeting which will be held at Thurles on 1 November to take steps for the formation of a Gaelic Association for the preservation and cultivation of our national pastimes and providing rational amusements for the Irish people during their leisure hours. The movement which it is proposed to inaugurate has been approved of by Mr. Michael Davitt, Mr. Justin McCarthy, M.P.; Mr. William O'Brien, M.P.; Mr. T. Harrington, M.P.; and other eminent men who are interested in the social elevation of the race. The place of meeting will be determined on, at the Commercial Hotel, Thurles, at 2 o'clock on the day of the meeting.

Maurice Davin, Carrick-on-Suir.
Michael Cusack, Dublin, Hon. Sec. protem.

Michael Cusack

N.B. – The favour of a reply is requested.
Michael Cusack'

In response to the circular a meeting was held at Thurles on Saturday, November 1, 1884 – as William Wordsworth put it 'one of those heavenly days that cannot die' – in the Billiard Room of Miss Hayes's Commercial Hotel. T F O'Sullivan recorded in *The Story of the GAA* that those present were:

Maurice Davin, Carrick-on-Suir
Michael Cusack, Dublin
John Wyse Power, Naas
John McKay, Cork
P J O'Ryan, Callan, Co Kilkenny
J K Bracken, Templemore
St George McCarthy, Templemore

T F O'Sullivan records that the Chairman Maurice Davin briefly explained the object of the meeting:

'He pointed out that the laws under which athletic sports are held in Ireland were designed mainly for the guidance of Englishmen, who promote the sports of their own country; that, as far as they go, these laws are good in their way, so long as they are observed; but that they do not deal at all with the characteristic sports and pastimes of the Gaelic race. It, therefore became necessary to form an association which would resuscitate our fast-fading sources of amusement, and draft laws for the guidance of those who were patriotic enough to devise schemes of recreation for the bulk of the people, and more especially for the humble and hard-working who seem now to be born to no other inheritance than an everlasting round of labour.'

At the meeting about sixty letters and telegrams were read out – all expressing warm support for the objectives of the promoters. Among them were letters from the Rev J Cantwell, Adm Thurles, Rev P Kiernan, P P Carron, Co Clare, Michael Davitt, Mr McLoughlin, Derry, Mr M Miller, Dublin, Mr Maher, Clonmel, Mr Crowley, Bandon and Mr D J Hishon, Dublin.

Maurice Davin was elected President and Michael Cusack, John Wyse Power and John McKay were elected Honorary Secretaries.

It was agreed at the meeting to submit the objectives of the Association to Dr Croke, Archbishop of Cashel, Charles S Parnell and Michael Davitt, with a view to having them as patrons.

In some quarters it has been suggested that others also attended the first meeting in Thurles. The reason given for the absence of their names on the record is the fact that they were members of the Irish Republican Brotherhood and did not wish to be identified as such. That, however, is difficult to understand when one considers the subsequent show of strength shown by the Physical Force men at the famous Convention of 1887 held in Thurles.

T F O'Sullivan in *The Story of the GAA* is very definite that only seven attended this first meeting as he comments:

' . . . not withstanding the fact that Mr Cusack placed a few etceteras after the names of those attending in Thurles, only seven persons whose names were given were present.'

A plaque at the entrance to Hayes's Hotel commemorates the historic occasion. As *Conor Cruise O'Brien* later commented:

"More than the Gaelic League, more than Arthur Griffith's Sinn Féin, more even than the Transport and General Workers Union and, of course, far more than the movement which created the Abbey Theatre; more than any of these the Gaelic Athletic movement aroused the interest of large numbers of ordinary people throughout Ireland. One of the most successful and original mass-movements of its day, its importance has, perhaps, not even yet been fully recognised.'

The subject matter of the first meeting was all about athletics. In a little while, however, football and the revival of hurling would become a priority. At this point it is worth noting that following the recognition of the Irish Free State in 1922 by the International Olympics Committee the GAA handed over control of athletics to the newly formed National Athletics and Cycling Association and thereafter concentrated entirely on its games.

Follow-up meetings took place at the Victoria Hotel, Cork on December 27 and at Hayes's Hotel, Thurles on January 17, 1885.

The door to a new future was now open. At the follow-up meetings the key items discussed were the spread of the new Association throughout the country and the formation of a club, if at all possible, in every parish – each club to be presided over by a President, Vice-President, Secretary, Treasurer and a committee of six members.

The grip of Anglicisation was about to be loosened. In time it would be undone altogether. The following paragraphs, written by my brother Paddy, Lecturer at Mary Immaculate College, Limerick, deal with the history of Anglicisation.

The foundation of the GAA was the first in a series of national organisations set up to revive an Irish identity that had been under attack for centuries but was under immense pressure from the beginning of the nineteenth century.

The significance of the foundation of the GAA, and the impact it has had on Ireland since its inception, has to be seen in the context of how

Anglicised Ireland had become in 1884. This Anglicisation process dates back to King John's visit to Ireland in 1210 when he compelled the Norman barons to swear that the *English* legal system only, would be observed and applied in Ireland.

However a century and a half later it was evident that the total conquest of Ireland was impossible. The Anglo-Normans then adopted a defensive colonial attitude and the Statutes of Kilkenny attempted to create what was in effect an apartheid system in Ireland. Marriage or the fostering of children between the two races was illegal. The Anglo-Normans were forbidden to use the Irish language, use Irish names, dress like the Irish, observe Irish law and custom or play Irish games. While these Statutes had little effect on Ireland as a whole, nonetheless they are important, as they are indicative of the attitude of the conqueror to the conquered.

The Statutes of Kilkenny were introduced at a time when Norman control of Ireland was at its weakest. Hurling was seen as distinctly Irish – attractive to play and watch. It was singled out for special mention. The greatest fear of the Monarchy was that the Normans would go native.

The plantations of the sixteenth and seventeenth centuries, which saw Irish landowners replaced by English settlers, may be seen from the perspective of a continuous attempt to change this country into the image and likeness of England.

The patently unjust and harsh Penal Laws of the eighteenth century, designed to keep Irish Catholics poor, uneducated and powerless, is another painful manifestation of one race believing in its superiority over another.

Michael Cusack as a footballer – before The GAA was founded – The Phoenix FC 1st XV of 1881–82. **Back** (*left to right*): C S Bowles, R W Ellis, E H Waring, R H Lowry, W M Russell, F E Rainsford, E J O'Reilly and E O Bailey. **Sitting**: V Guerrini, M Cusack (Founder of the GAA), R Code, G A Drought, T Askin (capt.), G Paton, M Sweeney.)

[Established over a Century.]

THE COMMERCIAL AND FAMILY HOTEL,

AND POSTING ESTABLISHMENT,

THURLES.

LIZZIE J. HAYES, Proprietress.

Hayes' Hotel as depicted in 1884.

However, despite all the oppression and upheaval, Irish was still the spoken language of the people and hurling was still being played and possibly some form of football.

The nineteenth century, however, would witness the most comprehensive and sustained attack on all things Irish and on all aspects of Irish life.

Looking back at the century from the vantage point of 1884 it must have been difficult for the founding fathers of the GAA to see grounds for optimism from a nationalist perspective. At the beginning of the century the Irish Parliament, infamously, voted itself out of existence, as it passed the Act of Union. Ireland was now to be governed from Westminster.

The next eight decades of the century were marked by military and constitutional attempts to undo the Union. The rebellions of Emmet (1803), The Young Irelanders (1848) and the Fenians (1867) were all doomed to failure.

On the constitutional front the national euphoria of Daniel O'Connell's success in gaining Catholic Emancipation (April 1829) turned to bitter disappointment at his failure to repeal the Act of Union. The humiliating back down when O'Connell cancelled the monster meeting planned for Clontarf on Sunday, October 8, 1843, marked the beginning of the end to an illustrious career. O' Connell's death in 1847 coincided with the most calamitous event in our entire history. The Great Famine or more correctly The Great Hunger was to have disastrous consequences. Death and suffering stalked the land. It marked the beginning of a mass emigration and began the decline of the Irish language. Hurling, too, declined, as indeed did all pastimes since people were pre-occupied with survival. Historians chronicling famine times don't mention games as they weren't a priority.

As the century moved on, the country now put its hope in Parnell, and in his parliamentary party in Westminster, to secure Home Rule for Ireland. The late 1870s were a particularly depressing time in Ireland. The country was in the grip of an economic depression brought about by the importation of cheap wheat from America and cheap frozen meat from Australia and New Zealand into the European market. The excessive heavy rains towards the end of the decade exacerbated an already miserable situation.

In 1878, John Devoy and Michael Davitt saw the need for a grand coalition between the Fenians, the parliamentary party under Parnell, tenant farmers, priests and Irish people at home and abroad, all working together to win justice for Irish farmers in their struggle against the landlords. This was "The New Departure" which initially gained Parnell's approval but which he later repudiated when he abandoned open rebellion under the terms of the Kilmainham 'treaty' in 1882.

By 1884 and the foundation of the GAA, Home Rule had not been achieved and the Land Question was far from being settled. Indeed the struggle for daily survival in the face of a successive litany of disasters brought about a steady decline in Irish culture throughout the nineteenth century. And following the principle that nature abhors a vacuum, Irish culture was being replaced by an English one.

The GAA became immensely popular in a remarkably short time. Within the first year of its existence more than a thousand clubs were affiliated. With hindsight it is easy to explain this phenomenal success. The Irish enthusiasm for sport and especially the love of hurling attracted immediate and huge support. But it was also a way of expressing a cultural identity that was uniquely Irish. As the GAA spread rapidly F S L Lyons in his book *Ireland Since the Famine* claims that it achieved three different purposes.

Firstly, it encouraged local patriotism. 'For the honour and glory of the little village', which patriotism is still as passionate today as it was in the 1880s.

Secondly, as well as fostering local pride it also fostered National pride:

'This, more than any other agency, the Gaelic Athletic Association achieved, and this was its chief contribution to the revival of national feeling in rural Ireland.'

Thirdly, and controversially, it encouraged a hostility to what were termed 'foreign games' culminating in a ban on all English games. This prohibited all members from playing, attending or associating in any way with such games.

However it is important to bear in mind that not everybody in Ireland was pre-occupied with the issues of Home Rule, land reform and the decline of Irish culture. We were part of the largest empire the world has ever known. If the sun was never to set over the British Empire it needed an enormous workforce to ensure its continued existence. Administrators, civil servants, medical personnel, teachers, soldiers, sailors and police, to name but some, were all needed to sustain this empire. Irish people working in different capacities from New Delhi to Nairobi served this empire and many rose to the highest ranking positions. The more recent recognition of the exploits of people such as Tom Crean and his contribution to the history of the exploration of the South Pole has gone some way in redressing their omission from Irish History. How much of their Irish culture they retained and how much of a British culture they embraced is impossible to calculate. In all probability many of them played English games. 'The peaceful penetration of Ireland' as Michael Collins once described it. Of course they may have played Gaelic games as well.

It is interesting that over a hundred years later the question as to whether Croke Park should be made available for international soccer and rugby fixtures has arisen. Obviously people will hold different views, but regardless of the position one takes, the request to make Croke Park available must be seen as a tribute to the remarkable success achieved by the GAA.

General Sean MacEoin prepares to throw in the sliotar in a match in Croke Park between Tipperary and Laois in September 1921. In 1945 he contested the Presidential election which was won by Eamon de Valera. (Courtesy Frank Burke, Clare Galway)

4

The Founding Fathers

JOHN WYSE POWER

John Wyse Power

A native of Waterford, he was connected with the Fenian Movement and was editor of *The Leinster Leader* in 1884. A year later he went to reside in Dublin where he joined the staff of the *Freeman's Journal* and became prominently connected with politics.

He was one of the first Honorary Secretaries of the Association and was also Chairman of the Dublin County Committee.

John was a fluent Irish speaker and an official GAA handicapper for many years. In the early days he took a pessimistic view of the Association's prospects of success.

JOHN McKAY

He was a member of the reporting staff of *The Cork Examiner* and one of the first Hon Secs of the Association. He furnished his paper with reports of the meetings of the Association, which he attended. He pursued his journalism in Belfast and Dublin, following which he took up residence in London before returning to Cork.

John McKay

JOSEPH KEVIN BRACKEN

J K Braken, Templemore

He was a contractor – a stonemason – as T P Flanagan commented 'the radical stonemason from Templemore'. He erected a number of '98 Memorials throughout the country and his business also included building and road contract work.

He took a keen interest in athletics and was a member of the Irish Republican Brotherhood. He was elected Vice President of the GAA at the Annual Convention of 1886 and was President of Tipperary County Committee in 1893. He was also the first Chairman of Templemore Urban District Council.

J K Bracken presided over the meeting of the GAA's Executive which excluded members of the RIC and he was also a strong supporter of the 'Ban' on games associated with the British garrison in Ireland. He died at Kilmallock, Co Limerick in May 1906 and is buried in the nearby cemetery of Tankardstown where a Celtic Cross marks his grave.

A tribute after his death stated – 'He was one of the old guard, or as better known, one of the Fenian Band'.

J K Bracken was father of Brendan Bracken, founder of *The Financial Times* and a close associate of Sir Winston Churchill and a member of his wartime government in the capacity of Minister for Information.

THOMAS ST GEORGE MCCARTHY

He was a native of Kerry residing in Templemore who later became a District Inspector of Constabulary. He took no further part in GAA affairs after the first meeting. As well as being an Irish rugby international player he was also a keen athlete and had known Cusack since he attended his Academy in Dublin prior to sitting for his police examination. He died in 1942.

In his ageing years he attended matches in Croke Park. When the GAA held its golden jubilee celebrations in 1934, he was the only surviving founder member – a fact that apparently escaped the attention of the GAA authorities.

P J O'RYAN

He was a young solicitor who practised in Callan and Thurles. After the Thurles meeting his links with the new Association were quite limited. Pádraig Puirséal in his book *The GAA In Its Time* had this to say:

> 'He helped to organise some of the early events sponsored by the GAA. But, except for an occasional letter to the papers proffering calm counsel at times of controversy, he never became prominent in the Association's early history.'

MICHAEL CUSACK

> 'Michael Cusack was determined to create a sporting organisation which suited the Irish rural poor especially the labourer, artisan and small farmer. Gaelic games would emancipate them from the tyranny of the existing athletic clubs. Cusack's genius was to meet this social need while retaining the territorial allegiances which typified the older games . . . its social base came especially from journalists, school teachers, priests and publicans.'
> (Dr Kevin Whelan)

Michael Cusack

Michael Cusack was born in Carron in the Burren in County Clare on September 20, 1847. He was the second son of Matthew and Bridget who had three other sons and one daughter. Michael grew up in an Irish speaking household and as he grew to manhood developed into a versatile athlete. He was particularly keen on cricket, rugby, football, handball, hurling and rowing. He was destined to become known as the 'Father of the Gaelic Athletic Association'.

In 1864 he became a pupil teacher in the Model School in Enniscorthy. After that he trained as a teacher at Marlborough St Dublin. In December 1866 he became a teacher at Lough Cutra NS near Gort, County Galway where he stayed until 1871.

Michael Cusack's home at Carron, Co Clare

Subsequently he taught Mathematics and English at St Colman's College, Newry and later at Blackrock College, Dublin. He then went to St John's College, Kilkenny and from there to Clongowes Wood, County Kildare.

In 1877, he established his own private academy in Dublin which for a decade proved to be a highly successful venture. His workload in the decade 1877 to 1887 was enormous and his output phenomenal – running his Academy, sitting on various committees, raising a young family, writing, setting and correcting exam papers while also serving as GAA Secretary from 1884 to 1886. Little wonder then that he found himself dismissed from his post as Secretary by 47 votes to 13 at a meeting of the Association in Thurles on July 4, 1886 for allegedly neglecting administrative work.

Cusack, while observing the Ireland of his day, became alarmed at the cultural decline in the country; the aimlessness of youth and the extent to which apathy had gripped the people.

He set about correcting matters by promoting the language, reviving hurling and organising athletics under Irish rules and nationalist control. He said, 'The strength and energy of a race are largely dependant on the national pastimes for the development of a spirit of courage and endurance.' Cusack was a powerfully built man, full of patriotic resolve driven by the energy of an idealist, devoted entirely to the aspirations of the GAA.

Michael Cusack was acutely conscious of the extent to which so many of the ordinary people were excluded from sports and pastimes by the ruling classes of the day. He was also aware that traditional Irish games, pastimes and certain athletic events were in decline and in danger of disappearing altogether. The solution, he believed, lay in the creation of a new organisation, open to all classes and creeds, that would promote and foster games, athletics and traditions that would give Irish people a sense of pride and identity.

Brother Liam P O'Cathnia, writing in the GAA Centenary Supplement of *The Irish Times* described Cusack as 'a most persuasive man, ruthless and calculating, determined and clever'.

Above all, however, Michael Cusack was a visionary, a cultural crusader, full of drive and enthusiasm. Unfortunately, qualities of aggression and arrogance made him difficult to get on with. As such, it would have to be said that he was deficient in leadership qualities.

Despite all, this colourful and controversial character captured the imagination of James Joyce. He depicted Cusack as 'The Citizen' in *Ulysses* and named him in *Portrait of the Artist as a Young Man* and twice in *Finnegan's Wake*.

The following description of Michael Cusack is given in *The Story of the GAA* by T F O'Sullivan:

'Here is a vivid pen-picture of the Founder of the GAA written by a Dublin gentleman (Mr Joseph Maguire BL) who was personally acquainted with him:

"In the closing years of the last century a striking figure would sometimes be met with in the streets of the Irish metropolis, and one that seldom failed to attract the attention of the passer-by, whether citizen or stranger. It was a man of middle height, with handsome features, dark eyes, black hair and a beard, and with a scholarly roundness of the shoulders, which combined with their great breadth, detracted from the apparent height of their owner, making him look shorter in stature than he really was. He usually wore a broad-rimmed soft hat, and in defiance of the prevailing fashion, always wore knee breeches instead of trousers. The habitual expression of his face was serious, and his stride, as he walked, self-reliant, even combative – an effect which was heightened by the large blackthorn he invariably carried. Those familiar with the main thoroughfare of Dublin at the period referred to, may easily recognise in this brief description the figure of the late Michael Cusack, a man of intensely Irish character and sympathies, a scholar, an athlete, and an Irish-Irelander of the most pronounced type . . . Cusack who had a magnificent constitution from his early boyhood took a keen interest in athletics. As a member of the Leinster Football Association he played a good deal of rugby and also competed in weight-throwing competitions at athletic meetings.

Cusack was a Nationalist of a robust, healthy type, and all the sympathies of his early manhood went out to the unselfish Irishmen identified with the '67 Movement. Long before the establishment of the Gaelic league, he was an earnest worker in the cause of the language revival. He was a trenchant writer, and a ready and fluent public speaker – qualities which he utilised to the full in the momentous campaign in which he was entering at this stage of his career – the establishment of the Gaelic Athletic Association".'

P D Mehigan (Carbery) – hurler, athlete and journalist – who greatly admired Cusack, was introduced to him by P J Devlin (Celt) and he had this to say:

'. . . without doubt, Ireland's woes and the possible remedy were ever in Cusack's innermost thoughts. In athletics as in all others things he saw Anglicisation in control . . . He saw his people were becoming serf-like in soul and body. He almost despaired of them . . . He never lost his serenity of soul . . . He was a realist and a dreamer at once . . . He conceived a great and noble mission and sacrificed his all.'

In 1926, Pat Davin, a brother of Maurice Davin, the first President of the GAA, wrote in his memoirs as follows:

'In his later years Michael Cusack used to claim credit for being the sole founder of the Gaelic Athletic Association, though Maurice Davin had a big hand in the formation of the organisation and should rightfully be entitled to at least an equal share of the honour. He never took the trouble of trying to assert his right to such a title and Michael's name may go down to posterity as that of the man in whose brain the idea of starting an All-Ireland Association first took shape; yet there are people still living who well know that such was not the fact.

In the year 1884, Michael Cusack's influence as far as athletics were concerned, was practically nil outside Dublin, and even there he was anything but popular; elsewhere he was quite an unknown quantity and could not hope to achieve wonders had he attempted to start even a 'Munster Athletic Club', as he first proposed.

As a matter of fact the first steps towards the formation of an Association for the revival of Irish games was well under consideration before Michael Cusack ever came into the picture.

However, there is no denying the fact that during the early years of the Gaelic Athletic Association, when owing to internal dissension and virulent opposition from a quarter where nothing else could be expected, and the very existence of the Association hung in the balance, Michael Cusack was the man who stood in the breach and fearlessly met all opposition.

His fluent pen, wielded with rapier like effect, never rested until the Gaelic ship had successfully avoided the shoals and quicksands in which her course abounded and safely arrived in smooth water. As there are few people who do not possess some fault or failing which might be termed a peculiarity, Mr Cusack was surely no exception to the general rule. Anybody who did not seem to fall in with his views, even in matters not quite within the ambit of the Gaelic code, was never safe from his sword-thrusts when in a fighting mood – even his colleagues in the GAA had occasionally cause of complaint in this respect.'

Although Michael Cusack was removed from his position as Secretary in 1886 – a position which he almost returned to in 1901 when he lost narrowly to Luke O'Toole by 19 votes to 17 – he remained supportive of the GAA for the rest of his life.

Michael Cusack died in relative poverty, on November 27, 1906, in Whitworth Hospital, a little over two months after his fifty-ninth birthday. He was buried on Sunday December 2, 1906, in Glasnevin Cemetery.

Fittingly, the prayers at his graveside were delivered in our native tongue.

MAURICE DAVIN

'Irish football is a great game and worth going a long way to see when played on a fairly laid out ground, and under proper rules. Many old people say just hurling exceeded it as a trial of men. I would not care to see either game now, as the rules stand at present. I may say there are no rules, and therefore those games are often dangerous. I am anxious to see both games revived under regular rules . . . I will gladly lend a hand if I can be of any use.'

(October 13, 1884)

Yours truly

Maurice Davin

Maurice Davin was born in Deerpark near Carrick-on-Suir on June 29, 1842 to John and Bridget Davin. He was the eldest of the five surviving children – four boys and one girl. As he grew to manhood he developed into a magnificent physical specimen and became an outstanding all-round athlete who participated in a variety of sports. He played cricket and was an excellent oarsman. He even did some boxing. In his late twenties he began to concentrate on athletics, weight-throwing, jumping and running. In time his prowess as a sportsman was to earn him the title of 'Father of Irish Athletics'.

Maurice Davin

He took part in the Irish championships in Lansdowne Road from 1875 to 1879 and was without peer in hammer-throwing, slinging the 56lb weight and putting the 16lb weight.

In the first ever international match between England and Ireland at Lansdowne Road in 1876 he won the 16lb shot and he broke the world record in the hammer-throw with a distance of 131ft 6ins.

In 1881, at the age of 39, Maurice and his brother Pat, then in his twenty-third year, travelled to Birmingham for the English championships. They swept all before them. Pat held the world championship for years in the long and high jumps. He was a member of the American 'Invasion' team in 1888.

Politically, Davin was a moderate – a constitutionalist and a nationalist. At the same time he was acutely conscious that athletic sports in Ireland were carried out under English rules and that the majority of Irish people were excluded from participation. This was a reflection of the social conditions of the time. And you can't isolate games and pastimes from social conditions. There were distinct levels of society in Ireland and perceptions of distinct social classes. You were expected to know your place and you were kept in your place.

This was contrary to his concept of fair play. In 1877 he said, 'we are very much in want of some governing body for the management of athletics in this country'.

Maurice Davin was elected as the GAA's first President, on November 1, 1884 at Thurles. The common denominator of interest in games and athletics had brought Davin and Cusack together.

Davin drafted the rules for the new Association which were submitted and adopted at a subsequent meeting on January 17, 1885.

He was also one of the main contributors to the revised constitution, which was adopted at the second annual convention of 1886. A breach of those rules by the Executive Committee led to Davin resigning as President in early 1887.

However, this man of calm disposition and firm leadership, who tended to shun adulation and publicity, was back again to assist in the reconstruction of the Association in early 1888, following the tempestuous Convention of 1887 in Thurles where the Physical Force group attempted to seize control of the organisation.

His dramatic appeal for unity is worth noting:

> 'One of the objects of the founders of the Gaelic Athletic Association was to put down factions and make you good friends with one another. Do not allow your Association to be split in parties by anyone. There is no reason why it should. Union amongst Irishmen was never more wanted than at present.'

Unfortunately, Davin's return was to be short-lived. He resigned the Presidency at the Annual Convention of 1888 that was held in Thurles on January 23, 1889. He left the meeting, having been subjected to vigorous questioning over the 1888 finances of the Association, for which he was not at all responsible.

He never returned to the Association's councils. But his deep interest in GAA affairs lived on and his field at Deerpark was always available for games. The 1904 All-Ireland hurling final was played on his farm on June 24, 1906 – Kilkenny (Tullaroan) 1:9 Cork (St Finbarr's) 1:8.

Maurice Davin was sixty-five-years-old when William Fletcher visited him at his home in Deerpark, following which he wrote this account of him in the *New York Daily News*:

> 'As the old champion came down the walk he moved erect with an easy stride. He was so broad that his well-set shoulders and massive chest entirely filled the walk. He stood 6'1", weighed 225lbs and measured 48" round the chest. His hair and beard were snow white; his eyes were bright and sparkling and there was a rosy glow of health on his cheeks. His heart burns fiercely with love for Ireland and glows warm for any athlete who is devoted to the sports at which he excelled. He lets you know his home is yours when you visit him.'

Maurice Davin died on January 26, 1927 at his home in his eighty-fifth year. In recording his death Phil O'Neill (Sliabh Ruadh) wrote:

> 'One of the founders of the GAA and its first President. He was a member of the Fenian Brotherhood, and as an athlete held the world's hammer-throw from 1875 to 1880 and also held the world's record for the 56lbs weight.
>
> A man of giant strength and ability in the athletic arena, Maurice Davin possessed equally high qualities of mind and heart and his name will go down to countless generations as a model of the highest type of Irishman.
>
> Beannacht Dé le anam an Bhile!'

Most Rev Dr Collier, Bishop of Ossory, sets the ball rolling in the
1932 Kilkenny v Clare final.

5
The First Patrons

The endorsement through patronship of the ideals and aspiration of the GAA by men of the standing and popularity of Croke, Davin, Parnell, O'Leary and O'Brien gave a tremendous initial impetus to the Association. It ensured that the goals of the GAA would penetrate through to the ordinary people of Ireland and capture and grip their imagination.

DR THOMAS WILLIAM CROKE

'Thanks to his great gift of oratory and his strong personality, Croke won for himself the lasting devotion and veneration of his flock. One could almost call him a superb showman.'
(Dom Mark Tierney)

His Grace the Most Revd. Dr. Croke, Archbishop of Cashel

Archbishop Croke was born in Castlecor near Mallow in County Cork in May 1824 and christened Thomas William. His father was a Catholic and his mother, Isabella Plummer, came of a Protestant family.

On reaching manhood T F O'Sullivan commented 'he stood over 6ft and was a fine specimen of vigorous manhood – fond of a good joke, a good story, or a good song'. Dr Croke received his early education in Charleville before entering the Irish College in Paris at the age of 14 to prepare for the Sacred Ministry. He left the College in 1844 and spent a year at the College of Menin, Belgium as Professor of English and Mathematics. He then resided at the Irish College in Rome where he took his DD degree. In 1846 he was raised to the dignity of the priesthood.

His fame as a preacher – he preached at the dedication of Newman's College University Church, St Stephen's Green, in 1856 – organiser and man of talent reached the Vatican and in 1866 he was raised to the Episcopate as Bishop of Auckland where he spent four years. In the summer of 1870 he was appointed Archbishop of Cashel where he remained until his death on the night of July 22, 1902.

All his life this patriotic man was a nationalist at heart. In Rome he was perceived as the most militantly nationalistic of the Irish bishops. When Prime Minister Gladstone brought his first Home Rule Bill before the House of Parliament in 1886 Dr Croke said of him, 'I believe he has an English head and an Irish heart'.

The principles of the Young Irelanders made a deep impression on him and he was influenced by James Fintan Lalor's call, 'for the land of Ireland for the people of Ireland'. He was an ardent supporter of the Home Rule Movement and worked for the re-establishment of our native parliament. He was a supporter of the Tenant League in the 1850s and Michael Davitt's Land league of 1879 – causing him to be known as 'the Land League Archbishop'.

The choice of Dr Croke as patron proved to be an inspired one. When inviting him to be patron, following the meeting in Thurles on November 1, 1884, the objects of the Association were submitted to him. These had his full support.

His Grace's famous letter of December 18, 1884, accepting the patronage of the Association, displayed overleaf, was one of the greatest factors in developing the infant organisation. In the days and years that lay ahead, his guiding hand, support and wise counsel were of inestimable value.

The letter was reproduced in the hurling programme of the Munster Final July 28, 1940 – Cork v Limerick. It must be read in the context of the times in which it was written. It gives an expression of patriotism by a man of peace, desirous of Home Rule and possessed of a passion for the promotion of all games, customs and pastimes Irish. In reading his letter it is interesting to note that he condemns no sports – rather espouses the cause and primacy of Irish games and pastimes. Interesting too, is the fact that in mentioning 'foreign sports' he makes no reference to rugby, soccer or hockey.

Archbishop Croke

DR CROKE'S LETTER

(Now known as The Charter of the GAA.)
At the founding of the Association the following letter was received from the Most Rev. T W Croke, Archbishop of Cashel & Emly:

The Palace, Thurles,
December 18, 1884

My Dear Sir,

I beg to acknowledge the receipt of your communication inviting me to become a patron of the Gaelic Athletic Association, of which you are, it appears, the Hon Secretary. I accede to your request with the utmost pleasure.

One of the most painful, let me assure you, and, at the same time, one of the most frequently recurring reflections that, as an Irishman, I am compelled to make in connection with the present aspect of things in this country, is derived from the ugly and irritating fact that we are daily importing from England, not only her manufactured goods, which we cannot help doing, since she has practically strangled our own manufacturing appliances but, together with her fashions, her accents, her vicious literature, her music, her dances, and her manifold mannerisms, her games also and her pastimes, to the utter discredit of our own grand national sports, and to the sore humiliation, as I believe, of every genuine son and daughter of the old land.

Ball playing, hurling, football-kicking, according to Irish rules, casting, leaping in various ways, wrestling, hand-grips, top-pecking, leap-frog, rounders, tip-in-the-hat, and all such favourite exercises and amusements amongst men and boys may now be said to be not only dead and buried, but in several localities to be entirely forgotten and unknown. And what have we got in their stead? We have got such foreign and fantastic field sports as lawn tennis, polo, croquet, cricket and the like – very excellent, I believe, and health-giving exercises in their way, still not racy of the soil, but rather alien, on the contrary, to it, as are, indeed, for the most part, the men and women who first imported, and still continue to patronise them.

And, unfortunately, it is not our national sports alone that are held in dishonour and are dying out, but even our most suggestive national celebrations are being gradually effaced and extinguished, one after another as well. Who hears now of snap-apple night, pancake-night, or bonfire night? They are all things of the past, too vulgar to be spoken of, except in ridicule by the degenerate dandies of the day. No doubt, there is something rather pleasing to the eye in the get-up of a modern young man, who arrayed in light attire, with parti-coloured cap on and racquet in hand, is making his way, with or without a companion, to the tennis ground. But, for my part, I should vastly prefer to behold, or think of, the youthful athletes, whom I used to see in my early days at fair and pattern, bereft of shoes and coat, and thus prepared to play at handball, to fly over any number of horses, to throw the 'sledge' or 'winding-stone', and to test each other's mettle and activity by the trying ordeal of 'three leaps', or a 'hop, step and jump'.

Indeed if we continue travelling for the next score years in the same direction that we have been going in for some time past, contemning the sports that were practised by our forefathers, effacing our national features as though we were ashamed of them, and putting on, with England's stuffs and broadcloths, her masher habits and such other effeminate follies as she may recommend, we had better, at once, and publicly abjure our nationality, clap hands for joy at sight of the Union Jack, and place 'England's bloody red' exultantly above the green.

Deprecating, as I do, any such dire and disgraceful consummation, and seeing in your society of athletes something altogether opposed to it, I shall be happy to do all for it that I can, and authorise you now formally to place my name on the role of your patrons.

In conclusion, I earnestly hope that our national journals will not disdain in future to give suitable notices of these Irish sports and pastimes which your society means to patronise and promote, and that the masters and pupils of our Irish Colleges will not henceforth exclude from the athletic programmes such manly exercises as I have just referred to and commemorated.

I remain,
My dear Sir,
T W Croke
Archbishop of Cashel

To Mr Michael Cusack,
Hon. Sec. of the Gaelic Athletic Association.

Dr Croke saw the foundation of the GAA as a cultural revolution, a national awakening, an opportunity for all Irish people to participate in sport. For up until then a large section of Irish people was excluded from taking part in competitions. He was opposed to any divisions in Irish life.

He was at all times close to his flock and he understood his people in the context of the times. When he was returning to Ireland from New Zealand he met with the Fenian John Devoy in America. He also knew that other and unrepentant Fenian, Charles Kickham and arranged for him to be reconciled to the sacraments. He visited Michael Davitt in Portland prison. As a prelate he spoke out fearlessly on social matters to a degree that caused concern in Rome.

Following a most disruptive convention held on November 9, 1887, the GAA was on the verge of collapse. But thanks to the good offices of Dr Croke unity was restored. On November 22, 1887, a meeting was held at Dr Croke's residence attended by Michael Davitt and Maurice Davin with a view to reconstructing the Association. This meeting paved the way for a special general convention on January 4, 1888 to reconstruct the Association on lines laid down by the Archbishop of Cashel. The result was that County Boards replaced the Central Executive Committee, thus bringing all clubs under county management.

In 1896, Dr Croke presented two silver cups to the GAA to be competed for by the counties in hurling and football.

The contribution of Dr Croke to the GAA is best exemplified by the following words of Michael Davitt.

> 'The name of the Archbishop of Cashel was connected with it [the GAA] from the outset. His patronage was a tower of strength to the organisation from its infancy. His pen was frequently employed in its support. When, later, the Gaelic ship was on the point of sailing into troubled waters, and the enemies of our name and race rejoiced over the fact, it was his advice and his disinterested mediation that steered the Association into a haven of security and peace, where it now moves free and fearless with well-trimmed sails, its colours mast high, and plain for all good folk to see.'

When Dr Croke died he was widely mourned by Gaeldom. Up to the time of his death he had taken a keen interest in the GAA as he watched its steady growth with pride and pleasure.

In 1913 the grounds at Jones's Road – now known as Croke Park – were dedicated to his memory.

Charles Stewart Parnell

CHARLES STEWART PARNELL

Parnell was born of an Irish father and American mother of Irish descent
in 1846 in County Wicklow into a well-off Protestant family. From his
parents he inherited the seeds of Irish nationalism. He was elected an MP
for County Meath in 1875 at the age of 29. Shy and reserved, no one
anticipated that he would in 1879 be chosen as Chairman of the Irish
Party. Parnell's main political objective was Home Rule. He grew in
political stature to such a degree that he was perceived as 'The Uncrowned
King of Ireland' and 'Leader of the Irish Race at Home and Abroad'.

TW Moody writing in *The Course of Irish History* said:

'Parnell had a matchless genius for leadership. His aloofness and
his self-restraint concealed a passionate nature of exceptional
intensity and strength of purpose.'

Politically, Parnell was a constitutional nationalist. He supported Davitt's land reform and became President of the Irish National Land League in October 1879. Four months earlier at a great land meeting in Westport on June 8 he spoke to the vast gathering, urging those present to 'hold a firm grip on your homesteads and land. You must not allow yourselves to be dispossessed as you were dispossessed in 1847'.

Parnell's indomitable sister Fanny wrote a poem *Hold the Harvest* which Davitt called *The Marseillaise* of the Irish peasants.

Hold the Harvest

Oh! By the God who made us all
The seignior and the serf –
Rise Up! and swear to hold this
day your own green Irish turf;
Rise Up! and plant your feet like
men where now you crawl as slaves.
And make your harvest fields
your camps, or make of them
your graves.

The birds of prey are hovering
round, the vultures wheel and
swoop –
They come, the coroneted
ghouls; with drumbeat and with
troop –
They come to fatten on your
flesh, your children's and your
wives:
Ye die but once – hold fast your
lands, and if you can, your lives.

Three hundred years your crops
have sprung, by murdered
corpses fed;
Your butchered sires, for ghastly
compost spread;
Their bones have fertilised your
fields, their blood has fallen like rain;
They died that you might eat
and live. God! Have they died in vain?

Parnell responded as follows on December 17, 1884, to the invitation from Michael Cusack to become a patron of the GAA from Irish Parliamentary Offices, London.

'Dear Sir,

I have received your letter of 11th inst. It gives me great pleasure to learn that a "Gaelic Athletic Association" has been established for the preservation of National pastimes, with the objects of which I entirely concur.

I feel very much honoured by the Resolution adopted at the Thurles meeting, and I accept with appreciation the position of patron of the Association which has been offered to me.

I need not say that I shall do anything I can to render the working of the movement a success.

I am yours very truly,

Charles Stewart Parnell

Charles Stewart Parnell

Unfortunately, Parnell's affair with Katharine O'Shea led to the Parnell 'split' in 1891 and the course of Irish history was altered. The GAA almost disintegrated, as you will read in a later chapter. Later that year, in the month of October, Parnell died unexpectedly.

Early on the morning of Sunday October11, the coffin containing the remains of Parnell arrived at Kingstown (now Dun Laoghaire). From there it was borne by train to Westland Row where a large crowd waited silently in the rain and the brass bands present, played *The Dead March* from *Saul*.

A Guard of Honour, with draped camáns, was formed by members of the GAA as the coffin was placed on the hearse. People cried openly for the man who had served them so well as the cortege proceeded to St Michan's in Church St, the burial place of Parnell's father and grandfather and from there to City Hall for the lying-in-state.

From 10 a.m. to 1 p.m. about 30,000 people filed past the bier.

Over an hour later the hearse, drawn by four horses, set off through the crowds for Glasnevin Cemetery followed by Parnell's favourite horse, the twenty-five-year-old 'Home Rule', led by a groom.

Writing on Parnell's funeral in *The Story of the GAA*, T F O'Sullivan described it as follows:

> 'In Parnell's funeral to Glasnevin on October 11, 2000, Gaels, with camáns draped, took part, and presented a very striking appearance. At the great conference in Dublin in July representatives of the Gaels of Ireland declared their adhesion to Parnell's principals, and no section of Irishmen more deeply mourned the great Leader's tragic and untimely death than the members of the organisation to which Parnell extended his patronage at its foundation. All the city clubs and several clubs in the provinces were represented in the huge funeral procession to Glasnevin. "Close on 2 o'clock," we read "the Gaels, leading the procession from Stephen's Green, appeared in Dame Street. There were not less than 2,000 of them – stout, brawny fellows, each supplied with a camán draped in black. Right through the thick of the vast crowd they marched, six abreast, with splendid military precision, headed by Messrs. Thomas Lee (Chairman, Dublin County Committee), A Murphy, P Gregan, W Briscoe, J Boland, W A O'Shea, P Tobin, P P Sutton, *Sport*, and the people, hitherto quiescent pushed and swayed and surged to make room for this irresistible body.'

MICHAEL DAVITT

The patronage of Michael Davitt, 'Father of the Land League', was immensely beneficial to the GAA. He led an organisation whose membership grew to 100,000 people. As Michael McInerney, former political correspondent of *The Irish Times* put it, it was 'a great popular front of leaguers, revolutionaries, nationalists and parliamentarians'.

According to Dr Donal MacCartney, Dean of Arts at UCD,

'the land league was one of the most powerful democratic movements in all of Irish history and its influence, both social and
political was profound.'

T P O'Neill wrote:

'the battles of Irish History, like Irish songs, are sad. Few ended in
victory. The Land league won not alone the battles but also the war.'

Michael Davitt was born in Straide,
County Mayo, on March 25, 1846. His
parents were small tenant farmers and in
1851, unable to pay the rent, they were
evicted and their cottage burned down. It
was a memory that never left Michael
Davitt. His father, Patrick, emigrated to
England in search of work and two years
later he was joined by the rest of the
family.

To supplement the family income
Michael went to work in a Lancashire
Cotton Mill in Haslingdon, near
Manchester. He was nine years of age and
worked a twelve-hour day. Two years later
at the age of 11 he lost an arm at work on
a machine he was minding.

Now industrially useless, he attended
Wesley school where he added French and
Italian to his Irish and English languages.

Michael Davitt

At 22 he became a commercial traveller. That was 1868. He was
arrested in 1870 on charges linking him to Fenian activities and sentenced
to 15 years penal servitude in Dartmoor. He was released on 'a ticket of
leave' in 1877 and returned to Ireland. There he immersed himself in the
Land Question – in the words of the Young Irelander James Fintan Lalor,
trying to secure 'the land of Ireland for the people of Ireland'. To this end,
Davitt visited the US in 1878 where he met with the Fenian John Devoy to
garner support for his campaign. The following year The Land League was
born – born against a background of 482,000 evictions between the years
1849 and 1882. Davitt was now an avowed enemy of English rule in
Ireland.

Though a Fenian he was, however, critical of their methods and dogmatism. As T W Moody commented:

> 'A Catholic who had been taught by a Wesleyan school master, he accepted religious diversity as a social fact and not a ground for estrangement among men . . . Above all he had passion for social justice that transcended nationality.'

Michael Davitt responded to the invitation to attend the Thurles Meeting of November 1, 1884, from London on October 30, as follows:

> 'Dear Mr Cusack,
>
> Sorry I cannot attend the meeting which you announce for Thurles on Saturday. In any effort that may be made to revive a national taste for games and pastimes such as once developed our Gaelic ancestors, I shall be most happy to lend a hand. Why should we not have our athletic festivals like other peoples – I mean on a national scale? In this, as in so many other matters, we ought to cut ourselves adrift from English rules and patronage, and prevent the killing of those Celtic sports which have been threatened with the same fate by the encroachment of Saxon custom, as that which menaces our nationality under alien rule.
>
> Why not make an effort for the revival of the Taltine games? A grand National Festival could be organised to come off at some historic spot, at which prizes could be awarded for merit, not only in the various athletic sports peculiar to the Celtic people (and in this expression I would include the Scotch, Welsh and Manx), but in music, poetry, oratory and other kindred accomplishments.
>
> To throw the prizes open to the Celtic race throughout the world and give a couple of years in which to organise the first grand National competition, would I am confident, ensure a great success. There are, of course, many others reasons why the physique of our people is not developed as it ought to be, but there is no doubt that one reason for the degenerate gait and bearing of most of our young men at home is to be found in the absence of such games and pastimes as formerly gave to Irishmen the reputation of a soldier-like and self-reliant race.
>
> Yours very truly,
> Michael Davitt'

Michael Davitt

This is Michael Davitt's response to his invitation to become a patron. It was written from the Imperial Hotel, Dublin on December 21, 1884.

'I accept with great pleasure the position of patron which has been assigned me by the Gaelic Athletic Association, though I am painfully conscious of how little assistance I can render to you in your praiseworthy undertaking. Anything, however, it is in my power to do to further the objects of the Association I will most willingly perform, as I cannot but recognise the urgent necessity which exists for a movement like that which you are organising with such zeal.

I have already explained to you my views upon Gaelic sports, and hinted at plans by which a Nationalist taste for them might be cultivated. I have, therefore, only to express my obligations to yourself and friends for the honour conferred upon me, and to repeat the assurance of my entire sympathy with the objects of the Gaelic Athletic Association.'

Michael Davitt was a most enthusiastic supporter of the US 'Invasion' of Irish athletes and hurlers in 1888 and, following its failure financially, he made available a sum of £450 ' . . . in order to meet hotel and other expenses incurred by the teams'. In 1901, he agreed to forego his claim in full, as the GAA struggled with its burden of debt.

After 1888 he ceased to be prominently identified with the GAA but his patronage in the early days was a most important asset to the promoters.

When he died on June 1, 1906, 100,000 passed his bier in Clarendon Street, Dublin.

He deserves to be commemorated in some special way in Croke Park.

JOHN O'LEARY

At a meeting of the GAA in Thurles on September 27, 1886, it was proposed and seconded that John O'Leary be appointed a patron.

This is his letter of acceptance written from Dublin on November 12, 1886:

'Gentlemen,

I need scarcely say that I am grateful to the Gaelic Athletic Association for the honour they have done me – an honour the more highly prized in that I am in such thorough sympathy with the aims and objects of the Association.

There are many societies and associations in Ireland about which good Irishmen may perhaps fairly differ, but your Society seems to me one about which there can be no difference of opinion amongst right-thinking and well-feeling people. The main object is, as I understand, to make our young men healthier and stronger, and to seek, by the attraction of manly Irish sports, to prevent young men from devoting their leisure time to less manly and possibly less moral pursuits. It is, of course, a very great additional merit in my eyes that the Gaelic Athletic Association devotes much of its energies to the cultivation (and sometimes, I believe, the revival) of special Irish sports as hurling and the like . . . we can always get "light and leading" from the pages of our prophet and guide, Thomas Davis:

"Mind will rule and muscle yield,
In senate, ship and field;
When we've skill our strength to wield,
Let us take our own again"

Sincerely yours,
John O'Leary'

His letter was read at a meeting in Thurles on November 15, 1886, and received with loud applause.

John O'Leary was born into a Catholic middle-class family in Tipperary town in 1830. At the age of 17 he went to Trinity College, Dublin, to study law. He became hugely influenced by Thomas Davis and was soon in the ranks of the Young Irelanders. He didn't have an opportunity to participate in the rebellion in Tipperary because it was crushed almost as soon as it began. However, he tried to revive the rebellion the following year and for his part in this he was imprisoned in 1848. Following his release he went

John O'Leary

back to his studies. He transferred from law and studied medicine at Queen's Colleges Cork and Galway but never qualified.

After a series of travels that took him from Dublin to Paris, to America and back to Paris, he finally settled in Dublin.

In 1863 he was appointed to the editorial board of *The Irish People* by James Stephens, the Fenian leader. Most of the articles in the newspaper tried to counteract the damaging criticism of the Fenian movement as a secret society, which was emanating from the Irish Hierarchy. Charles Kickham and John O'Leary in column after column repeatedly disagreed with clerical interference in politics. Also as a man of some literary taste, O'Leary tried to ensure that the paper maintained a certain literary standard and he deplored the poor quality of many of the patriotic poems submitted to the paper.

Although a convinced and trusted Fenian he refused to take its oath of allegiance. As a man of honour totally committed to the cause of Irish Nationalism, he saw no good reason for taking this oath. His stance on the matter was respected, which goes to show the measure of the man and the high esteem in which he was held.

The British Government set out to crush the Fenian movement and in 1865 *The Irish People* was suppressed. O'Leary and Kickham were arrested and tried. O'Leary spent the next nine years in prison. Under the Balfour Amnesty he went into exile in Paris and was finally permitted to return to Ireland in 1885.

Following his return he took a keen interest in the Irish literary revival and had a profound influence on Yeats, cultivating in him a love of Irish history, legend and folklore. Yeats also came to admire O'Leary's stoicism. As Professor Lyons recorded in his book *Ireland since the Famine* John O'Leary once said to Yeats, 'there are certain things a man must not do to save a nation'. When Yeats asked what these were O'Leary replied – 'to cry in public'.

To show their high regard for him a group of Anglo-Irish writers, including Yeats and Douglas Hyde, collaborated in the production of a volume of poems and ballads dedicated to the Fenian, John O'Leary.

As an old man, honours were heaped on him. To celebrate the centenary of the 1798 rebellion, O'Leary was made President of the executive committee. He unveiled the Memorial to Charles J Kickham at Tipperary on November 27, 1898.

In 1900, Cumann na nGael was founded. Among the aims of the organisation was the preservation and cultivation of Irish games. O'Leary was chosen as its President.

He had the honour of speaking at the grave of James Stephens on March 31, 1901. On the occasion of the Emmet Centenary in September 1903, he delivered an oration to a huge multitude outside St Catherine's Church, Thomas St – the 'scene of Emmet's martyrdom'.

John O'Leary died on March 16, 1907 and was buried in Glasnevin Cemetery beside his old friend James Stephens – a private ceremony, in deference to the wishes of his relatives.

> *Romantic Ireland's dead and gone,*
> *It's with O'Leary in the grave.*
> W B Yeats

WILLIAM O'BRIEN

A meeting was held in the Victoria Hotel in Cork on December 27, 1884. At the meeting Michael Cusack stated that William O'Brien MP – whose popularity with nationalists in rural Ireland was second only to that of Parnell – had agreed to give space every week in his paper, *United Irishman*, for articles on GAA matters.

At the Convention in Thurles in January 1888 it was decided to ask William O'Brien to become a patron.

He replied as follows from Dublin on 5 April 1888:

William O'Brien

'My dear Sir,

You are right in assuming that your communication must have been lost in (I am sorry to say) the very large number of letters, which I was utterly unable to acknowledge after my release from prison. I take the opportunity now of acknowledging very gratefully, the resolution of the Thurles Gaelic Convention. Of their sympathy with the struggle against Coercion I never entertained a moment's doubt, and, although I am most unwilling to increase the prominence, which undoubtedly the exigencies of the struggle has forced upon me for the moment, I cannot resist the voice of the young Gaelic Athletes that they should add my name to those of their well-wishers in any capacity they may choose.

Sincerely yours,
William O'Brien'

William O'Brien (1852-1928) won fame as a nationalist and journalist especially in the 1880s. He represented various Cork seats in Parliament 1883-95 and 1900-18. Although he came from a Catholic family he was educated at a Church of Ireland seminary and at Queen's College, Cork.

William O'Brien was one of Parnell's most trusted lieutenants. In 1882, Parnell replaced The Land League with a new movement called the Irish National League. He appointed O'Brien as editor of his newspaper, *United Ireland*.

On October 23, 1886, the newspaper published an article entitled 'A Plan of Campaign' setting out the tactics which tenants should follow in order to force landlords to reduce the rent. 'The Plan' was first tried out at Woodford, County Galway on the estate of the Earl of Clanrickarde. Four hundred tenants, led by bands and banners, marched to Portumna to hear William O'Brien and John Dillon explain their campaign. What was at issue was the question of a Fair Rent – one of the three Fs (Fair Rent, Fixity of Tenure and Freedom of Sale). The tenants then went to the Agent's Office and demanded a 40 percent reduction in their rents. When this was refused the tenants paid over the money to O'Brien and Dillon –

making them, in effect, trustees of their funds and proof that they were prepared to pay a fair rent rather than exorbitant rent.

By the end of the year 'the Plan' was in operation on 116 estates. Parnell, fearing a new Land War, ordered the campaign to be ended. O'Brien protested that the tenants now depended on him and he would not betray them. Parnell finally agreed that it could continue on the estates where it was already in operation but should not spread any further.

During the 'Plan of Campaign', O'Brien defied secular and ecclesiastical authority. He went to prison and was prepared to sacrifice his health and his life. His identification with the just cause of the tenant farmers won him huge popular support.

In the Parnell split, O'Brien tried to stay out of the controversy, but this wasn't possible in the climate of politics at the time. Although he publicly condemned the stance taken by Tim Healy, the leader of the anti-Parnell faction, he reluctantly decided he couldn't stay on the side of Parnell. He tried to be the moderate voice of the anti-Parnell MPs – and failed.

His greatest contribution to Irish politics was setting up The United Irish League in 1898. The aim of the League was the redistribution of land in Connaught, where the 6,000 largest farmers held the same amount of land as the 70,000 smallest. It soon became a national movement. Its membership increased from 33,000 in 1899 to 63,000 in 1900 and had reached almost 100,000 by 1901. Almost 1,000 branches were established nationwide and its policy had developed from a simple redistribution scheme to the demand that landlords be bought out by compulsory purchase.

Although compulsory purchase was never embarked upon, the efforts of The United Irish League were eventually responsible for the Wyndham Land Act, 1903, enabling the Irish tenants to purchase entire estates from the landlords.

In that same year O'Brien split with John Redmond, a Wexford man who was MP for Waterford and Leader of the Irish Party, because of the latter's continued conciliation with Southern Unionists. He later founded the All-For Ireland League, which won eight Parliamentary seats in County Cork. These were all to be wiped out later, by the advent of the Sinn Féin candidates in the 1918 general election.

William O'Brien was in agreement with the Sinn Féin call for armed rebellion. He was involved in talks with Arthur Griffith and James Connolly that a rebellion must go ahead with or without aid from Germany, even though it is reported that Connolly said to him 'we are going out to be slaughtered'.

And so, as predicted, it came to pass when the men of 1916 gave their lives 'in bloody protest for a glorious thing' (Pearse). William O'Brien saw the fruits of their sacrifice with the signing of the Anglo-Irish Treaty on

December 6, 1921, which established the Irish Free State but it didn't satisfy him. He resented the partition of his country. As a consequence, in late 1922 he declined the offer of a sea in the Senate.

In his final years he was in failing health. He died in 1928 and is buried in Mallow where a monument to his memory was erected.

One has to conclude that there was foresight and insight attached to the selection of Croke, Parnell, Davitt, O'Leary and O'Brien as patrons. Here you had five strong characters, diverse in many ways, differing on occasions politically, but united in their love of Ireland, its people, its customs, and its pastimes. They were all close to their people and respected and revered by them. And those who invited them to be Patrons knew that well.

Dr Croke

John O'Leary

Glen Rovers v Sarsfields 1936 Cork County Final

6
The Initial Impact of the GAA Recalled

It began a revolt against degradation, leading to submission;
A recall to the past so that its glories might again animate us;
A tocsin for the present so that the future should find us
united and strong and fit to be free men.
(Celt, P J Devlin)

Fr James B Dollard, poet and scholar, was a Kilkenny man who served in the priesthood for many years in the North American continent. He was born in August 1872. Writing in the Gaelic Athletic Annual of 1907/08 he recalled how the spirit of the people was electrified and enlivened following the establishment of the GAA.

'Though still young at the time, I well remember the great change that came over the country, and the vivid and lasting impression it made on me. Until then everything was lonely and stagnant in the land, and the young men in their idle hours loitered in dull fashion by the street and fence corners. In a few months how different things became!

The country was soon humming with interest and activity, the ambitions of the young men were aroused. Every parish had its newly formed hurling or football team, prepared to do or die for the "honour of the little village".

Anon, the war of the championships was on! We followed armies of Gaels many miles along the country roads to the field of combat, where as many as eight or ten teams, gaily clad in their coloured jerseys, struggled for supremacy before our dazzled and delighted eyes! How we cheered our beloved heroes on to victory, and what pride we felt in looking on the stalwart and athletic forms! To play on the first team was, indeed, the greatest honour a youth could hope for, and many of us looked forward to that day with swelling hearts!'

Little wonder then that, shortly after the foundation of the GAA, Michael Cusack was able to say that the organisation had 'swept the country like a prairie fire'.

On June 21, 1908, Fr Dollard, then a Monsignor home on holiday from Canada, was in Dan Fraher's field in Dungarvan for the All-Ireland hurling final of 1907 between his native Kilkenny and Munster champions Cork. And what a contest it turned out to be; an epic that set a benchmark by which subsequent contests were measured; a thriller that ended when, on the call of time, Jimmy Kelly of Mooncoin met the sliotar on the drop to secure the winning point – score 3:12 to 4:8.

The game got under way with Monsignor Dollard throwing in the ball. There was a strongly held conviction in Kilkenny at the time that if one of their priests threw in the ball they would win. For them the result, and the timing and dramatic nature of the winning point, bore this out. Faith can move mountains.

The Hurler

Upon his native sward the hurler stands
To play the ancient pastime of the Gael,
And all the heroes famed of Inisfail
Are typified in him – I see the bands
Of the Craobh Ruadh applauding with their hands,
The Fianna shouting over Clui-Mail,
Oisín and Finn with eager faces pale,
Caoilti and Goll are there from fairy lands.

And fierce Cú Chulainn comes, his Godlike face,
With yearning wild to grip in hand once more
The lithe camán and drive the hurtling ball.
In Walsh's, Kelleher's, and Semple's grace
He sees again his glorious youth of yore,
And mourns his dead compeers and Ferdia's fall.
(Rev James B Dollard, D Litt)

As Fr Dollard recalled his youthful memories of almost a quarter of a century earlier, he must surely have reflected too on the events of the interim relating to the Gaelic Athletic Association.

There was the ambitious trip of 1888 to the US that was idealistic rather than wise. Followed by the terrible set-back of the Parnell 'Split' that almost rend the GAA asunder. There was the ever-present support and guiding hand of Archbishop Croke until his death in 1902.

Fr Dollard must too have reflected on the dedication of so many patriotic and altruistically driven individuals, the magnetic qualities of parish pride and the establishment of Provincial Councils and the founding of Camogie clubs.

And there was, of course, the great Football Final of 1903 (played 1905) between Kerry and Kildare. It took three games to decide the issue with victory going to Kerry. These games put Gaelic football on the map and swelled the coffers of the GAA as they attracted huge crowds.

The third game in Cork on October 13 broke all records in championship contests. Word of the quality of earlier meetings in Tipperary July 23 and Cork August 27 had spread and caused rugby and soccer enthusiasts to flock to the final game in Cork.

Father James B Dollard
(Canada)

Mick Mackey wears special protective headgear at Thurles in the 1939 Munster championship. He had suffered an injury in a tournament match a week previously that necessitated eleven stitches.

7
The All-Ireland Championships Begin

Initially, as the organisation got off the ground, there was much emphasis and concentration on athletics. Of course some hurling and football matches were played, but it took until 1887 before the All-Ireland hurling and football championships got underway.

1887 was a stormy and extraordinary year in many respects. It witnessed the formation of county committees and disputes over matches and fixtures. It was the year Maurice Davin resigned as President for the first time and there was a struggle for control of the Association between the Constitutionalists and the Physical Force men. Following the stormy convention in Thurles, which was attended by two delegates from each of 800 clubs, the Association spilt and there was the prospect of the GAA being torn asunder and destroyed only three years after its formation. But the same year also saw the reconstruction of the Association and the healing brought about through the influence of Dr Croke.

It was against this turbulent background that the All-Ireland championships were initiated, and understandably, in the year that was in it, the games didn't reach a conclusion until April of the following year.

THE RULES

The attire as stated in the Rules was as follows: 'the dress for hurling and football to be knee breeches and stockings and shoes or boots'.

A few of the hurling rules applicable at the time make interesting reading today:

> 'A player should not catch, trip, or push from behind, or bring his hurley intentionally in contact with another player.'

For each breach of this rule the referee was empowered to order the offender to stand aside during the whole or part of the balance of the game.

> 'The ball must not be lifted off the ground by the hands when in play. It might be struck with the hand or kicked. It might be caught when off the ground, and the player so catching it might puck it in any way he pleased, but he *must not carry it* (except on the hurley) or throw it.'

In other words, no steps allowed with the ball in the hand.

In football it was quite common to see players striking the ball with the arm. And it wasn't unusual to see them sending the ball a distance of almost fifty yards by this method. The practise gradually died.

Only twelve counties had formed county committees and only those counties were eligible to compete. For the first and only time the championships were run on an open draw basis – the club that won the county title progressing to represent the county.

The draws for both hurling and football, made at a meeting of the Executive in Dublin on Sunday, February 27, 1887, were as follows:

Wicklow v Clare – Tuesday, July 19, Athlone
Wexford v Galway – Sunday, July 24, Dublin
Dublin v Tipperary – Saturday, July 30, Mountrath
Cork v Kilkenny – Sunday, July 24, Dungarvan
Waterford v Louth – Thursday July 21, Dublin
Limerick v Meath – Monday July 25, Maryboro

In hurling, Wicklow, Dublin, Louth and Waterford didn't participate for a variety of reasons. Disputes within the counties of Cork and Limerick led to neither county fulfilling their hurling engagements. There is no record of a game played by Meath.

So in the end only five counties, Clare, Wexford, Galway, Tipperary and Kilkenny, actually participated in the hurling championships.

Tipperary (Thurles) defeated Clare (Smith O'Brien's) in a re-fixture at Nenagh and followed with a victory over Kilkenny (Tullaroan) in a re-fixture at Urlingford.

Galway (Meelick) overcame Wexford (Castlebridge) at Elm Park.

Thus for the final, Tipperary, represented by Thurles, and Galway, represented by Meelick, met at Birr, on Easter Sunday, April 1, 1888. Victory went to the Premier County on the score Tipperary 1 goal, 1 point and 1 forfeit point to no score for Galway. A forfeit point was the equivalent of a 70 in today's game.

Jim Stapleton captained the winners in a 21-aside contest played on a pitch measuring about 200 yards by 140 yards. The game was refereed by P J White of Offaly.

In the football championship Wicklow, Dublin and Galway did not field teams.

Mr Patrick Larkin, Kiltormer, Ballinasloe, played for Meelick in the first All-Ireland hurling final and represented his county at several conventions. He was President of the Galway County Committee for years and a member of the Central Council.

The following games are recorded:

Kilkenny (Kilmacow) 0–4 Cork (Lees) Nil
Tipperary (Templemore) 1–8 Clare (Newmarket-on-Fergus) 0–3

Limerick (Commercials) 3–2 Meath 0–2
Limerick (Commercials) 1–10 Kilkenny (Kilmacow) 1–10
Limerick won the replay.

Limerick lost to Tipperary and following an objection a replay was ordered which Limerick went on to win.

Louth (Dundalk Young Irelands) 1–8 Waterford (Ballyduff Lr.) 0–4
Louth (Dundalk Young Irelands) 0–7 Wexford (Castlebridge) 0–5

The way was now clear for a final between Limerick and Louth. It was played at the grounds of the Benburb Club at Donnybrook, Dublin, on Sunday April 29, 1888, on a pitch that would have measured 140 yards by 84 yards. Teams would have consisted of 21-aside.

Limerick, captained by Denis Corbett, won on the score 1:4 to 3 points in a game refereed by John Cullinane of Bansha, County Tipperary.

Limerick Commercials, All-Ireland Champions, 1887 – **Back row**: F Fitzgibbon, E Nicholas, E Casey, T McMahon, Phil Keating. **Middle row:** D H Liddy, P S Reeves, J Mulqueen, M Slattery, P Kelly, T Kennedy, J Hyland, R Normoyle, D Corbett (captain), W Gunning, W Cleary, R Breen, P Treacy. **Front row:** T McNamara, P J Corbett, Malachi O'Brien, Tom Keating, J Kennedy.

The outstanding man of the day, and indeed of the championship, was Malachi O'Brien of Limerick – a mighty kicker of the ball, and acclaimed by many as the star footballer of those days.

A report on the game in *The Freeman* described it as follows:

'A splendid exhibition of skill, science, speed and stamina; it was a model in every respect, the feeling between the combatants being of the friendliest nature. It was a game won fair and square and without fluke or fortune by the Commercials . . . the hand-play, punting and general knackiness of the Dundalk men, of whom Louth may well be proud, could hardly be excelled, but they were unable to withstand the fast, determined charging of the boys from Garryowen . . . Mr John Cullinane refereed with great judgement and tact and scrupulous exactness.'

John Cullinan, MP

According to T F O'Sullivan in *The Story of the GAA*, 'Thurles or the Commercials did not get their medals until over a quarter of a century later'.

As an aside, it is interesting to note that in June 1887, at Kilkenny Castle, the highest temperature ever recorded in Ireland reached 33 degrees celsius.

Of interest, too, is the fact that on January 1, 1887, *The Celtic Times* – a Gaelic games' newspaper edited by Michael Cusack – made its first appearance. It was a weekly publication but only survived until January 14, 1888. In 2003, Clasp Press, Ennis, County Clare, published facsimile editions of the only known surviving issues, covering the period February 19 to December 31, 1887.

The inter-county championship contests generated much interest and attracted enthusiastic supporters. Arrangements, however, for the contests, were not always the best. After all, this was an Association in its infancy. Teething problems and growing pains were inevitable. You had pitch invasions by spectators; disputes between players and referees; spectators interfering with play; internal dissension in counties.

Media interest in GAA affairs ranged from minimal to non-existent at the time. We don't really know how many attended those first finals. Compared to present day attendances the figures would have been modest. But great days lay ahead.

Bíonn gach tosnu lag.

1947 Kilkenny v Cork
A Hurling Classic

8

A Financial Misadventure

Idealism tends to breed noble aspirations. And so it was with the infant GAA organisation when it decided to send a team of crack athletes and hurlers to America. There had been much discussion on the matter throughout 1887 and finally on July 6, 1888, at a Central Council meeting at Limerick Junction the proposal was given the go ahead. It was estimated that £1000 would be required to pay the expenses. In the GAA world the trip has become known as the US 'Invasion'.

There was enthusiastic support for the undertaking at home and among the Irish in America. Subscriptions were received from clubs and individuals. Dr Croke wrote in its support and personally subscribed. Maurice Davin, himself a famous athlete and founder member of the GAA, was its most active promoter and the person most closely identified with the venture.

The trip had a number of key objectives:

To promote international Gaelic games' competition

To establish GAA branches in the US and promote the image of the young Association

To present to a wider audience the skills and thrills of Ireland's unique game of hurling

To enhance the image of Ireland

To display the prowess of our athletes on a larger world stage

To gain financially and significantly enhance the coffers of the GAA

Michael Davitt, too, was most enthusiastic. He saw the trip as:

' . . . a means to an end – the end being a projected international Gaelic festival here in Ireland in August 1889 . . . to re-establish the old Tailtean Games . . . an international Celtic festival every five years . . . prizes could be offered not alone for excellence in athletics but for music in song and composition, harp recitals, band contests, etc., all thrown open to our Highland, Welsh, and Manx kindred, as well as those of our own race from all parts of the globe. Prizes could likewise be offered for essays, plans, etc., in connection with subjects more material – improvement of agriculture, butter-making, artisans' dwellings, development of industries, . . . an occasion on which all that would tend to develop the physique, the mind, and the material well-being of our country might be honoured and stimulated by national recognition and reward.'

John Cullinane of Bansha, County Tipperary, who refereed the All-Ireland football final of 1887 and who later became an MP travelled to the

States some weeks before the main party to finalise arrangements for the athletic events and the hurling contests. There were no football competitions organised.

The team of hurlers and athletes sailed for the States in *The Wisconsin* on September 16, 1888 and arrived in New York to scenes of great enthusiasm. They were warmly welcomed and lavishly feted in every city they visited. There were bands, banquets and speeches. In a way it was a case of home from home. For they were in a land where one in every five, 20 per cent of the population, were either Irish or of Irish descent.

The trip had its successes and failures. On the plus side the hurling exhibitions were popular and generated much enthusiasm with the Americans freely admitting that they had no game to equal hurling. The athletes demonstrated their prowess, though all didn't come up to form – too much feasting perhaps? At the end of the trip the foundations of the establishment of the GAA in America were laid.

Mr Patrick Davin, solicitor, Carrick-on-Suir (brother of Mr Maurice Davin) held the World Championship record for years in the long and high jumps. He defeated the American athletes in Dublin in 1888 in the individual athletic championship, and was a member of the US 'Invasion' teams. Taken in 1882, when Mr Davin was in his twenty-fourth year.

However on the minus side the trip, contrary to expectations, was a financial failure – a disaster really as it left the infant organisation in a worse financial state after the event than before. (It wasn't until after the memorable three All-Ireland football games of 1903 – played in 1905 – between Kerry and Kildare that the finances of the GAA were placed on a sound footing again.) Michael Davitt, had to advance £450 in order to meet hotel and other expenses incurred by the athletes.

The financial failure was due in the main to the fact that the States were in the throes of a Presidential election and the hustings attracted people who might otherwise have watched the athletes. The weather was also for the most part wet and militated against large attendances. The advertising programme was not as efficient or as effective as it might have been. The fact that a war was waging between the two athletic organisations of America – the National Amateur Athletic Association (NAAA) and the Athletic Union (AU) – both of whom were anxious to exploit the 'invaders' did not help matters. The Gaels held their exhibitions under the auspices of the Manhattan Athletic Club which was affiliated with the NAAA, with the result that the AU refused to allow their athletes to compete in any of the meetings in which the Gaels participated. With hindsight, it would seem that advance planning, preparation and marketing lacked the professional touch and that idealistic motives took priority over realism.

There was, however, further negative fall-out. About twenty of the athletes remained in the US and some of those who had sailed home from New York on October 31 on the *City of Rome* later returned to the States – all lost to the GAA in its infancy.

The trip also indirectly caused the departure of Maurice Davin from the Association. At the annual convention of 1888 held in Thurles on January 23, 1889, Maurice Davin occupied the Chair. Having outlined the financial state of the Association he was vigorously questioned by some delegates. He left the meeting, never to return to the council chambers.

His loss was immense.

There were no more Atlantic crossings by any unit of the GAA until 1926 when the Tipperary hurling team – All-Ireland champions of 1925 – boarded the *SS Bremen* in early May and set forth on a most successful tour of the States. They travelled from coast to coast and returned home undefeated after playing seven games – two each in New York and Chicago and the others at Boston, San Francisco and Buffalo.

Maurice Davin of Carrick-on-Suir lived to see this successful venture. It would have pleased the great athlete.

Thurles of the thrills. His Grace Most Rev. Dr. Kinane, Archbishop of Cashel, Patron of the G.A.A., throws in the ball to start the Tipperary-Limerick Munster Championship semi-final at Thurles Sportsfield in July 1951. Tipperary won by 3–8 to 1–6. Mr. V. O'Donoghue, president of the G.A.A., is on Archbishop Kinane's left

The Tipperary and Limerick teams parade just before the game commenced

His Grace Most Rev Dr Kinane, Archbishop of Cashel, Patron of the GAA, throws in the ball to start the Tipperary-Limerick Munster Championship semi-final at Thurles Sportsfield in July 1951. Tipperary won by 3–8 to 1–6. Mr V O'Donoughue, President of the GAA is on Archbishop Kinane's left. The Tipperary and Limerick teams parade just before the game commenced.

9
The Parnell 'Split'

The political genius of Charles Stewart Parnell as displayed in his leadership of the Irish party at Westminster made him in his time the greatest Irish politician since Daniel O'Connell – revered and respected throughout the land.

In March 1887, *The Times* newspaper began publishing a series of articles 'Parnellism and Crime', with a view to destroying Parnell's reputation and also that of Gladstone and the Liberal Party, who were supporting the Home Rule cause. The object of the articles was to establish a connection between Parnell and terrorism. The most damning link appeared to be a letter purporting to be written by Parnell on May 15, 1882, in which he allegedly expressed his regret for having to denounce the murders of Chief Secretary Lord Frederick Cavendish and Under-Secretary Thomas H Burke in the Phoenix Park in 1882. Parnell, in the House of Commons, protested his innocence and denounced the letter as a forgery.

A special commission of three High Court judges was appointed to inquire into the matter. Finally in February 1889 Richard Pigott, a Dublin journalist, cracked under cross-examination in the witness box and admitted forgery. He fled to England and from there to Madrid where he committed suicide.

Parnell's popularity, which for some time had been somewhat on the wane, was restored to its former glory. Unfortunately, however, dark clouds were gathering on the horizon. For a while rumours were about regarding Parnell's private life. In December 1889, Captain William H O'Shea filed a divorce suit against his wife, citing Parnell as co-respondent. Parnell told several people that he would emerge from it without a stain on his reputation. But it wasn't to be. In November 1890 the case came to trial. Parnell's adultery with the wife of Captain O'Shea was revealed in the Divorce Court. Politically, it was the beginning of the end for Parnell.

Gradually, throughout 1891 things began to badly unravel. All attempts to get Parnell to step aside as leader failed. Political reality as distinct from any moral judgement saw Gladstone demand Parnell's temporary retirement from the leadership. Parnell refused.

The Irish Parliamentary Party 'Split'. Most of the members now saw Parnell as unfit to be leader – among them were Michael Davitt, John Dillon, William O'Brien and Tim Healy.

The Irish people then split, breaking up into Parnellites and anti-Parnellites.

The Hierarchy, guided by 'that sagacious man', Archbishop Walsh of Dublin, remained silent and awaited developments before eventually calling upon him to stand down from the leadership.

Parnell then lost the support of *The Freeman* newspaper, heretofore a great ally.

T W Moody writing in *The Course of Irish History* gives this interesting insight:

'Parnell's fall deprived the Irish party of a leader whose genius was irreplaceable and seriously injured the Home Rule cause among the British public. It was all the more tragic because, in the supreme crisis of his life, Parnell abandoned the stern realism that had hitherto governed all his political conduct and allowed his passion and his pride to overmaster him. He refused to admit for a moment that his own personal conduct was in any way involved, and insisted that the only issue was whether the Irish party was to remain loyal to his leadership or surrender to dictation from Gladstone and the liberals. In fact, the crux of the matter was whether he was to continue as leader of the party at the cost of depriving Home Rule of a large and decisive section of its liberal supporters. His refusal to contemplate even a temporary retirement forced an excruciating decision on a majority of his party.'

The whole affair ended tragically when Charles Stewart Parnell died unexpectedly at the age of forty-five on October 6, 1891 in the arms of Katharine, his wife since June 1891.

The Parnell 'Split' impacted severely and adversely on the GAA in 1891. Indeed, it almost destroyed the Association.

P P Sutton writing in Sport commented:

'The Association would have made wonderful strides this season in most of the districts in which it has been for a long time in a moribund condition had not the present deplorable crisis [The Parnell 'Split'] arisen, and caused our people to devote all their attention in the majority of rural districts to politics and to fighting one another.'

T F O'Sullivan captured the mood in *The Story of the GAA*:

'In the intense political excitement which prevailed throughout the country, and from which members of the organisation were not, of course, free, men's minds were turned from our national pastimes and the terrible conflict which divided the closest personal friends, resulted in the breaking-up of clubs in every county. At a Representative Convention held in Dublin, the Gaels decided unanimously in favour of Mr Parnell's leadership and this action had the effect of alienating the support of others who were not in favour of the "uncrowned king" retaining his position as Chairman of the Irish party which he had created.'

In 1892 the Association was in a poor state. The number of affiliated clubs fell significantly, torn by political dissensions and a bitterly contested general election. Only three counties took part in the All-Ireland hurling championship – Cork, Kerry and Dublin. The football entry wasn't much better with only Cork, Kerry, Waterford, Roscommon, Kildare and Dublin contesting the title.

Efforts by the Central Council to keep political controversy outside GAA affairs proved impossible in many cases. Feelings ran deep and the intensity of those feelings made it extremely difficult for those holding opposing views to meet as friends under the banner of the GAA.

Matters got worse in 1893 with the Association becoming almost completely disorganised. Only Dublin, Cork and Kerry were represented at the annual convention and the number of affiliated clubs fell to an all-time low. In the All-Ireland championships only Kilkenny, Cork and Limerick contested the hurling while Cork, Kilkenny, Wexford and Westmeath, were the only counties with teams in the football.

Happily, there were unmistakeable signs of revival in 1894. With wise counsel advocating the elimination of political discussion from the deliberations of the Association at all levels, the people of Ireland again found a common cause and purpose in the aims and aspirations of the GAA that rallied them and bonded them together from 1894 onwards.

Referee Jack Mulcahy of Kilkenny throws in the ball for the
Oireachtas Final of 1953 between Clare and Wexford at
Croke Park. (Photo courtesy of Billy Rackard)

10
The Provincial Councils

As the twentieth century dawned, men's minds began to turn to new structures for the Association. There was an influx of young men at various levels of the organisation and their enthusiasm and ability engendered new life into the GAA. The language crusade brought a further dynamism. The appointment of a full-time Secretary of the GAA was another positive step.

The Annual Convention of 1900 was held in September of that year. Delegates attended from Cork, Kerry, Limerick, Tipperary, Galway, Kilkenny, Wexford and Dublin. Michael Deering from Cork, President of the Association, occupied the Chair. Also in attendance were Michael Cusack and Mr Douglas who represented the London County Board.

Resolutions were passed in favour of the establishment of provincial councils. Earlier in August of that year concern had been expressed in Wexford and Kilkenny at the need for reform, with both county boards threatening to break from the GAA. Nick Cosgrave, Vice-President of the GAA, and Watt Hanrahan, both of Wexford, were to the fore in advocating reform. They came up with the idea of provincial councils or provincial committees and had it unanimously passed by Wexford County Board with promises of support from other counties.

The structure of the organisation as we know it today was about to take shape. The primary functions of the provincial councils were:

To ensure the smooth operation of the championships in the province

To deal with the finances within the province

To present a set of accounts and balance sheet at the Annual Convention

To take steps to establish an 'Action Plan' to deal with long outstanding debts

To work on bringing championship games up to date (It took them until 1909.)

Matters began to move quickly.

MUNSTER PROVINCIAL COUNCIL

A meeting was held in Tipperary on October 14, 1900, attended by delegates from Munster counties with a view to electing officers for the newly-appointed provincial council.

Delegates present were Patrick McGrath, Tipperary, P J Hayes, Limerick, J T McQuinn, Kerry and Thomas Dooley, Cork. Also present were Frank B Dinneen, Secretary of the Association and Michael Deering, President.

Patrick McGrath of Tipperary was elected President with P J Hayes of Limerick elected Secretary.

It was later decided, however, at a meeting of the Central Council held in Thurles on January 6, 1901 that the October meeting was not properly constituted. Accordingly, another meeting was held at Limerick Junction on January 27, with the following result:

Patrick McGrath, Tipperary

Patrick McGrath – Tipperary – elected President.
Thomas Dooley – Cork – elected Secretary

Controversy still continued and on June 30 another meeting of County Committee representatives was held. The following elections ensued:

President – Richard Cummins – Tipperary
Secretary – Thomas Dooley – Cork
Treasurer – Dan Fraher – Waterford

Finally in July Kerry joined in with the Munster Council.

LEINSTER PROVINCIAL COUNCIL

On Sunday, October 13, 1900, on the direction of Frank Dinneen, General Secretary, a meeting of representatives of Leinster counties met to form the Leinster Provincial Council. The meeting was adjourned to November 4 and at that meeting the following were elected to the Leinster Council:

President – Alderman James Nowlan – Kilkenny
Secretary – Watt Hanrahan – Wexford

By mid-January 1901, Kilkenny, Dublin, Wexford, Louth and Kildare had promised to affiliate to the Leinster Council.

CONNAUGHT PROVINCIAL COUNCIL

It was not until November 9, 1902, that delegates from Mayo, Galway and Roscommon met at Ryan's Hotel in Claremorris with a view to forming the Connaught Council. The following elections took place:

Chairman – Joseph McBride – Mayo
Treasurer – Michael C Shine –Galway
Secretary – Frank Dorr – Roscommon

ULSTER PROVINCIAL COUNCIL

Ulster was the last province to form a provincial council. This was done on March 22, 1903, at a meeting in Armagh. The following elections took place:

President – George Martin – Antrim
Vice President – Michael Victor Nolan –Tyrone
Secretary – L F O'Kane – Derry
Trustees – Messrs Power of Belfast and O'Reilly of Cavan

It is interesting to note that at the 1903 Annual Convention, provincial councils were directed to award gold medals to the hurling and football champions when funds were available. No doubt, the purpose was to add status and eminence to a provincial title. Heretofore, provincial councils didn't exist to honour provincial winners.

The establishment of provincial councils streamlined the structure of the Association. It was a logical step really in the structural development of the GAA. It was also a move of great vision. For it introduced to the Association a very worthwhile increase in man-power and brain-power. The provincial council structure has now been in place for a century and has certainly served the GAA very well. In recent times there were suggestions that this structure should be reviewed. Only time will tell what the future holds.

All-Ireland final, Cork v Wexford. The old style throw-in with forwards
and midfielders all lined up at midfield 1954.

11

Dr Douglas Hyde and the Gaelic League
(Conradh na Gaeilge)

Dr Douglas Hyde

D ouglas Hyde, son of a Church of Ireland Rector, was born in Sligo in 1863 and raised in French Park, County Roscommon.
On July 31, 1893, he, together with Eoin MacNeill, Fr Eugene O'Growney and others met and founded Conradh na Gaeilge.

One of its advertisements defined its objectives as follows:

> The preservation of Irish as the National language of Ireland and the extension of its use as a spoken tongue
> The study and publication of existing Irish Literature and the cultivation of a modern literature in Irish
> The support of Irish industries

Conradh na Gaeilge was strictly non-political and non-sectarian. Its official organ was *An Claidheamh Soluis*. It attracted members from all walks of life – ranging, on the political spectrum, from the staunchest Nationalist to the most steadfast Orangeman. By 1916 it boasted upwards of 1,500 branches.

In 1902, Douglas Hyde was appointed a patron of the GAA. Writing of him Donal McCartney said:

'Hyde argued that the practical steps taken by the Gaelic Athletic Association to revive the National games had done more good for Ireland in five years than all the talk in sixty.'

Both organisations had much common ground. Before setting off for America, in November 1905 to raise funds for the Language Movement, Douglas Hyde said he was one of the original members of the GAA when it started and he was still a boy in Trinity College. He felt that the GAA was the compliment of the Gaelic league and believed one was working for the physical and the other for the intellectual development of Ireland. The Gaelic League was a great ally of the GAA.

Douglas Hyde had a very deep-rooted sense of patriotism and nation-hood. He was a member of the Anglo-Irish literary movement led by William Butler Yeats. In 1937 he became President of Ireland under the new Constitution. In this capacity he attended an International Soccer game in Dublin in 1938. This led to his suspension by the GAA authorities from his office as Patron. He was never reinstated. His suspension caused a sense of outrage both within and without GAA circles. To have dealt with a man of his stature, in such a manner, in his ageing years, then seventy-five-years-old – a man who had worked unceasingly all his life for the promotion and preservation of all things Gaelic – hurt many people very deeply.

His name is perpetuated in Roscommon where the GAA county grounds are named Dr Hyde Park as a tribute to him.

Douglas Hyde wrote under the pen name An Craobhín. The following article appeared in *The Gaelic Athletic Annual 1908/9*. It gives a deep insight into the man.

'All good Irishmen desire to see Ireland a self-reliant nation. Nobody, I think, would wish to see the old Irish nation classed as an English County, nor to see the men inhabiting it fall into the ranks of imitation Englishmen. This, however, was very near happening, and no one seemed to know how to prevent it. Now, however, our eyes are open and it is plain to all men that there is really and truly only one possible way of preventing Ireland from falling into a second-rate English County, and her men from becoming second-hand imitation Englishmen, and that this way is the vigorous revival throughout Ireland of all the different marks of nationhood.

They may vary a little with time and place, but practically they are pretty much the same in every country.

The marks of nationality are language, manners and customs that distinguish a particular people inhabiting a particular country from the different people that inhabit other countries.

These manners and customs include the national games, sports, music, plays, dances and, of course, above all the language of the country.

When I was a gasún these things were not recognised; or, at least, no conscious attempt was made to act upon them. The establishment of the Gaelic Athletic Association by my old friend Michael Cusack – I was one of its earliest members – was an enormous step in the direction of Irish nationhood. I knew that Michael felt it so himself, and hence his remarkable power and enthusiasm to the last day of his life – an enthusiasm which was something more than a mere game as a game could ever have evoked.

Later on an even more important step towards nationhood was taken in the formation of the Gaelic League. Both bodies have so much in common that it has been a perpetual source of astonishment to me that there has not been anything of a real union or drawing together between them.

No Gaelic Leaguer that I ever knew of cared to lend his support to foreign games in preference to the native ones encouraged by the GAA. Have the members of the GAA reciprocated to anything like the same extent in aiding the ideals of the Gaelic League, or in running clear of foreign songs, dances music and language? . . .

. . . One Society is improving the intellect, the other the physique of Ireland. Neither of them is complete without the other . . . Well-developed Irish brains in well-developed bodies is the true ideal of the Gaelic League. Well-developed bodies with well-developed Irish brains ought to be the ideal of the GAA . . . And some day, too, it will help in its primary struggle for the revival of Ireland's language, without which the Irish Nation will remain like a half-plucked fowl.'

In the words of Thomas Davis, the Young Irelander, 'a Nation without a language is only half a Nation.' – Ní tír gan teanga.

Speaking at a Meeting of the Literary Society in Dublin on November 25, 1892, Douglas Hyde said that Ireland must de-Anglicise. And that this must be done through 'The Language, The Music and the National Games', but especially through the Language and the speaking of the Language. His motto at all times was 'labhair gaeilge le céile'.

Douglas Hyde died in July 1949. Louise Fuller in her book *Irish Catholicism Since 1950* recalled the occasion.

'At both Diocesan and National Synod level in the second half of the nineteenth-century, legislation was passed prohibiting Catholics from participating in worship with non-Catholics, under pain of mortal sin. The new Code of Canon Law promulgated in 1917, however, distinguished between active participation, which was illicit, and participation or presence at such ceremonies as Protestant weddings or funerals for a good reason as a matter of civic duty or courtesy, provided that there be no danger to faith or scandal to others. The Dublin Diocesan Synod of 1927 and the Maynooth Synod of 1956, in keeping with the new Code of Canon Law, omitted the relevant prohibitions.

However, this relaxation of the law did not find its way into practise. The event that most graphically illustrated this was the occasion of the funeral service of Douglas Hyde, the first President of Ireland, in St Patrick's Cathedral, Dublin, on July 14, 1949. Leading political figures could not see their way in conscience to be even passively present at the funeral of the Head of State. Austin Clarke has immortalised the occasion as follows:

> *At the last bench*
> *Two Catholics, the French*
> *Ambassador and I, knelt down.*
> *The vergers waited. Outside.*
> *The hush of Dublin town,*
> *Professors of cap and gown,*
> *Costello, his Cabinet,*
> *In government cars, hiding*
> *Around the corner, ready*
> *Tall hat in hand, dreading*
> *Our Father in English. Better.*
> *Not hear that 'which' for 'who'*
> *And risk eternal doom.*

The Convention of the day held that attendance at a Protestant service, be it baptism, marriage or a funeral, was sinful for Catholics. The funeral of a President was no exception and, in keeping with the tenor of the times as described above, Government ministers gave the lead in upholding the Catholic ethos. Catholic practise was in strict conformity to this principle until the late 1960s.'

(My thanks to Gill and Macmillan for their kind permission to reproduce this text)

Thus did the soul and spirit of Douglas Hyde – poet, scholar and patriot pass from this mortal life to their eternal reward.

As I write, my mind goes back to my schooldays and I recall that lovely poem of his, *An Gleann 'Nar Tógadh Mé*, that we learned by heart. He wrote it in his old age. I visualise him with his eyes closed as he reflects on his departed youth and yearns to be young again in the Glen in which he was reared.

The last verse always particularly appealed to me:

> *Ní hamhlaidh tá sé liom anois,*
> *Do bhí mé luath is tá mé mall,*
> *Níl fhios agam cad é do bhris*
> *Sean-neart an chroidhe is lúth na mball:*
> *Do rinne mé mórán 's fuair mé fios*
> *Ar mhórán – och! Níor sásadh mé, –*
> *Mo léan, mo léan, gan mé airís*
> *Óg san ngleann 'nar tógadh mé!*

Douglas Hyde was the first President of Conradh na Gaeilge – a post he occupied for twenty years. It isn't widely known that in 1915 he resigned from the Gaelic League. This followed on a resolution in 1915 at the Dundalk Ard Fheis, carried by a majority, to include the political independence of Ireland among the League's objectives.

Founded as a non-political group, Douglas Hyde and other moderates felt they had no option but to resign from the league.

Today, the Gaelic League (Conradh na Gaeilge) is still in existence. Sadly, the fervour engendered by this literary movement in its early days gradually waned. It is now but a shadow of its former glory.

Wexford v Galway, 1955

12
Frank Brazil Dinneen and the Purchase of Croke Park

'In the early part of the last GAA century every GAA pie had Frank Dinneen's fingers in it. He was the sort of hustle and bustle merchant that the Association could never have survived without. A handicapper, a journalist, a businessman and the owner of a splendidly unkempt moustache.'

(Tom Humphries)

Many of the spectators who enter the magnificent stadium that is now Croke Park have probably never heard of Frank Brazil Dinneen. And yet but for his vision and altruism Croke Park might never have become GAA property.

Frank Dineen

Frank was born in Ballylanders, County Limerick in 1862, and from early in his youth developed a keen interest in athletics. On May 3, 1885 the first big athletic meeting under GAA rules was held at Blarney and attracted a large gathering. The high jump was won by Frank as was the 100 yards handicap in which he clocked in a time of 10.6 seconds – a feat that caused him to be rated the best 100 yards man in Ireland at the time. Efforts by those opposed to the GAA to get Frank not to compete at Blarney failed.

Reporting on the meeting *The Cork Examiner* said:

'The GAA can at present lay claim to having under its banner the best 100 yards man in Ireland, Frank Brazil Dinneen, of Ballylanders. An attempt was made by one of those opposed to the GAA, to get him not to run but, like "the true man he is, he scorned such meddlesomeness and boldly stuck to his resolution to throw in his lot with the Nationalist athletes of Ireland".'

A month later on June 3, a meeting was held in the Mardyke Cricket Grounds. Thousands attended. Frank failed at the high jump. However, in the 100 yards handicap he again clocked a time of 10.6 seconds but was beaten into second place by T J O'Mahoney of Roscarbery who had a two-yard start.

In 1886 at the second annual convention of the GAA held at Hayes' Hotel, on November 15, in Thurles, Frank was appointed as handicapper.

In his time he held the posts of Vice-President and President of the Athletic Council. In addition he was President of the GAA from 1895–1898, succeeding Michael Deering of Cork, and was General Secretary 1898–1901

– the only man in the history of the Association to hold both posts. He also served as Vice-President.

In 1906 he published *The Irish Athletic Record*.

Politically, he was a Fenian at heart and was prominent in the Land League movement. 'Sliabh Ruadh' said of him ' . . . in the early days of the Association he took sides with the Physical Force Party against the Constitutionalists'. The Physical Force Party consisted of those who were prepared to take up arms, if necessary, to achieve what they believed to be a just cause, after all other efforts had failed. In contrast the Constitutionalists were those who believed in the supremacy of the law as expressed through the will of the people. 'Sliabh Ruadh' also comments that:

> ' . . . earlier, [Dinneen] was imprisoned as a 'suspect' under "Buck-shot" Foster's regime'. "Buckshot" Forster was Britain's Chief Secretary in Ireland and the instigator of two coercion acts.'

Frank was, however, conscious of the need to eliminate politics from the Council Chambers of the GAA if it was to thrive. He took concrete steps in this direction at a Central Council meeting held in Thurles on February 26, 1893, at a time when the Association was still reeling from the shock-waves of the Parnell affair. Frank, then Vice-President, took the Chair. He outlined to those present the depth of damage being done to the Association by the discussions on politics, which were taking place at club and Central Council level. He indicated that, while the GAA would always be national in outlook, as an organisation it should divorce itself from politics and concentrate on the ideals that inspired its foundation. The response to his call was positive.

A letter was read at the meeting from the Treasurer, William Field MP – a Parnellite – who wrote from the House of Commons urging the elimination of politics from the deliberations of the Association.

In November 1908, Frank made what turned out to be an inspired move. He purchased the grounds at Jones's Road which had been used by the GAA since 1895 for its games – a holding slightly in excess of 14 acres – for £3,250 plus fees, after he had tried, it would seem without success, to interest the Association in such a move. He then proceeded to effect very considerable improvements.

In 1910, with a view to reducing indebtedness, Frank sold 4.5 acres, located behind the Cusack Stand side, to the Jesuit Order for £1090. This site was subsequently repurchased by the GAA in 1991, as they embarked on their new development to modernise Croke Park.

In December 1913 Frank conveyed his interest in the property to the Trustees of the GAA, who following bonanza gates from a drawn and replayed Croke Memorial football final between Kerry and Louth, were in a good financial position to make the purchase.

Initially, but only for a very short period, the grounds were called Croke Memorial Park.

Frank made no profit from the transaction. In reality, from the moment he made the purchase in 1908, he had held the property in trust for the GAA. He perceived himself merely as a caretaker.

Frank was one of the great pioneers of the early days of the GAA. He died suddenly on Good Friday 1916 while working at his desk in the *Sport* office where he was Gaelic games' editor.

He deserves to have his memory commemorated in some special way at Croke Park.

Wexford v Cork 1956 (Photo: P.A Crane Collection. © Ibar Carty LMPA)

13
The Ban

'The Ban's origin is somewhat obscure . . . There is no recorded
reason for introducing the games ban . . . '
(Tom Woulfe)

The Ban was dealt with under Rule 27 of the GAA. In brief, the rule
stipulated that attendance at, involvement in, or promotion of
foreign games – in reality what were known as British army games,
such as rugby, soccer, cricket and hockey – rendered one liable to a
suspension, the term of which could vary depending on the nature of the
offence.

The Ban wasn't introduced at the establishment of the GAA. It could be
said to have gradually evolved before eventually being formulated.

Let's now look at the Resolutions, debated and passed, on this subject at
the various meetings of the GAA in its early years.

At a meeting of the Association in Thurles on September 27, 1886 a
rule was adopted, ' . . . that only hurling, football, handball, and athletic
clubs, including gymnasiums, could be affiliated with the Association'. It
was further proposed and passed, ' . . . that persons playing under rugby or
any other non-Gaelic rules cannot be admitted as members of any branch
of the GAA'.

And yet a certain level of tolerance prevailed. At an Executive meeting
in Limerick on April 11, 1887 letters were read from the Rosanna and
Tipperary Commercial Clubs asking permission for members to continue
playing rugby for a few weeks longer until the Munster Cup final had been
disposed of. Permission was given.

At the Annual Convention in Thurles on January 4, 1888, it was agreed:

' . . . that no member of the Constabulary, including Dublin
Metropolitan Police be eligible for membership of any affiliated
club, or be allowed to compete at any Gaelic sports'.

This rule was probably introduced because as servants of the Crown they
might operate, or be perceived to operate, as spies.

At the Convention in Thurles on April 16, 1893, the aforementioned
rule was rescinded and deleted from the rules of the Association.

Then at a meeting of the Central Council in Dublin, in July 1896, it was
confirmed that at an adjourned meeting of the Convention that had been
held in Thurles, 'it was decided that the rugby men could compete in
Gaelic matches'. A decision thereon was left to each county committee.

Between the 1896 meeting and 1901 the records are silent on the matter.
Then at the Convention in Thurles, held on September 22, 1901, a reso-

lution, against imported games, was proposed by T F O'Sullivan of Kerry and seconded by Denis O'Keeffe of Tipperary:

> 'That we, the representatives of the Gaels of Ireland in Convention assembled, pledge themselves to resist by every means in our power, the extension of English pastimes to this country as a means of preventing the Anglicisation of our people. That County Committees be empowered to disqualify or suspend members of the Association who countenance sports which are calculated to interfere with the preservations and cultivation of our own distinctive national pastimes. That we call on the young men of Ireland not to identify themselves with rugby or Association football, or any other form of imported sport, which is likely to injuriously affect the national pastimes while the GAA provides for all self-respecting Irishmen, who have no desire to ape foreign manners and customs. That we call on the Newspaper Press of the country, which does not profess to support alien rule, and all our public representatives and Nationalist organisations to sustain the Association in its struggle to crush English pastimes; and in its patriotic effort to make our young men more thoroughly and essentially Irish and self-respecting.'

The resolution was passed after considerable discussion.

At the Annual Convention in Thurles on November 30, 1902 the relevant rule was then amended as follows:

> 'Any member of the Association who plays or encourages in any way rugby or association football, hockey, or any imported game which is calculated to injuriously affect our National Pastimes, be suspended from the Association; and that this resolution apply to all counties in Ireland and England.'

Previously the rule was optional and at the discretion of the county committees.

At the adjourned Convention in Thurles on January 11, 1903, the following motion was carried by 24 votes to 12:

> 'That police, soldiers, and sailors on active service be prevented from playing hurling or football under GAA laws.'

At the Convention in Thurles on December 13, 1903 it was resolved:

'That police, soldiers, sailors in the navy, militia men, and pensioners in the navy be prevented from playing hurling or football or competing at athletic meetings under GAA laws.'

The Rule suspending members for playing foreign games was, by 25 votes to 24, left optional with county committees. In other words it was no longer compulsory on county committees to enforce the rule.

At the Annual Convention held on January 8, 1905 at Thurles, the following resolution was passed:

'That persons who play rugby or association football, hockey or cricket, or other imported games shall be suspended for two years from the date of playing such games; this rule to take effect on and from February 1, 1905 . . . and to be applied to all counties affiliated to the GAA. . . .'

A motion in 1906 to have the Ban on playing 'foreign' games left optional to county committees was defeated.

Again in 1908 motions proposing that no office or profession be a bar to membership of the Association and that the rule on playing foreign games be rescinded were defeated by a large majority – a response, it is believed, brought about by the influence of the Irish Republican Brotherhood.

In summary, therefore, it would appear that the main purpose of the Ban was to create an organisation devoted exclusively, through its membership, to the promotion and preservation of Ireland's games and pastimes.

The build-up to the Ban came at a time when it was clear to nationally-minded people that the Irish nation was in great danger of being subsumed totally into the British Empire, with a consequent loss of everything that denotes identity and independent nationhood – customs, games, sports, traditions, culture and language. The Ban certainly wasn't born of bigotry or bias. After all, Maurice Davin played cricket and Michael Cusack was associated with cricket and rugby.

It is important to note that resolutions on the Ban would appear in those early days to have been well-debated and rarely passed unanimously. In some respects the Ban could be viewed as a form of protectionism – an instrument of identity, born of a nationalistic outlook.

Down through the decades as the GAA grew in strength there was many a blind eye turned to Rule 27 – some counties were more zealous than others in enforcing it. Many a Gaelic player tried his hand at rugby or soccer; many, too, attended these games. The unlucky ones were caught and paid the penalty.

The two most notorious cases happened in 1938: Douglas Hyde was suspended from his position as GAA patron for attending an international soccer game in his capacity as President of Ireland; Jimmy Cooney, a great Tipperary hurler, was suspended for attending a rugby match. I dealt with this case in detail in my book, *Off the Field and On*.

The Ban on 'attending and promoting', was imposed in 1918 by Central Council, without reference to Congress. Similarly in 1923 Central Council initiated the setting up of vigilance committees.

Following the Anglo-Irish Treaty of 1921 there was a significant body of support advocating the abolition of the Ban at the Congresses of 1923–1926 incl. They took the view that the Ban had served its purpose and should end. It is interesting to note that two Presidents of the GAA of that era were openly and emphatically anti-Ban.

However, the motion before Congress in each of those years failed to find the necessary level of support and in 1926, Congress – probably weary of the annual debate – decided that thereafter the Ban could be discussed only every three years. The years rolled on but the subject never really died.

It is worth recording that at the Golden Jubilee Congress in 1934 power was given to County Boards to '. . . extend pardon to all suspended persons except those suspended under the foreign game rules'.

In the 1960s, when motions to remove the Ban failed heavily at the Congresses of 1962, 1965 and 1968 there was no indication that its end was in sight. And that despite the efforts of Tom Woulfe – a Kerryman, associated for many years with the Civil Service Club and the Dublin County Board.

He 'went public' on the Ban in December 1959. At his suggestion the Civil Service Club submitted a motion to the Dublin Convention asking that Congress set up a commission of enquiry into the Ban. As a result of the 'three year' rule the motion didn't reach congress until 1962 – 'there it got a hot reception and an emphatic rejection'.

In 1965, the Civil Service Club sponsored a motion calling for the removal of the Ban. It was passed at Dublin County Board level but was rejected at Congress after a record 65 minute debate and received 52 votes from an attendance of 285 delgates. Tom Woulfe had this to say:

'. . . the motion produced a remarkably even-tempered debate . . . it showed that, for the first time in forty years, the Ban could be debated without rancour at Congress'.

Then something happened at the 1968 Congress that paved the way for the removal of the Ban. Tom Woulfe wrote about it in the GAA Centenary Supplement of *The Irish Times* in 1984.

'At the same Congress, an innocuous Mayo motion, professionally packaged and plausibly presented, was swallowed without as much as a hiccup. It asked that a committee be set up to set out the present day reasons for the Ban; that the committees report be published in the National Press within two years to give every club member a chance to make up his mind on the subject by the time the Ban came up for discussion in 1971.

The passage of the motion represented light at the end of the tunnel for those of us on the anti-ban wavelength. For the opposition, they obviously didn't suspect danger – it represented the headlights of an oncoming train. There was an even more significant development at Congress in 1970 that gave the nod to a Meath-sponsored motion asking that Congress order a club-by-club referendum on the Ban the following winter. The press and RTÉ gave the Referendum massive publicity in due course.

The report sought by Mayo was published in the National Press early in November 1970. It recommended retention of the Ban on grounds which were manifestly untenable. The Referendum produced a very high pole. The results revealed a massive vote for deleting the rule. At the end of the day, 29 county conventions had voted it out. By the time congress came round on Easter Sunday 1971 in Belfast, deletion was a mere formality. The late Lar Brady of Leix protested alone. Rule 27 had passed away with the ease and elegance of a movement whose time had come.'

Rule 29 – the Ban on 'foreign' dancing was also dropped. Rule 15 which excludes members of the British Army, Navy and Police remains. According to Tom Woulfe:

'. . . there was a motion on the 1971 Congress agenda to delete it. Amazingly, the Rule 15 motion was not moved at Congress. Had it been put to the meeting it is likely that it would have been passed in the ecumenical climate of the day'.

Thirty-three years later in an interview with Enda McEvoy of *The Sunday Tribune*, Pat Fanning reflected on the removal of the Ban which took place during his presidency.

He described its removal as 'painful'. He would like to have held back the tide but he couldn't. As President and in the interests of the GAA it was very important for Pat that he would get the abolition of the Ban through Congress at Queens' University without a bloodbath.

'The best way of doing that, I thought, would be to have no discussion, to say that the counties had spoken, the decision taken and we had no alternative. Except for one interruption, that was agreed.

There was never such a media presence at Congress. The reason was the fear or the hope – take it as you will – that the Association would tear itself apart. We didn't. That was a happy day for me.'

Kerry v Armagh 1953

14

The Development
of Competitions

'Bhí uaisle na cathrach ar ardán
An t-easpag, an bardas, an maor
Ag comhairliú don slua bheith foighdeach
Is ag achainí orthu brú siar.
Nuair a crochadh an corn in airde
Corraíod go gliondrac gach croí
Is cuireadh gáir mholta go spéarta
Nach ligtear i ndearmad a choich.'
(Micheál Ó h-Eidhin)

At the present time All-Ireland championships take place at the following levels in hurling and football: Senior, Junior, Minor, Under-21 and, in hurling only, Intermediate.
However, as we shall see, such was not always the case.

1904 All-Ireland Hurling Trophy

THE SENIOR CHAMPIONSHIP 1887

For the first quarter-century of the Association (1887–1911) there was only one All-Ireland inter-county competition. That was at senior level. Initially, the club that won the county title went on to represent the county in the All-Ireland championship. That was the position until 1892 in which year the county champions were allowed, if they so wished, to select players from other clubs with a view to strengthening their ranks for the All-Ireland campaign.

The first championships took place in 1887 three years after the foundation of the GAA, and for the first and only time were run on an open-draw basis. Tipperary won the hurling title with Limerick winning the football title.

Only once, in 1888, was the senior championship not finished. This was due to the US 'Invasion' of Irish athletes and hurlers.

The political climate that prevailed from 1917 to 1922 caused the junior competitions to be abandoned – only the senior competition was played in those years.

The impact of World War II on the country caused the junior competition to be abandoned from 1942 to 1945 and the minor competition from 1942 to 1944. Only the senior competition was played in those three years.

Even in 1941, when the Foot-and-Mouth was raging, steps were taken by the GAA authorities to ensure that the senior championship progressed.

At the present time twelve counties, including London, have shared the senior hurling titles. There has been a better spread of the football titles. Nineteen counties have been successful.

THE JUNIOR CHAMPIONSHIP 1912

Competition at this level was introduced in 1912 with a view to giving more players the honour and opportunity of playing at County level and, for some, the glory of All-Ireland success. The competition was suspended in football and hurling during the war years, from 1917 to 1922 and again from 1942 to 1945.

The junior football was suspended from 1974–1982 inclusive.

The structure of the hurling competition, in terms of eligibility to participate, changed from time to time over the years.

Only three counties, Carlow, Donegal and Leitrim have failed to capture a junior title in either hurling or football.

Entering the second half of the 1920s, political stability had returned to the nation. The GAA had seen forty years of inter-county All-Ireland activity, but only two major competitions existed – senior and junior. If our games were to flourish it was obvious there was an ever-increasing need for more competition, more activity and more involvement.

One of the hallmarks of the GAA has been its capacity to look to the future and take appropriate action. Thus was born three more major competitions in the 1920s.

New Competitions

THE NATIONAL LEAGUE 1926

The introduction of this competition in 1926 gave players an increased opportunity to wear the County jersey. It took a number of years for the National League to generate interest among both players and spectators. It fell to the two glamour teams of the 1930s – Mayo in football and Limerick in hurling – to bring status and attractiveness to a competition that in its infancy had failed to ignite or capture the public imagination.

Mayo won their first of six successive titles in the 1933/4 competition and in the same year Limerick won their first National League title and went on to win five in a row. Both counties set records that still stand. Stamina, endurance and consistency are key qualities in National League victories.

The National League is the marathon of the field games world. Its format has also changed from time to time over the years.

During World War II the competition was suspended from 1942 to 1945.

The structure and operation of the football league and hurling league are reviewed and revised from time to time. At present, they both operate on the basis of different divisions with promotion and relegation a feature of the arrangement.

THE RAILWAY CUP 1927

The purpose of the Railway Cup competition was to add a further dimension to the opportunities available to Gaelic players. There already existed the glory of playing for your parish and county. Now, an elite of players would have the honour of playing for their province.

P D Mehigan 'Carbery' – player, author and journalist and a native of Cork – had this to say about playing for a Munster hurling team:

> 'It is every hurlers ambition to win an All-Ireland medal but the greatest honour of all was to get on Munster's chosen twenty – to be chosen for your province – the proudest feather in any hurler's cap.'

The first Railway Cup finals were played at Croke Park on St Patrick's day 1927 and attracted an attendance of 10,000 people. In hurling, Leinster captained by Wattie Dunphy of Kilkenny defeated Munster in a thrilling game by 1:11 to 2:6.

Garrett Howard, a native of Croom who played with Dublin, Tipperary and his native Limerick, played that day on the Leinster team and recalled the game as follows:

> 'It was my most memorable inter-provincial game. Both teams were star-studded. The game was a thriller right through – great hurling and very sporting. It was considered by many to be one of the best games ever in the Railway Cup series.'

Munster represented by an all-Kerry selection defeated Connaught 2:3 to 0:5 in the football. They had in their ranks some of the greatest names in football lore –among them Johnny Riordan, John Joe Sheehy (Capt), Joe Barrett, Johnny Walsh, Paul Russell, Con Brosnan and Bob Stack.

The Railway Cup finals grew in popularity and Croke Park became the mecca of ever increasing numbers of hurling and football fans on St Patrick's Day. Fans travelled not just for a day out; not just to see the St Patrick's day parade in Dublin but primarily to see Ireland's leading hurlers and footballers in action.

Attendances reached the 30,000 figure in the 1930s but it was in the '40s and '50s that the competition reached its peak of attractiveness with the hurling final of 1955, which was played on April 3, attracting over 52,000 spectators.

The name Christy Ring is synonymous with the Railway Cup competition. Selected at centre forward in 1942 he became an automatic choice every year up to and including 1963. He wore the Munster jersey on 44 occasions over a 22-year period and won 18 Railway Cup medals. His scoring feats were remarkable.

Des Foley of Dublin created a personal record by winning Railway Cup medals in hurling and football with Leinster on the same day. This happened on St Patrick's day 1962 – victory over Munster in hurling 1:11 to 1:9 and victory over Ulster in football 1:11 to 0:11. Both medals were won playing at midfield. Fellow province-man Pat Dunny of Kildare achieved the double in 1974 but on that occasion the games were played on successive days.

In the early days of the GAA it wasn't unusual for teams to walk off the pitch following a dispute. However, it isn't widely known that such a happening occurred in the Railway Cup semi-final of 1928. It took place in the game between Munster and Ulster played at Croke Park on February 26. Ulster scored a goal from a sideline ball that should have been awarded to Munster. With the score then standing at 2:8 to 2:6 in Ulster's favour the Munster team walked off the pitch in protest.

Unfortunately, the once great competition went into decline in the early '70s. Efforts to revitalise it proved unsuccessful. At present it is but a pale shadow of its former glory with its games often attracting a mere handful of spectators.

Is fíor a rá go bhfuil a ré reatha.

THE MINOR COMPETITION 1928

A further step towards promoting and popularising our games was taken in 1928 with the introduction of an under-age competition. It was available to players under 18 years of age on January 1 in the year of competition.

In the early stages of the competition there was considerable abuse of the age limit. So much so, that consideration was given to abandoning the competition altogether. Fortunately, good sense prevailed and the age requirement was adhered to and a competition that has produced some wonderful games down the decades flourished.

It was only during World War II that the competition was suspended from 1942 to 1944.

Subsequent Competitions

INTERMEDIATE 1961

This grade was introduced in 1961 for hurling only. Football was widespread and well-established. Hurling on the other hand needed every incentive and encouragement possible.

The competition was discontinued in 1974, following the introduction of the Senior 'B' competition. It was, however, revived again in 1997 when the Senior 'B' competition was abandoned.

The Intermediate grade, which was not age related, bridged a gap between junior and senior level.

The first winners of the competition were Wexford who after a thrilling 5:6 apiece draw with Tipperary won an equally exciting replay on the score 4:11 to 3:9

THE UNDER-21 COMPETITION 1964

So as to bridge the gap that existed between minor and senior level the under-21 competition was introduced in 1964. It has produced many outstanding and memorable encounters.

Success in football has been shared by fifteen counties, with Cork and Kerry heading the list with nine titles each. Hurling success has been

Datapac Hotshots – Hurling Team Selection

1. Richie O'Neill
UCC (Kilkenny)

2. John Tennyson
UCC (Kilkenny)

3. Ken Coogan
Waterford IT (Kilkenny)

4. JJ Delaney
Waterford IT (Kilkenny)

5. Tom Kenny
UCC (Cork)

6. Stephen Lucey
UCD (Limerick)

7. Keith Rossiter
Waterford IT (Wexford)

8. Michael Walsh
Waterford IT (Waterford)

9. Tommy Walsh
UCC (Kilkenny)

10. Kieran Murphy
Cork College of FE (Cork)

11. Conor Phelan
Waterford IT (Kilkenny)

12. John Phelan
Waterford IT (Kilkenny)

13. James Fitzpatrick
UCC (Kilkenny)

14. Eoin Kelly
Limerick IT (Tipperary)

15. Rory Jacob
Waterford IT (Wexford)

Larry Banville, General Manager, Datapac with hurling Hotshot nominees, John Phelan and Conor Phelan from Kilkenny and Waterford IT.

Datapac Hotshots – Football Team Selection

1. Paul Durcan
IT Sligo (Donegal)

2. Eamonn McGee
IT Sligo (Donegal)

3. Dan McCartan
QUB (Down)

4. Brendan Ó hAnnaidh
UCD (Wicklow)

5. Eamonn O'Connor
Cork IT (Cork)

6. Sean Kelly
QUB (Antrim)

7. Kevin Cassidy
IT Sligo (Donegal)

8. Michael Moyles
IT Sligo (Mayo)

9. Billy Joe Padden
QUB (Mayo)

10. Christy Toye
IT Sligo (Donegal)

11. Paul Finlay
IT Sligo (Monaghan)

12. Nickey Joyce
IT Sligo (Galway)

13. Brian Sheehan
Cork IT (Kerry)

14. Joe Sheridan
UCD (Meath)

15. Aidan Fegan
QUB (Down)

Larry Banville, General Manager, Datapac with football Hotshot nominees, Paul Durcan (Donegal) Sligo IT and Paul Finlay (Monaghan) Sligo IT.

confined to seven counties – all hurling strongholds – Cork 11, Tipperary 8, Kilkenny 8, Galway 7, Limerick 4, Wexford 1 and Waterford 1.

SENIOR 'B' – 1974(HURLING) AND SENIOR 'B' – 1990 (FOOTBALL)

For hurling, this competition replaced the Intermediate competition in 1974. It was run specifically for the so-called 'weaker' counties with a view to developing the game and rewarding those who couldn't hope for success at senior level against the established hurling counties. It was abandoned after 1996 following the re-introduction of the Intermediate competition.

The football competition in this grade had a short life – it lasted only from 1990 to 2000 inclusive.

THIRD LEVEL

Two prestigious Third Level competitions in hurling and football have operated for almost a century. These Third Level competitions have been further enhanced under the sponsorship of Datapac. Following the 2003/2004 games the company initiated a honours selection, entitled Datapac Hotshots – the Combined Colleges version of the All-Stars.

THE FITZGIBBON CUP 1911

The credit for this hurling competition, now open to all Third Level Colleges, goes to Dr Edwin Fitzgibbon. He was a Capuchin Priest, a native of Dungourney, County Cork, who was Professor of Philosophy in UCC from 1911 to 1936. The inaugural games took place in 1912. UCD captained by J Dwan became the first holders of the trophy. It was of course a 17-aside affair. From 1913 onwards teams lined out 15-aside. The competition, with a few exceptions, was played on a league basis up to 1948.

Down through the decades UCC and UCD have dominated the competition. Many of the finals between them were of fierce physical intensity. Rivalry was desperately keen. Glory and honour were at stake. Victory evoked pride. 'I shall never forget the Fitzgibbon Cup matches when I played with UCC' wrote the late Dr Jim Young of Cork when I interviewed him for my previous book *Giants of the Ash*. And this from a man who won several Munster, All-Ireland and Railway Cup medals.

Brian Lohan of Clare fame, talked in a similar vein. He recalled the 1994 success, the college's second title, with the University of Limerick:

'definitely one of my greatest moments in hurling . . . every time Daragh O'Neill, he was captain, and myself meet we end up talking about the Fitzgibbon Cup win.'

UCG won the occasional title, their first in 1919. Queens' University Belfast entered the competition in 1946 and won the title in 1953 with a team of 14 Antrim-men and one from County Down. In 1973 St Patrick's Maynooth won the title for the first time and repeated the success in 1974.

In the century to date victory has gone to UCD, UL and WIT on two occasions.

THE SIGERSON CUP 1911

Dr George Sigerson presented this trophy in 1911 for football competition between the universities. He was a native of Strabane, a poet, life-long nationalist and Professor in UCD. The first title, a 17-aside affair, was won by UCC captained by W Riordan at Jones's Road, on May 12, 1911. From 1913 onwards sides were reduced to 15-aside.

In the early years of the competition only UCC, UCD and UCG took part. Queen's University, Belfast, participated for the first time in 1923. They didn't compete again until 1933 – thereafter on a permanent basis. Their first success came in 1958 when captained by Hugh O'Kane of Antrim they defeated UCD by 10 points to 9 at Ballybay following a drawn game of 2:7 each.

Nowadays, the competition is open to all Third Level Institutions. In the century to date victory has gone to UUJ, Sligo IT twice and NUI Galway.

Where victory is concerned in both the Fitzgibbon and Sigerson Cups 'The old order changeth, yielding place to new' (Tennyson).

Competition and attractive contests are the lifeblood of all sports. The GAA provides for its members a wide range of different grades at club and county levels; also competition at every educational level.

Despite the attractiveness of international games such as rugby and soccer, which now have world-wide appeal, Gaelic games continue to flourish and attract large followings. Tickets for the big occasions are like gold dust.

Wexford v Tipperary 1960 (Photo: P.A Crane Collection. © Ibar Carty LMPA)

15
Far Foreign Fields

The Gaels Beyond the Wave
("Air: The Dawning of the Day")

Whilst love and praise we'er accord
The men of might and brawn,
Who foot the leather o'er the sward,
And wield the stout camán:
We'll not forget the exiled ones,
Our brothers stout and brave,
Who plod and toil on foreign soil –
The Gaels beyond the wave!

In English fields and mills and mines,
You'll find our young men there,
And where the burning sunlight shines,
On Pampas broad and fair;
And 'mid the deep Canadian woods,
And where the wild beasts rave,
In every sphere, where 'er you steer –
The Gaels beyond the wave!

Amongst the cities famed and fair
Of Europe, they'll be found:
Some hold the highest honours there,
Some thread the cloistered ground;
And down by where the Tiber sweeps,
Where lies our princes' grave,
They are loyal and true, and not a few –
The Gaels beyond the wave!

Upon the barren African veld
You'll find our lads today,
And in Australia too, the Celt
Has nobly won his way;
And 'neath the friendly 'Stars and Stripes',
That oft they died to save;
They are here and there and everywhere –
The Gaels beyond the wave!

Phil O'Neill "Sliabh Ruadh"

Wherever the Irish emigrated in large numbers they took with them our National games. For them, the games were an ever present link with the homeland: they played them; they cherished them.

The presence of teams at the Tailteann games in 1924 from England, the United States, Canada, Australia, South Africa, New Zealand and a shinty team from Scotland, bear testimony to what our games meant to our exiles.

In 1934, the jubilee year of the GAA, the annual congress was held on April 1. At it, messages were read from Gaels in America, Britain, The Argentine, Australia and South Africa.

The affiliated clubs in far flung fields in 2002 as published in the Congress Report of 2003 read as follows:

England	79
Scotland	7
New York	51
Nth American Board	61
Australasia	49
Canada	8
Europe	16

Let's now look briefly at our Gaelic games in some of those foreign lands.

SCOTLAND

In the early days of the GAA emigration to Scotland, especially from Ulster, was quite significant. At the Annual GAA Convention of 1904, held on 8 Jan 1905 in Thurles, Scotland was made a province of Ireland for GAA purposes.

The records show that Glasgow played a quarter-final game against Antrim in the 1905 hurling campaign, losing narrowly on the score 3:13 to 3:11.

In 1908, Glasgow earned the right to play Tipperary in the All-Ireland hurling championship but opted to concede a walkover.

On July 31, 1910, Glasgow travelled to Belfast and defeated Antrim by 1:13 to 7 points in a quarter-final game. In the semi-final at Jones's Road on October 2 they performed remarkably well before going under to Dublin on the scoreline of 6:6 to 5:1.

Glasgow's last appearance would appear to have been in the 1913 championship – the year of the first 15–aside competition. They lost a quarter-final game to Kilkenny at Glasgow on 21 June 10:6 to 5:2.

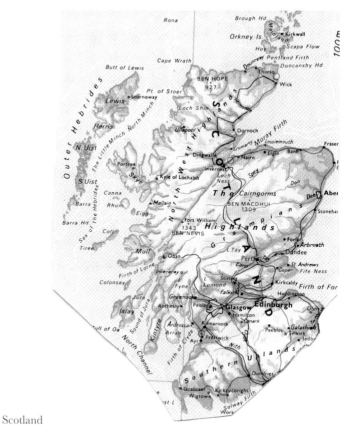

Scotland

It is fascinating to note the fact that it was in hurling rather than, as one might have expected, football that the Gaels of Scotland participated in our National games. The explanation, I believe, is fairly simple. Pockets of hurling strongholds existed in Ulster, chiefly in Antrim and Donegal, and the preference of these emigrants would certainly have been for the game of hurling.

AUSTRALIA

On a continent where 30 per cent of the population is of Irish descent it is not surprising to find our games played there.

Writing on the Association in 1905 T F O'Sullivan had this to say:

'Irish games also made great headway in Australia during the year, though reports of the contests seldom found their way into the Irish papers. In October, New South Wales' hurlers visited Bendigo, Victoria, to play the local team. They were received by

Australia

Dr Burke Gaffney, President, and W Jeffrey, Secretary of the Bendigo Hurling Association; James Brady, of the St Kilian's Branch of the H.A.C.B.S., and other prominent supporters of the game. The visitors were driven in drags to the Town Hall, where the Mayor, (Mr Luke Murphy) extended to them a cordial welcome to the City. M P Furlong captained the visiting team, and A Myers Flat acted as captain of the local team. The visitors won easily by 11 goals and 13 "behinds" (overs) to 1 goal and 6 "behinds". In the evening the players were entertained by the Bendigo Association at a banquet at the City Club Hotel, Dr Gaffney presiding. The principal toast, "Ireland's National Game" – was proposed by the Chairman, and responded to by E F Ryan, President of the Victorian Hurling Assoc.'

Several decades ago, an article by Stocaire in *An Dord Féinne*, the organ of the Gaelic league in Australia, described the game of hurling as follows:

'Hurling is more than a game; it is a National institution, and par excellence the pastime of the Gael. It has survived through long centuries and has borne with it noble traditions. Its origin is shrouded in antiquity. In its own sphere it is as true an expression of Irish temperament and mentality as the Gaelic language, traditional music, or national dancing. The national character is written largely across it. It is the creation of the Irish mind and it has evolved and developed with the growth of the Irish Nation.'

Many Irish players get invited to play in the Australian hurling and Gaelic football Championship. "Sambo" McNaughton, an Antrim hurling stalwart, tells the story that he was in Melbourne in 1982 to play with Sinn

Féin against Young Irelands in the Australian States Championship. To his amazement, when he took up his position before the throw-in, who did he find himself marking but Hugh Gilmore of Ballycran, Co Down, against whom he had played the previous Sunday in Ireland.

A perusal of the winners of the Australian Championships in hurling and football from 1971 onwards presents an interesting picture. New South Wales and Victoria are the strongholds for both, but Auckland, South Australia, Western Australia and Queensland have also had successes.

A Minor Football Championship was started in 1978. Success has been well spread with victories going to Victoria, Auckland, South Australia, West Australia and Queensland. The Queensland victory was its first success in any Gaelic grade.

In 1995 a ladies football competition was inaugurated. So far camogie doesn't appear to have made its mark.

In a continent where the local games of Australian Rules football and rugby dominate, Gaelic games are likely to always remain minority sports.

ARGENTINA

Irish emigrants took root in the Argentine in the early 1800s. Unlike their counterparts who settled in the US, the Irish who went to the Argentine settled in the country not the cities and over time acquired large tracts of land. They settled mainly in the province of Buenos Aires, about 70 miles to the west of the capital city.

They took with them the game of hurling. An Offaly man named William Bulfin played a major role in promoting the game, when he emigrated to the Argentine in 1884. He is credited with officially organising it there in 1900.

Reporting on the affairs of the Association in 1905 in *The Story of the GAA*, T F O'Sullivan wrote:

> 'Irish pastimes made great progress during the year, not only in Ireland, but in Great Britain, the US, Australia and in the Argentine Republic, where they were introduced by Señor Bulfin, editor of *The Southern Cross*, and some Irish friends.'

The Southern Cross, a newspaper of the Irish community, gave the game good coverage. The religious orders too played their part in spreading its popularity – the Palatine Fathers, the Passionists and the Christian Brothers.

The advancement of hurling suffered a setback at the start of World War I due to the shortage of hurleys which could no longer be imported from Ireland. In the 1920s and 1930s a possible revival was halted by the advent of World War II when, again, hurleys could not be imported. There was, however, a greater contributing factor to the decline of the game. Irish emigration to the Southern Continent had all but ceased at this stage.

In *The GAA In Its Time*, Pádraig Puirséal records that Canon Hayes of Bansha, Co Tipperary, who founded Muintir na Tíre in 1937, once attended a hurling match in Buenos Aires. He had been attending the Eucharistic Congress and had remained on for a short holiday. To his surprise, he was invited to throw in the ball at a game in the Gaelic Park. This is what the good Canon had to say about the game:

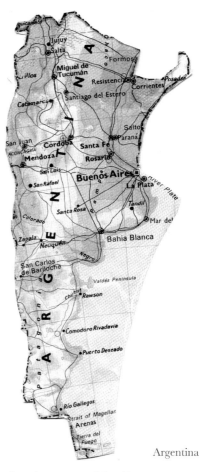

Argentina

> 'A better game I never saw at home. There was a great spirit of sport combined with enthusiasm. When the game was over the exiles gathered for a ceilí in a beautiful hall which stood in the grounds . . . far away in the land of the Southern Cross were these Gaels carrying on the grand traditions of our native games.'

For the Missionaries who went to the Argentine the game of hurling was a link with the homeland. Words do not adequately describe their feelings. From his school in Buenos Aires, Brother T N O'Briain, a Christian Brother, wrote to me on March 5, 1992 after he had read my book *Giants of the Ash*. It sent him reminiscing as this excerpt from his letter demonstrates:

> 'I can still recall vividly Bobby Rackard's majestic display at fullback when Nick O'Donnell had to go off injured [1954].
>
> I never knew Lory Meagher was Lorenzo – we always called him Lowry as kids. I can still see Shem Downey lording it against Tipperary in that league final; was it '50. I have never known anybody to dominate a game to such an extent, for so long a period, as Shem did on that occasion. After a long bout of great hurling in which Shem seemed to have taken on Tipp. single-handed I heard somebody behind me saying, more or less to himself "isn't he a great little man".

You may recall the incident which lost the '61 All-Ireland for Dublin. I believe the sending off of Lar Foley and Ryan (Tipp) turned the tide against Dublin. The Boothman brothers were flying at that stage and the writing was on the wall for Tipp. Two very doubtful frees against Snitchy Ferguson for picking the ball off the ground gave Tipp. two golden points which made all the difference at the end. I would place Snitchy among the great dual players of the GAA.

I left Ireland in March '62 (I come from Cappamore, Co Limerick) and haven't seen an All Ireland since. I saw every All-Ireland from '47 to '61, hurling and football (except the Polo Grounds). Since then I have been following the games on video tapes and have seen some of them over an over again . . .

The league final of a few years ago, Galway v Tipp., was a beautiful display of crisp hurling, with great continuity, first time pulling and outstanding individual displays.

We used play a bit of hurling here on the beach during holidays, just pucking about.

The Association grew from the common people of Ireland. The little men in the towns and villages supported it when it hadn't the prestige which it enjoys today. The common people have always been on the side of just and noble causes. God bless them.

Chaith mé fhéin mo óige ag féachaint ar fathaigh na fuinseoige in Oirthear Luimní nuair a bhí muintir Athán i mbarr a réime. Tá cuid acu ar shlí na fírinne agus an chuid eile ag feitheamh, ag cleachtadh, le h-aghaidh an chluiche deiridh.

Bua is beannacht.'

The game could be said to have flourished among the Irish community in the Argentine for over a century. In 2002, a group of hurlers went from Ireland to the Argentine to play an exhibition game. Unfortunately, political unrest placed limits on the success of the occasion.

I have come across no record of any effort to introduce Gaelic football to the Argentine by Irish immigrants. Given that it's a land where the international games of rugby and soccer in particular are now played with almost fanatical fervour, Gaelic football would never have survived even if it had got off the ground.

USA

Given the level of emigration from Ireland to America, it was inevitable following the US 'Invasion' of Irish athletes and hurlers in 1888 that the GAA would become established and firmly rooted there.

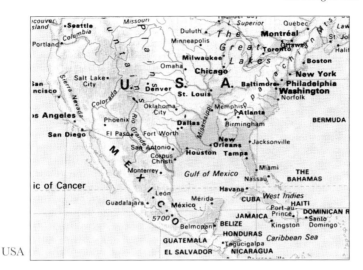

USA

As the year 1889 drew to a close there were about a dozen clubs in the US – among them, New York Gaelic League club, Yonkers Wolfe Tone club, Port Chester, Hastings and Newburgh. In Philadelphia there were three clubs – Thomas Francis Meaghers, C S Parnells and Limerick Guards.

On April 20, 1890, an Irish American athletic club was established in New York. It was to be governed by the rules of the GAA. The following November exhibition football matches were played in New York and on December 13, 1890, a great athletic gathering was held in Madison Square Gardens, New York. Among the events was a football match between New York Gaelic and Port Chester Sarsfields that thrilled the gathering of five thousand spectators.

In September 1891 the Gaelic Athletic Association of America was formally established. It followed from a convention held in New York attended by delegates from all the branches of the Association in the states of Jersey and New York. Its objective was to popularise and promote Gaelic sports.

Fourteen teams entered for the football championship and the opening rounds were played throughout the month of October. It was a 15-aside contest and the draws were as follows:

Sunday, October 4, 1891
Irish-Americans of New York City v Stars of Erin, Hastings
Farley Emmets, Jersey City v Kickhams, New York

Sunday, October 11, 1891
Gaelic, Jersey City v Shamrocks, Jersey City
Emmets, Brooklyn v Rangers, Yonkers

Sunday, October 18, 1891
Mitchells, Brooklyn v Barrys, Jersey City
The Faughs, Brooklyn v Irish Americans of Newark, NJ

Sunday, October 25, 1891
Volunteers, Yonkers v Sarsfields, Portchester

The prize was a set of gold medals and a gold cup for the winners. The runners-up were to receive a set of silver medals. Unfortunately the records don't tell us their names.

Throughout 1892 games continued to be played involving the following teams: Early Emmets and William Barrys; San Francisco Emmets and Shamrocks; Irish-American Athletic club and Emmets; C J Kickhams of Harlem and Farney Wanderers; Irish-Americans of New York and William Barrys; Wolfe Tones and the Irish-Americans; Irish-Americans and Shamrocks of Jersey City; the Gaelics, New York and Innisfails – also Garryowns; Emmets of San Francisco v Sarsfields, Porta Costa.

By 1893, Gaelic clubs were also flourishing in Chicago, which boasted 14 clubs, Kansas city and San Francisco. By 1903, a provincial council was established in California.

The progress of Gaelic games in the US is reflected in the fact that throughout the summer and autumn of 1905 matches were played on almost all Sundays between the various Irish counties represented in the major cities.

At the Annual convention in Thurles on February 24, 1908, it was decided that America be considered as a province of Ireland for GAA purposes.

As the annual flow of Irish emigrants continued down through the years and as they played Gaelic games the games flourished. The standard of play was high. In 1927, mighty Kerry toured America and lost two games: one at Celtic Park, NY; and the second at the Polo Grounds, before an attendance of 50,000 people.

A great Mayo football team followed in Kerry's footsteps in 1932 and they too lost their game to the Gaels of New York.

New York came to Ireland in 1950 to play Cavan in the National Football League final. They created a mild surprise by winning on the score 2:8 to 12pts.

New York repeated that success on two subsequent occasions: in 1964, they accounted for Dublin on the score 2:12 to 1:13 in New York; and in 1967 in a two leg affair in New York they defeated a Galway team that had won three All-Ireland titles in a row. The aggregate score was 7:8 to 1:16 – a 10 point winning margin.

New York's most cherished hurling victory over a Home side was achieved in 1958 when in a St Brendan's Cup final they defeated National League winners Wexford by 1 point – 3:8 to 3:7.

Every year, for over forty years, the North American Board Championships have taken place in hurling and football with successful teams emerging from San Francisco, Los Angeles, Montreal, Boston, Chicago, Toronto, Cleveland, Hartford, Detroit and Philadelphia.

Nowadays teams from New York take part in the All-Ireland senior hurling and senior football championships each year.

Fr Pat Doody CS SP wrote to me on March 10, 1992, from Norfolk, Virginia.

'I have just finished reading your book *Giants of the Ash*. It was a wonderful trip down memory lane for me. Living here in the US for the past seven years, I savoured it all the more.

Willie Hough was my teacher in Monagea, NS in the early fifties. He took a few of us to our first Munster hurling matches when he was Treasurer of the Munster council. Later a few of us worked the gates (turnstiles) going into the sideline seats. They got filled early, so we saw most of the matches. It was wonderful for us teenagers to soak up the atmosphere of Thurles on a Munster final day.

I was lucky enough to see Christy Ring play at the end of his career. I even saw Donal Broderick of Drom hold him scoreless for most of a game.

I am passing on the book to friends of mine in New Jersey. They have been in the US for over thirty years, but their love of the GAA has never waned.'

ENGLAND

Clubs under GAA auspices were formed in Wallsend and Newcastle-on-Tyne in 1885 and a club was also established in Manchester.

On September 6, 1896 the following teams participated in a hurling tournament for a set of hurleys – O'Connells, Hibernians, Exiles of Erin, Ireland United, Robert Emmets and Sons of Erin.

In 1900, England for the purposes of GAA competitions, was given the status of a fifth province. The arrangement was that the winners in England would play the winners of the Home Final to decide where the All-Ireland title would rest. The thinking behind this arrangement was to encourage, promote and strengthen Gaelic games among our exiles and at the same time create a link with the homeland. The opportunity to compete at the highest level was, of course, an added bonus.

England

There was one glorious moment on August 2, 1903 when London (Emmets) defeated Cork (Redmonds) at Jones's Road, in the final of the 1901 championship, on the score 1:5 to 4 points. In so doing, as "Carbery" put it, they took 'the hurling title beyond the four seas of Eireann for the first time in history' and as we now know, the only time. The victorious London team was comprised of men from Kerry, Tipperary, Limerick, Clare and Cork.

A year earlier on October 26, 1902, at Jones's Road, the exiles London (Desmonds) came within three minutes of what would have been a sensational result when they faced Tipperary (Two-Mile Borris) – perceived at the time as well nigh invincible – in the final of 1900. The score stood at London 6 points Tipperary 5 points. Then disaster struck. Dan Horgan accidentally touched the sliotar on the ground after it stuck in a rut. From the ensuing free the sliotar was rushed to the net. Disgusted at their hard luck, a poor puck out followed from the exiles. Tipperary forwards gained possession and thundered through en masse for a second goal. Thus in the space of three minutes the game was won and lost.

It is hard to credit that this London hurling team disembarked on the North Wall at 2 a.m. on the Sunday morning of the match. A few hours sleep and then to hurling action – and incredibly almost pulled off the sensation of the decade against a crack Tipperary outfit.

It is interesting to note that in both 1903 finals, played on November 12, 1905 at Jones's Road, Tim Doody, a native of Limerick took part in the two contests – unfortunately losing both.

Sam Maguire, after whom the All-Ireland football trophy is named, captained London in the 1901 and 1903 finals and played on the 1900 team.

The structure whereby the English champions gained direct access to the All-Ireland final was discontinued for hurling after 1903 and for football after 1908.

The Intermediate Hurling Championship, which was introduced in 1961, discontinued in 1973, and revived again in 1997, was won by London exiles in 1967 and 1968.

The Junior Hurling competition, which began in 1912, was won by London teams in 1938, '49, '59, '60 and '63. Warwickshire won three titles, 1968, '69 and '73.

A Senior 'B' Championship came into being in 1974 with a view to promoting hurling in the weaker counties. It was discontinued in 1996 following the re-introduction of the Intermediate Championship. London won five Senior 'B' titles – 1985, '87, '88, '90 and '95.

In junior football London recorded All-Ireland successes in 1938, '66, '69, '70, '71 and '86.

A glance at the hurling and football results of the British Championship over the past forty years shows that London is the major centre of success with teams from there capturing the vast bulk of the titles. Other centres of success are Warwickshire, Hertfordshire, Lancashire and Yorkshire.

At the present time football and hurling teams from London take part in the All-Ireland Senior Championships.

Fr P J Madden was an exile who corresponded with me on a number of occasions between December 1991 and August 1993, from Norfolk in England.

From his fascinating letters I give the following excerpts:

> 'Among the things I enjoyed about *Giants of the Ash* was the praise lavished by some of your contributors on opponents for their skill and sportsmanship.

My first introduction to hurling was the final of 1935. I was then an avid supporter of Limerick. I was standing behind the goalposts waiting to catch the ball when my great idol, Mick Mackey, took the last minute free that would level the scores. It was the point that never was and Limerick lost. I had to return alone on the train to Belfast very disappointed but elated by the skills and good sportsmanship of all 30 players. Since then hurling has been my favourite game and reading about the great players I saw in action (1935–1945) has brought back many memories.

Since 1946 I have been mostly out of Ireland: first as a Columban Missionary in Burma; then in the USA and England. At present I am convalescing from a rather severe stroke. Under Mick Mackey you write, "God gave us memories so that we could have roses in December". I am enjoying those roses now thanks to your book. If I ever get well enough to get back to active ministry I would like to use that quotation in my first sermon . . .

I had the pleasure in 1938 of meeting Micheál O'Hehir the day after he made his first broadcast. We were altar boys at the Mass of Final Profession of my sister as a Carmelite nun. I am sure in a later book you will be mentioning him and might like to use these concluding words of one of his last radio commentaries. It came at the end of a nail-biting game between Cork and Limerick which ended in a draw. Micheál ended his broadcast with: "Thank God for the hurlers of Cork; Thank God for the hurlers of Limerick. Thank God for the game of hurling." The date was, I think, June 12, 1983.

God has been very good giving me seventy years blessed with good health and now in the December of my life there are many roses to enjoy.

My father was from South Derry where there is a small pocket of Maddens, My mother was an O'Hara. She came from South Antrim, where there is a small group of O'Hara families. My first cousin is Paddy O'Hara who frequently broadcasts on RTÉ and BBC Sports programmes . . . He played football for Antrim in the early forties . . .

A second cousin to us both is Alf Murray of Armagh.

My only brother, also a priest, was Curate in Dunloy (1934–39). His housekeeper was from the neighbouring parish of Loughgiel. Both are small Nationalist oases in a territory almost 95% Unionist, and are GAA strongholds.

I have all the time in the world as I gradually recuperate from the stroke. It does me good just to write about my favourite game, which, of course, is unknown to the kind people here in Norfolk. I have a large framed colour photograph of Loughgiel, the 1983 Club champions hanging on the wall in my room. It arouses a certain amount of interest among visitors and staff but no one is quite sure whether the game is curling or a new brand of hockey.

I saw Noel Campbell play in 1943 in the All-Ireland quarter-final against Galway at Corrigan Park, Belfast. My own memory of Noel was of a very skilled clean player who would have made his name in a Kilkenny or Tipperary jersey if he had been born in one of those counties.

Several of my Columban colleagues made it to the top on GAA fields. Fr Tom Kennedy, the Bursar in Navan when I was in the seminary, played some games with Limerick just before the Mackey era. Fr Des Maguire, who died a few weeks ago, was on the victorious Cavan team of 1952. Fr Peter Tierney, still going strong in Korea, was on one of the winning Mayo teams. At County level, Fr Peter Campbell (Tyrone) and Fr Dan McGeown (Armagh) were well known footballers during the War years.

In hurling, our solitary All-Ireland medallist, was Fr Mick O'Dwyer. He played with Tipperary in 1908. Sixteen years later, he became Superior of the Columbans. Our present SG is Fr Nicholas Murray. He had several games with his native Galway during his student days in the mid-fifties. As A N Other, he also played illegally at Intermediate level, for Roscommon against Antrim. Two or three other Galway students also, were on the "Roscommon" team. The game ended in a draw. In the replay Antrim had a facile win – the students were back in College and couldn't get permission to travel to Belfast.

My general condition remains as it was except that walking has become more difficult. However, some kind local friends, have volunteered to take me to Ireland for five days at the end of this month. We fly to Belfast and then drive to Downings in Donegal, where my sister has a bungalow overlooking the sea. It will be a wonderful break, after two and a half years in this small room.'

1962 Football Final Kerry v Roscommon

16
Line-out Formats

Hurling games of the eighteenth century produced a tough, exciting physical contest between two disciplined outfits.

The manner in which the teams lined out, shown below, was published in an article by Liam P O'Caithnia in Part Five of *The Book of Gaelic Games*.

Line-out of eighteenth century hurling teams

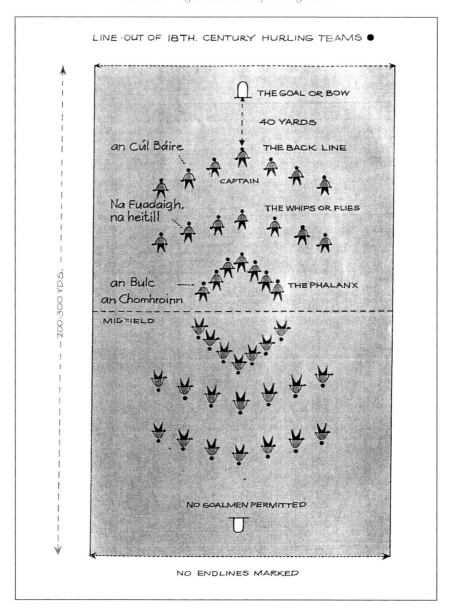

LINE·OUT OF 18TH. CENTURY HURLING TEAMS ●

THE GOAL OR BOW

40 YARDS

an Cúl Báire

THE BACK LINE

CAPTAIN

Na Fuadaigh,
na heitill

THE WHIPS OR FLIES

an Bulc
an Chomhroinn

THE PHALANX

MIDFIELD

200·300 YDS.

NO GOALMEN PERMITTED

NO ENDLINES MARKED

Teams lined out 21-aside; and a contest was often the best of three games. The duration of time was agreed beforehand.

The goal scoring areas were two to three hundred yards apart. The goal area was three feet wide and about six and a half feet high. The ball had to be carried through on the hurley from either side, to effect a score. The score was a goal as there was no such thing as points, goalkeepers, wides, seventies or puck outs. The first goal won the match.

When no goal was scored the side that succeeded in bringing the ball nearest the opponents goal, won.

The captain was responsible for the behaviour of his men – there was no referee.

In the Phalanx – consisting of big strong men with heavy hurleys – only right to left pulling was allowed. The task of the Phalanx was to get the ball to the Whips or Flies who would then try to outwit the opposition, by speed of carrying, with back-up support from colleagues. Or by a calculated puck ahead with a speedy follow up that might, if lucky, catch the opposition unprepared.

A player wasn't allowed to stand between the ball and the opponents' goal. Neither the captain, who generally played on the 40 yards mark, nor any other player, could advance nearer his goal than 40 yards, unless the ball had gone inside the 40 yards mark.

Wrestling was allowed but the ball could not be handled.

Lying on the ball was strictly forbidden.

Umpires decisions were at all times final.

Betting on contests was a common practice.

> *'In consultation now they stand,*
> *The captains move thro' either band,*
> *Hither and thither marking round*
> *The order of the game and ground;*
> *Appointing those, with footsteps light,*
> *Who are to bear the ball to flight;*
> *Who shall pursue, and who remain;*
> *Who shall wield hurlbat on the plain.'*

21-ASIDE 1887–1891 INCLUSIVE

The following diagram, as published in *The Story of the GAA* by T F O'Sullivan, shows how teams were usually placed under the old rule of 21-aside.

At the time of the first championship in 1887 teams consisted of 21-aside.
This continued until 1891.

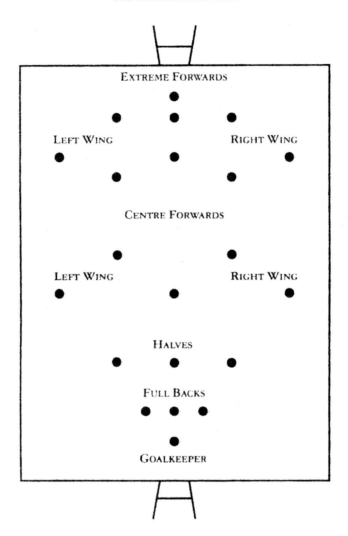

21-ASIDE

The format above was published in Joe Lennon's book T*he Playing Rules of
Football and Hurling 1884–1995*. It was taken from the Official Guide, 1889.

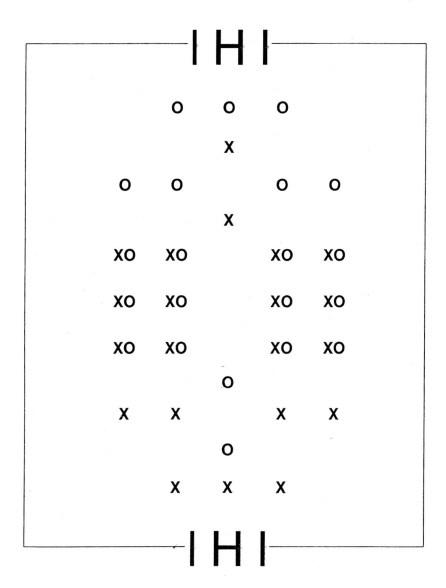

The 21-aside team line-out as shown in the Official Guide 1889.

There were only four 21-aside All-Ireland finals in both hurling and football.

The last of these finals (1891) were played at Clonturk Park on February 28, 1892 between Kerry (2:3) v Wexford (1:5) – after extra time – in hurling, and Dublin (2:1) v Cork (1:9) in football.

Victory went to Dublin in football by virtue of no number of points equalling a goal at the time.

The counties with 21-aside All-Ireland titles are Tipperary, Dublin, Cork and Kerry in hurling and Limerick, Tipperary, Cork and Dublin in football. Tipperary and Cork figured in both codes.

17-ASIDE 1892–1912 INCLUSIVE

The 17-aside line-out shown below was also taken from T F O'Sullivan's *The Story of the GAA.*

At the 1892 Thurles Congress, teams were reduced to 17-aside and this continued until 1912. The team's line-out is illustrated below.

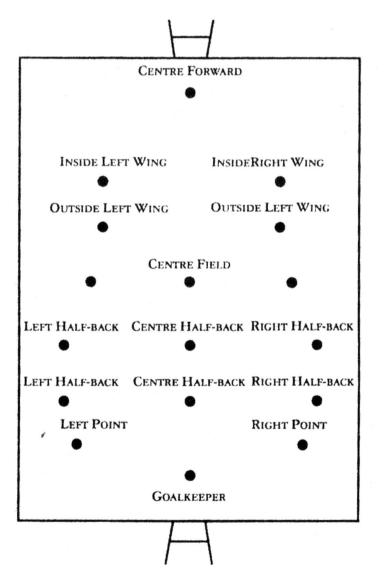

It consisted of five players down the centre and six on either wing as told to me by the late Mick Neville of Castlebridge who played for Wexford in the 1910 hurling final.

Twenty-one of the Senior Championships in hurling and football were played by 17-aside teams.

The hurling titles went to six different destinations:

Tipperary (7)
Kilkenny (6)
Cork (5)
Limerick (1)
London (1)
Wexford (1)

It will be noted that the strength of the game in those early years of the Association in Tipperary, Cork and Kilkenny is reflected in titles won – a trend that has continued to the present day.

Eight counties shared the football titles, with Dublin way ahead of the field, having accumulated 10 of their present day total of 22 titles in that era.

The football chart reads as follows:

Dublin (10)
Kerry (3)
Tipperary (2)
Louth (2)
Cork (1)
Limerick (1)
Wexford (1)
Kildare (1)

It is interesting to note that Tipperary, Cork, Limerick and Wexford figured in both codes.

15-ASIDE – 1913 ONWARDS.

GAA followers are very familiar with the 15-aside line-out which has been with us since it was introduced in 1913.

I have chosen to illustrate the format by publishing the lineout of the Kilkenny hurling team who won the All-Ireland title in 2003 – a success that brought them to a total of 28 titles and gave them shared first place with Cork.

Sean Ó'Siochain throwing in the ball

Limerick City Primary School Hurling Team

Michael O'Hehir starts football game –
Limerick City v Dublin City

Limerick City v Dublin City Primary Schools.
(Limerick Year Book 1972)

17
Some Key Rule Changes

1887

The revised rules for hurling and football were announced at the Second Annual Convention held on November 15, 1886, at Hayes's Hotel in Thurles. The new rules came into operation for the first All-Ireland hurling and football championships held in 1887.

It is interesting to note that the measurements of the ground for hurling were 196 yards by 140 yards, or as near as could be got; while for football, the size was 140 yards by 84 yards.

The goal posts were 21-feet apart with a crossbar that was 10.5 feet from the ground. Side point-posts were provided for the first time and were located 21-feet from either goal post.

No number of points equalled a goal. A forfeit point (five equalled a point) was awarded if a defending player was the last to touch the ball before it crossed the end line on either side of the scoring area.

Teams consisted of 21 players a side. Teams were selected from members of a parish and the team winning the county title advanced to represent the county in the All-Ireland championship. With a view to avoiding controversy a parish was defined as a district presided over by a parish priest.

All players with the exception of the goalkeeper lined up at midfield for the throw-in.

For the puck-out, no player from the striker's side could be further out from his own goal than the centre of the field, until the ball was pucked.

The score in the first All-Ireland hurling final was Tipperary 1 goal, 1 point, 1 forfeit point. Galway no score.

Given the extent of the scoring area and taking the final score into account, one can only speculate as to what type of game was played in those early days.

THE SCORING AREA

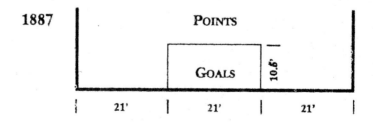

The scoring area in 1887

1888

At the Convention to reconstruct the Association, held in Thurles on January 4, 1888, the new Constitution drafted by Maurice Davin was approved.

Forfeit points were abolished. Instead a 40-yard free (later adjusted to 50) was awarded in both hurling and football.

The pitch measurements for both games were fixed at:

Minimum 140 yards by 84 yards
Maximum 196 yards by 140 yards

1892

Congress, held in Thurles on January 13, 1892, approved further changes with a view to developing our games and encouraging and rewarding the art of point scoring. To this end five points became the equivalent of one goal.

To open up play and lessen congestion teams were reduced from 21-aside to 17-aside.

To improve standards and increase skill levels the county champions, when representing the county, could if they so wished, select players from any of the other clubs in the county.

1896

As the progress of our games unfolded, their enhancement was very definitely under constant consideration by the governing body. Further dramatic changes were effected at Congress, held in Thurles on May 10, 1896.

Three points now equalled one goal.

The height of the crossbar was substantially reduced from 10.5 ft to 8 feet; thus reducing the area for goal scoring from 220.5 sq ft to 168 sq ft – a change that stands to the present day.

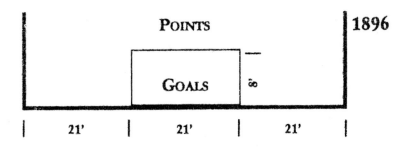

The scoring area in 1896

Pitch measurements were as follows:

Hurling:
Maximum 196 by 140 yards
Minimum 140 by 84 yards

Football:
Maximum 180 by 140 yards
Minimum 120 by 84 yards

1901

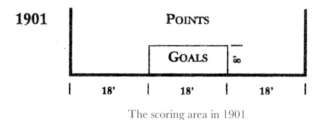

The scoring area in 1901

After two adjournments the Annual Convention was held on September 22, in Thurles. A sub-committee was appointed to revise the rules of hurling and football. They concentrated on the scoring area and decided to reduce the frontage by 9ft.

The goalkeeper had 24 sq ft less to defend in the goal area.

1903

The scoring area was again the subject under consideration.

A Dublin motion, at the Convention in Thurles on January 11, that the scoring area in hurling and football be reduced to 45ft in frontage, was approved.

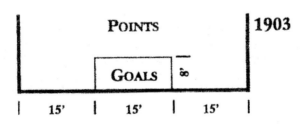

The scoring area in 1903

1910

After a quarter of a century that saw a variety of changes at regular intervals 1910 ushered in some radical adjustments that paved the way for the modern-day games of hurling and football.

The scoring area was completely overhauled:

- The side posts and the soccer-style goal-scoring area were abolished.
- Introduced in their place were two uprights, 21ft apart and 16ft high, with a crossbar located 8ft from the ground.
- Goals were scored beneath the crossbar; points above the crossbar.
- Nets were introduced behind the goal-scoring area
- A completely new feature was the introduction of a parallelogram 45ft by 15ft in front of goal – traditionally referred to as 'the square'. Goals were disallowed if attacking players were within the parallelogram before the arrival of the sliotar or football.
- Backs and goalkeepers were to take up their positions before the ball was thrown in.
- A 70-yard puck instead of a 50-yard was introduced in hurling.

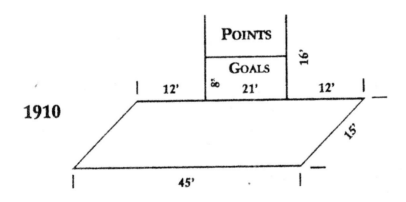

The scoring area in 1910 – the parallelogram in front of the goal was introduced that year. Any goals scored were only allowed if the opposing players were not in the parallelogram before the arrival of the ball.

The change wrought on scoring – particularly in hurling – was for some time to come quite remarkable.

If you look at the information overleaf note the swing from points to goals when the All-Ireland finals' scores from the decade before 1910 and the decade after are compared.

AGGREGATE ALL-IRELAND FINAL SCORE – HURLING

1899	4.16	1910	13.2
1900	2.11	1911	No Final
1901	1.9	1912	3.4
1902	2. 7	1913	3.6
1903	8.17	1914	6.1
1904	2.17	1915	10.3
1905	9.16	1916	8.6
1906	6.24	1917	9.6
1907	7.20	1918	10.8
1908	4.20	1919	8.8
1909	4.18	1920	8.12
		1921	11.7

1913

It was the twenty-seventh year of the championships. Teams were reduced to 15-aside and have remained so to the present day. The aim of reducing the teams in hurling and football was to enhance the spectacle of the games. The reduction in team numbers made an immediate impact on hurling. A sports journalist writing in the *Freeman's Journal* said, 'it was the fastest hurling final that we have ever witnessed'.

1931

A score direct from a sideline puck in hurling was allowed.

1933

The Association applied a ban on the playing of all 'foreign' games in its grounds. This move could be seen as adding another dimension to the 'Ban' – a dimension that still remains in force today.

1937

Pitch measurements for both games were defined as follows:

Maximum 160 yards by 100 yards
Minimum 140 yards by 84 yards

1956

Up to the mid-fifties there was no limit on the number of substitutions a team could make for injured players. Probably the most celebrated case in this regard was the 1938 All-Ireland Senior Football final replay between Galway and Kerry. In the dying moments, with Galway leading by 2:4 to 6 points, the referee blew for a free, which spectators took to be the final whistle. Suddenly the pitch was black with jubilant Galway supporters. Then there was an announcement over the loud speakers stating that the game had not ended and requesting people to please return to their seats.

The Galway players had not left the field and were to hand for the restart. However, when Kerry selector Jerry O'Leary went to recall the Kerry players he had a real problem on his hands. Prior to the game the Kerry players had togged out at the Central Hotel and Jerry discovered when he reached the dressing room that nine of them had departed to the hotel to tog in. The rest were gathered around Johnny Walsh who had been injured.

Jerry told those who remained, together with substitutes, to return to the field and finish the game. They did, and in the few moments remaining Kerry scored a point to leave the final score Galway 2:4 Kerry 7 points.

To this day I don't think anyone knows what Kerry players finished that game – nor, indeed, is it clear if they even had 15 players on the pitch.

From 1956 onwards three substitutions were allowed for injured players.

1966

The arrangement for the throw-in of the ball to start the game was altered as follows:

> Four players, two from each side, shall stand in two lines at the centre of the field – the other players to be in their respective positions behind the 50 yards line (football) and the 70 yards line (hurling).

1970

Substitution without injury was allowed.

1970 was also the year of the first 80 minute final – an arrangement which lasted until 1974.

1975

Radical changes were implemented:

- Protection of the goalkeeper. While the goalkeeper may be challenged within the smaller parallelogram for possession of the ball, physical contact with him is not allowed.
- Abolition of the third man tackle
- Larger penalty area (experimented with in 1974)
- 10-yards penalty for dissent
- Distinction between personal and technical fouls in the penalty area
- Seventy minutes game for Inter-County Championships introduced.

1979

The customs of singing *Faith of our Fathers* prior to major games; the kissing of the Bishop's ring by the captains; the throwing-in of the ball by a religious dignitary; were all discontinued in 1979.

1980 TO DATE

Key changes include:

- The abolition of the palmed goal in hurling
- The abolition of the fisted goal in football – with the exception of when the football is fisted while in flight.
- The increase in the number of substitutions allowed from three to five in both hurling and football.
- The 'blood' substitution.

Eudie Couglan kisses the ring of the most Rev Dr Hayden, Archbishop of Hobart, before the 1931 All-Ireland replay. Kilkenny's captain, Lowry Meagher, is on Eudie's right.

The Throw-in for the All-Ireland senior football semi-final replay of 1937, played at Waterford on August 29, between Kerry and Laois. Kerry won the game on the score 2:2 to 1:4.

18
The GAA Presidents

To date 34 candidates from 20 different counties have occupied the prestigious position of President of the GAA.

The Provincial representation is as follows:

Munster	12
Leinster	11
Ulster	6
Connaught	5

Maurice Davin is the only President to have been elected twice.

James Nowlan of Kilkenny was the longest serving President. He was in the position for 20 years, having first been elected in 1901. After his time, with just a few exceptions, a three-year term became the norm.

Members of the teaching profession have dominated the esteemed position of GAA President.

Below is a pen picture of each President.

1884 – MAURICE DAVIN – TIPPERARY

At the meeting in Thurles on November 1, 1884, on the motion of Michael Cusack, seconded by John Wyse Power, Maurice Davin was elected first President of the GAA.

A profile of Maurice appears in the chapter on 'The Founding Fathers'.

1887 – EDWARD M BENNETT – CLARE

Edward M Bennett, born in 1845, was a native of Newmarket-on-Fergus. He was elected President of the Clare Board at the county convention of 1887 held on February 14. He belonged to the Fenian tradition – took part in the abortive rising of 1867 – was active in the Land League and involved in

Maurice Davin

athletics. He was elected President of the GAA – the Fenian nominee – at the stormy convention in Thurles in November 1887 when he defeated Maurice Davin by 316 votes to 210 after the Constitutionalists had walked out.

He lost his position, however, at the convention to reconstruct the Association in Thurles on January 4, 1888, when he was succeeded by Maurice Davin.

Edward Bennett's reign as President was the shortest in the history of the Association.

He died on November 24, 1910.

1888 – Maurice Davin – Tipperary

At the Convention to re-construct the Association, held in Thurles on January 4, 1888, Maurice Davin was elected President for a second time.

1889 – Peter J Kelly – Galway

Peter hailed from Killeenadeema, near Loughrea, where he was born in 1843. He farmed for a living and was

Edward M Bennett

Chairman of the Loughrea District Council. He was also a member of Galway County Council.

He was active in the GAA from its early stages, was Hon Sec of the Galway County Committee in 1887 and was Chairman of the Galway convention in 1900. He was a member of the Fenian movement.

Peter died on April 18, 1908.

Peter J Kelly

1895 – Frank B Dinneen – Limerick

Frank is profiled in Chapter 12 which deals with the purchase of Croke Park.

Frank B Dinneen

1898 – MICHAEL DEERING – CORK

Michael Deering

Michael Deering was a native of Limerick where he was born in 1858. Prior to going to Cork, where he ran a business, he worked with Limerick Corporation. He was Chairman of Cork County Board for ten years. He took an active part in Gaelic League affairs. Following the controversy that arose after the 1894 football final between Cork and Dublin, when Cork refused to play a third game and the title was awarded to Dublin, he resigned from the Central Council. Michael died suddenly on March 25, 1901 – the only President to die in office.

A tournament was started to erect a Memorial over his grave. The Memorial, which took the shape of a Celtic Cross, was unveiled in St Joseph's Cemetery in October 1902.

The inscription read:

'To the Memory of Michael Deering, President of the GAA.
Died March 25, 1901.
Erected by the Gaels of Munster. God save Ireland.'

Croppy Pikes and the hurley and ball, entwined with shamrocks, and a raised harp were engraved on the Memorial.

1901 – JAMES NOWLAN – KILKENNY

This genial Kilkenny-man was an Alderman of Kilkenny Corporation for many years. He was a cooper by trade – a fluent Irish speaker and active in the Gaelic League. He was interned for a while in England after the Easter Rising of 1916.

James Nowlan

He was elected first President of the Leinster Council on November 4, 1900 and was there until 1904. He was the Association's longest serving President, having been unanimously elected in 1901. He was made a life member of the Central Council in 1921. James Nowlan died in Dublin on June 30, 1924, at the age of 69.

> 'He brought to the reconstruction of the Gaelic Athletic Association the healing influence of a genial nature, singleness of purpose and sound common sense . . . a wide vision and a practical sympathy with the younger generation of Gaels who sought an intellectual as well as a virile national resurgence.'
> P J Devlin (Celt)

In 1928, the Kilkenny county ground was dedicated to his memory and has been known as Nowlan Park since.

1921 – DAN MCCARTHY – DUBLIN

Dan MacCarthy

Dan was for years a leading figure in GAA circles in Dublin. To date, he has been the only Dublin man to hold the office of President. Dan served two terms as Chairman of the Leinster Council, 1909–1910 and 1919–1921. He was also Chairman of the Dublin County Committee and of the football league. For a three-year period he produced with P J Devlin (Celt) *The Gaelic Athletic Annual*.

In 1920, following James Nowlan's twenty year Presidency, Congress ruled that for the future, President and Vice-President should serve only a three year term. At the 1920 congress Dan had lost to Jim Nowlan by only one vote – 33 to 32.

Dan was a member of the Irish Republican Brotherhood. As an Irish Volunteer he was seriously wounded during the 1916 Easter Rising. He went on to serve his country as a TD in Dáil Eireann and voted to accept the Treaty.

Dan was opposed to the Ban on foreign games. He died in 1957, aged 74.

1924 – P D Breen – Wexford

P D Breen was a native of Carrig-on-Bannow and came to Castlebridge to teach when he qualified as a national teacher. He represented Wexford on the Central Council and on the Leinster Council from 1914 to 1952. He was Chairman of the Leinster Council from 1921 to 1923 and was a trustee of the GAA from 1930 to 1950. He was Chairman of Wexford County Board on many occasions, including 1921–1922 and 1941–1944.

In 1955, the Leinster Council of the GAA presented him with a special plaque to mark 25-years of unbroken service.

P D Breen

He won an All-Ireland senior football medal with Dublin in the 1902 championship – not completed until 1904 – beating Tipperary in the home final and London in the final. He won county titles in Dublin while studying to be a teacher.

He played senior hurling and football for his native Wexford and was on the 1914 football team that lost the final to Kerry by 3 points after a replay. He was County Secretary during the 1915–1918 football era when his native Wexford won four successive All-Ireland titles. He was opposed to the Ban.

He was born in 1883 and died in 1957.

1926 – William P Clifford – Limerick

William P Clifford was a native of Boher. He served a two-year term. He was Chairman of Limerick County Board from September 1921 to January 1939 and was Chairman of the Munster Council from 1932 to 1935. He served as player and an official with his club Fedamore.

In his time as President he initiated the development of Provincial grounds.

William P Clifford

He induced the Munster Council to give a grant of £1,000 towards the purchase of the Gaelic Grounds in Limerick – the first such move by any Provincial Council. William P, who was born in 1877 and died in 1949, was a Creamery Manager by profession. In 1936 he was appointed Chief Dairy Inspector with the Department of Agriculture.

My father, Jim, who was in the same profession as William P, came from a Longford family that was deeply involved with the GAA in that county. I remember him saying, when we were young, that he was approached when stationed in East Limerick to seek the Longford vote for William P, which he duly proceeded to do.

1928 – Sean Ryan – Dublin

At the Annual Congress held in Dublin at Easter 1928 William P Clifford did not seek re-election. He was succeeded in the Presidency by Sean Ryan who served a four year term. Sean, who had just turned 30, was the youngest President in the history of the Association. One of his first tasks was to officiate at the formal opening of Nowlan Park, Kilkenny, on the occasion of the All-Ireland Hurling semi-final between Cork and Dublin on August 26, when the grounds were blessed by Dr Collier, Bishop of Ossory.

Sean Ryan

So admirable was Sean's performance as President, that in 1931 – despite the three year rule – Congress unanimously decided that Sean should continue for a further year. He came from Bansha, Co Tipperary and practised as a solicitor in Dublin. Sean played hurling and football with UCD and was their Representative at County Board level in the 1920s. He maintained very close links with the GAA throughout his life.

He died in 1963 in his 68th year.

1932 – Sean McCarthy – Cork

Sean McCarthy was a teacher by profession and an ardent supporter of the Gaelic League. He was a native of Upton, Co Cork and played club hurling in Cork and Waterford, where he trained to be a teacher. After qualifying in 1911 he taught in Brooklodge School. He took part in the War of Independence.

Sean McCarthy

Sean was Chairman of the Munster Council from 1929–1932 and from 1938–1941. He also served as President of the Munster Council. He was at all times an uncompromising supporter of the Ban on foreign games. He also regularly advocated the provision of playing grounds for the youth.

Sean was a member of Cork County board for sixty years, having started as a club delegate for his native Knockavilla in 1913. He was a member of Cork County Council for 20 years; a member of Cork Corporation for 22 years; Lord Mayor of Cork on five occasions; represented Fianna Fáil as a Dáil TD for eighteen years.

He died in March 1974, aged 84 since the 22nd of the previous January.

1935 – BOB O'KEEFFE – LAOIS

Bob O'Keeffe was a Kilkenny man, born in Glengrant, Mooncoin, in 1880.

He trained as a teacher in De La Salle, Waterford, and while there won several hurling trophies. Following his graduation, he took up an appointment in Dunboyne, Co Meath. During his time in Meath he twice won the Long Puck Championship of Ireland.

Bob O'Keeffe

In 1908, Bob was a member of the Leinster selection that won the Railway Shield with a three point victory over Munster, 14 points to 2:5.

Around that time he took up a teaching post in Borris-in-Ossory, Co Laois and from then until his death in 1949 he was closely associated with the GAA in that county.

Bob was a very prominent figure in the GAA Councils. He held many posts including Secretary of Laois County Board and Secretary of the Leinster Council.

In the twilight of his hurling career he won Leinster titles with his adopted Laois in 1914 and 1915 – converting the second success into an All-Ireland title at Cork's expense.

This was the Laois team on that historic day, October 24, 1915, at Croke Park.

Pat Ryan

Jack Walsh   Joe Dunphy   Joe Carroll

Tom Finlay   **Bob O'Keeffe**   Jack Daly

Jack Finlay(Capt)   Ned McEvoy

Jim Carroll   Jack Carroll   Paddy Campion

John Phelan   Jack Hiney   Joe Phelan

Bob never played with his native Kilkenny. The declaration rule for non-residents didn't operate in Bob's time.

He was Chairman of the Leinster Council from 1924–1935, a position he vacated following his election to the Presidency.

Given the political atmosphere of the time, Bob, in his address to Congress, sounded a note of caution:

> 'Our national outlook has its dangers as well as its advantages, for there are within our ranks sincere and honest enthusiasts who may, without weighing up the consequences, unwittingly try to use the Association to shore up the power, influence and strength of a political party. There is ample scope for enthusiasts and absolute freedom of thought and expression for all members outside the business of the Association, but it must be clearly understood that our playing fields, committees and councils are not to be exploited in the interests of any outside body.'

The memory of Bob O'Keeffe is perpetuated in a magnificent trophy that is presented each year to the Leinster Senior Hurling Champions – the Bob O'Keeffe Memorial Cup. It stands at 3 ft 8 inches, weighs 564 ozs and has a capacity of 6 gallons. The Celtic Chase work has been taken from *The Book of Kells*. The hurler depicted on the top of the Cup is bare-footed.

(My thanks to Pat Dunphy of Carrigeen for his help with this article on Bob.)

1938 – PADDY MCNAMEE – ANTRIM

Paddy MacNamee

Paddy, a native of Armagh, was the first Ulster man to hold the post of President. His Presidential term of five years – an exception to the mandatory three years – was unanimously approved by Congress. All his life he was an ardent supporter of all things Gaelic – especially the language. He was Chairman of the Ulster Council 1935–1937 and 1943–1945.

In 1936 he was chosen to commentate on the All-Ireland football final between Mayo and Laois.

To Paddy fell the honour of formally opening the Cusack Stand in 1938 prior to the All-Ireland Senior football semi-final between Kerry and Laois on August 21.

During his presidency two very contentious issues were dealt with. They related to the suspensions, under the Foreign Games Rule, of Douglas Hyde, President of Ireland and of Jimmy Cooney, outstanding Tipperary hurler of those days.

When it was decided in 1947, by 20 votes to 17, to play the All-Ireland senior football final at the Polo Grounds, New York, the huge task of organisation and administration had to be dealt with. The skills and expertise of Paddy McNamee were called upon and he was one of an advance party that travelled to New York to prepare the ground.

He was Chairman of the GAA Commission from 1969–1971. This Commission was set up by Central Council following a motion, at Congress in 1969, initiated by Antrim, to investigate all aspects of the affairs of the Association with special reference to:

(a) structure of the Association at all levels
(b) finance management
(c) youth
(d) grounds
(e) communications
(f) hurling
(g) discipline
(h) sponsorship

A brilliant team was assembled under the Chairmanship of Paddy McNamee, then a joint trustee of the Association.

A first class report – one of the finest ever produced – was published in December 1971. In the years that followed, much of what was recommended in the McNamee Report, as it became known, was gradually implemented.

Paddy was also a member of the RTÉ Authority. By profession he was a lecturer and examiner.

Paddy, who remained a bachelor all his life, was born in 1896 and died in 1975.

1943 – SEAMUS GARDINER – TIPPERARY

Seamus Gardiner

Seamus was a native of Lisdoonvarna in Co Clare, where he was born on July 17, 1894. It was football territory and he showed his skills at the game in captaining UCD to a Sigerson Cup victory in 1923. He also played at senior level for his native Clare and lined out for Munster in the Tailteann games competition of 1924.

He trained as a national teacher at De La Salle College, Waterford and UCD. While in Dublin, he became involved in the administrative side of GAA affairs and represented UCD on the Dublin County Board.

Having qualified as a teacher, he took up a teaching post in Borrisokane, Co Tipperary in 1924. From 1931 to 1938 he was Chairman of the North Tipperary Board.

Seamus was Chairman of the Munster Council from 1941–1943, prior to which he served a term as Vice-chairman.

In his election to the presidency he defeated Dan O'Rourke of Roscommon, the man who was to succeed him in 1946.

Restrictions on travel due to the Emergency conditions associated with World War II made the term of his presidency a difficult one. He also had two other matters that required diplomatic handling. One was the controversy about the position of Gaelic games in the army. The second was more delicate. It related to tensions that had arisen between the Government and the GAA following the suspension of Douglas Hyde, President of Ireland, by the GAA in 1938, following his attendance in his capacity as President of his country at an International Soccer match.

After the election of Sean T O'Kelly in 1945 as President of Ireland, a series of meetings, initiated by the GAA, followed and a resolution acceptable to all sides was reached.

Seamus Gardiner died on January 10, 1976, after a lifelong association with the GAA in his adopted Tipperary.

His son, Fr Seamus, is at present actively involved with the Munster Council as their PRO.

1946 – DAN O'ROURKE – ROSCOMMON

Dan O'Rourke

Dan was a native of Tents, Co Leitrim, where he was born in 1887. He qualified as a national teacher in 1908 and taught in Warrenpoint, Co Down.

In 1911 he went to Tarmon in Co Roscommon, where he retired from the position as principal in 1955. Dan founded the local Tarmon club and served as its President, Secretary and Treasurer.

He played football for Roscommon for 15 years and is identified with the revival of football in the county. He was Chairman of the Roscommon County Board 1935–48 and 1954–56, enjoying the successful years of the forties. He travelled to New York with the Kerry and Cavan teams for the 1947 All-Ireland football final.

Dan was Chairman of the Connaught Council for two terms and was Secretary from 1915–1918.

He was in public life from 1917–1967 serving as a County Councillor, a Fianna Fáil TD and a Senator. His name is perpetuated in the local GAA field in Castlerea and the O'Rourke Cup which is presented to the winners of a league competition between the senior football teams of Roscommon.

Dan died in 1968.

I am grateful to my friend Gerry O'Malley – outstanding footballer and hurler with his native Roscommon – for information on Dan and also on Donal Keenan.

1949 – MICHAEL KEHOE – WEXFORD

Michael was a native of Enniscorthy – educated at Enniscorthy CBS, De La Salle College, Waterford and UCD where he played football and hurling. Having qualified as a national teacher he taught in Carrick-on-Suir before moving to Emo in Co Laois and while there he was a member of Laois County Board from 1922–1929.

Michael was appointed Principal teacher in Glynn, Co Wexford, in 1929. Later he became County Secretary and represented Wexford on the Leinster Council and the Central Council. He served as Chairman of the Leinster Council from 1942–44, a body of which he was a member over a period of 55 years.

He was a keen student of local history. His love of our native language led to him having a lifelong association

Michael Kehoe

with Ring College in Co Waterford – a college to which he won a scholarship in 1915 at Feis Charman.

The Leinster Council honoured Michael for his long years of service to the GAA in 1972 by presenting him with an inscribed silver plaque. Michael made two trips to the US – one of those was in 1950 when he accompanied the Tipperary hurling team.

Rugadh é 1899 agus dimigh sé ar shlí na firinne 1977.

1952 – VINCENT O'DONOGHUE – WATERFORD

Vincent was a native of Portumna, Co Galway, but his teaching profession led to him being a lifelong resident of Co Waterford – he taught in Lismore. He took part in the War of Independence, chiefly in West Cork and Cork City.

He was Chairman of Waterford County Board 1936–46 and was again Chairman in 1948 when the County won its first All-Ireland senior hurling title. Vincent was Chairman of the Munster Council 1950–52. He strove at all times to promote the Irish language within the GAA.

Vincent O'Donoghue

Even though his name isn't listed with the winning 15 that brought an All-Ireland junior hurling title to Waterford for the first time in 1931, he was part of the panel and may have played in some of their games.

He questioned the wisdom of playing the All-Ireland senior football final of 1947 in New York and made every effort to alter the decision. He died in 1972, aged 72.

1955 – Seamus McFerran – Antrim

My letter to Antrim Secretary, Eamon McMahon, was passed to Sean McGettigan, who very kindly supplied the following information:

'Seamus was born in Belfast city and educated at St Paul's Primary School in the Falls Road. He joined the Post Office at the age of 14 and progressed through various grades to senior level, before becoming Postmaster in Newcastle, Co Down, in 1960.

Seamus married Maura O'Callaghan and they reared a large family.

He was a founder member of the Geraldine Club – confined to post office workers. The club initiated annual games with Dublin post offices in hurling and football – usually winning the football – not a great hurling side.

Seamus was blessed with a fine singing baritone voice and was a member of the Belfast Gaelic choir that won the Welsh Festival competition against choirs from Wales, England, Scotland and various continental countries.

Seamus McFerran

He organised scenes on stage – before Riverdance was ever heard of – in the forties and fifties, that included long line of Irish dancing, singers and musicians. Seamus was also a fine MC at concerts and ceilís and was in great demand.

He was MC at a ceili in Belfast's Ulster Hall, attended by 1,600 people, on Easter Tuesday night 1941 – the night of the German blitz of Belfast. Artists that night were Delia Murphy, Jack Blaney and Liam Magee's Ceilí band.

The blitz started at around 11 p.m. – over 2000 people were killed. I remember that night as I was running a small ceilí in the Ard Scoil Hall and heard the sirens that told the Germans were on their way. I walked up Falls Road – beautiful clear starry night with a full moon, no one on the street, windows all blacked out – and went past Clonard Church where protestants from the Shankill flocked down into the Monastery vaults where all prayed and got tea. Bombs hopped all round our house that night in 1941.

In 1944 Seamus McFerran was elected Chairman of Antrim County Board. At that year's Convention I proposed from my club (Rossa) that a committee be set up to raise funds for the levelling of Corrigan Park – the then County grounds.

The motion was agreed and the County executive set up a committee with me as Chairman. Seamus McFerran became active in it from the start, becoming Publicity Officer and doing a wonderful job.

The Committee raised, in around ten years, £130.000. During that time a decision was taken to find an alternative to Corrigan Park. And so was born Casement Park, following plans drawn up by architect Danny McDaniels. The cost of the land in 1947 was £5000. Casement Park was opened in 1953, debt free.

Seamus was Antrim's and Ulster's second President. He was Chairman of the Ulster Council in 1949 and was the Antrim delegate to the Ulster Council for several years.

It goes without saying, had Seamus not been Antrim Chairman, there would be no Casement Park. I worked with him for around ten years. He gave me my head – let me get on with my ideas to make money for building Casement.

Along with making Casement, Seamus bought thirty acres at Shaw's Road. Now, three Belfast clubs have pitches. Thirty acres cost £20,000 in 1949 – no debt.

Antrim GAA owes a great debt to Seamus McFerran – the right man, at the right time – a great Chairman – and a great friend of mine. He died young (51), before his time.'

1958 – Dr Joseph J Stuart – Dublin

Joseph Stuart was born in Ogonelloe in East Clare in 1904, one of a family of 16 children. He pursued a career in medicine and was in his time Master of the Coombe Maternity Hospital.

He delivered into this world on a Whit Sunday afternoon the eminent cardiac surgeon, Maurice Neligan, as recounted in an *Irish Times'* article of February 24, 2004:

Dr Joseph J Stuart

'I was born in Booterstown, Co Dublin, in May 1937. I was a domiciliary birth – not uncommon then – and was delivered by Dr Joe Stuart, later President of the GAA and a friend of my parents.'

I decided to write to Maurice Neligan and to ask among other things if he had any link with 'The Spy in the Castle'. This was his reply:

'Yes, Joe Stuart delivered me at home, and I believe his incursions onto the pitch in Croke Park were often greeted with hilarity by the crowd in view of the nature of his speciality. You are quite correct too in your other conclusion. My Uncle David was "The Spy in the Castle" for Michael Collins. My grandfather, born in Kerry, became the NT in Templeglantine, Co Limerick, so I am a typical Irish mix – Dublin, Limerick, Kerry and on my mother's side Roscommon and Galway.'

Joe was a prominent referee for over a decade during which time he officiated at National League, Railway Cup, and championship games. He took charge of the 1943 All-Ireland senior hurling final between Cork and Antrim – which was won by Cork.

He survived a contest for the Presidency that included five candidates. Dr Stuart had a lifelong association with Gaelic games and athletics at UCD and as a student hurled with UCD in the Fitzgibbon Cup competition. He also hurled with St Flannan's College, St Joseph's of Ballinasloe and Croom in Co Limerick. He served for many years as Vice-Chairman of the Dublin County Board and was Chairman of the Leinster Council 1954–1956

The provision of medical attention for players at major games in Croke Park was pioneered by Joe Stuart – not surprisingly, I suppose, given the nature of his profession.

Joe was born in 1904 and died in 1980.

1961 – HUGH BYRNE – WICKLOW

'He started in the schoolyard in Rathcoyle, Rathdangan and worked his way via club, district and county to the top post in the GAA. He was a crack sprinter, a good club footballer and a Chairman who knew the rules backwards.'

Hugh Byrne

Kicking football at lunchtime in the national schoolyard, Hugh Byrne, son of P J Byrne, "the old Master", was known as "Hugh the Master" to distinguish him in a school that was full of Byrnes. He was educated at Patrician College, Ballyfin – my own Alma Mater – and later at St Patrick's, Drumcondra. In his youth he excelled at handball, football and athletics. He was a first class sprinter and won many events in the 100 yards and 220 yards.

He graduated from UCD with a BA and MA and took up a teaching post in Bray. There, in 1934 he won a Co Wicklow football title with Bray Emmets. Martin O'Neill of Wexford fame was a team-mate. The following year they made it two in a row.

Hugh then moved back to his native Rathcoyle to teach. With his three brothers Mick, Paddy and Nick he joined the Rathdangan team. On a Sunday afternoon in June 1936 they defied the odds in the county semi-final and recorded a shock victory over Bray Emmets before going on to defeat Donard in the final. For Hugh it was a historic three in a row. Later in the thirties he played on the county junior football team.

Hugh was club delegate at West Board and County Board meetings and actively involved in organising the youth competitions in his own area.

He spent a term as Chairman of the West Board and in 1947, at the County Convention in Bray, he replaced his namesake C M Byrne as Chairman of the County Board. Hugh served in that post for 22 years.

He is credited with having had a tremendous grasp of the rules and having brought great dignity and honour to every post he held in the Association.

Hugh was Chairman of the Leinster Council from 1957–1959, having served as Vice-Chairman from 1954 – a body of which he was a member for over 25 years. In 1966 he was elected Treasurer of the Leinster Council. He was a Trustee of the Association in the years 1968,'69 and '70.

At the election for the Presidency at the Gresham Hotel in Dublin on Easter Sunday, April 2, 1961, Hugh held off the challenge of Jack Barrett of Cork and Jack Fitzgerald of Meath, to become Wicklow's first GAA's President.

(My thanks and appreciation to Jimmy Dunne for his kind assistance with this article.)

1964 – ALF MURRAY – ARMAGH

Alf Murray was born in Miltown, Co Down. However, his name in the GAA world will always be associated with Co Armagh. With his adopted county he was an outstanding footballer and equally brilliant at Provincial level with Ulster.

His first taste of inter-county success came in 1935 when he was on the Armagh Junior Football team that defeated Derry by 3:6 to 3:2 in the Ulster final. From 1935 onwards he was on the Armagh Senior team.

Alf was a regular on Ulster Railway Cup teams from 1937– 1945. He played in five Railway Cup football finals and was successful on two occasions – 1942, when a Munster team consisting of 14 Kerrymen, many of them legendary, was defeated and 1943 when Leinster were overcome. The two wins were Ulster's first titles in the then very prestigious competition that began in 1927.

The 1942 Ulster team read as follows:

B Kelly
(Cavan)

E McLoughlin	Barney Cully	Tom O'Reilly
(Armagh)	(Cavan)	(Cavan)
G Smith	Jim McCullagh	Vincent Duffy
(Cavan)	(Armagh)	(Monaghan)

Columba McDyer   John Joe O'Reilly
(Donegal)   (Cavan)

Kevin Armstrong	**Alf Murray**	T P O'Reilly
(Antrim)	(Armagh)	(Cavan)
B Cullen	Simon Deignan	Hughie Gallagher
(Tyrone)	(Cavan)	(Donegal)

He won an Armagh senior football title with Lurgan in 1943. He was Secretary of Armagh County Board 1936–37 and 1942–43. He was a member of the Ulster Council for 26 years from 1938 and was Chairman from 1946 to 1949. Alf who was a teacher by profession was an ardent and tireless worker in the language movement and a strong supporter of the Ban.

Many would place Alf among the 'All-time Great' footballers. In 1986 he was honoured with the All-time All-star football award.

Alf Murray

1967 – SEAMUS O'RIAIN – TIPPERARY

Seamus O'Riain – born April 2, 1916 – is a native of Tipperary and now resides in Moneygall. He won a Waterford County hurling medal with De La Salle in the mid thirties as he trained to be a teacher. He taught at Cloughjordan, Newcastle West, Borrisokane and finally at Dunkerrin NS.

He played at inter-county level with his native Tipperary in junior hurling and junior football. He was an accomplished all-round athlete, specialising in the 440 yards and the long jump. During his two years in De La Salle College Waterford, he won the Gold Medal each year for the best all-rounder.

He held a wide variety of GAA posts including Chairman of the Munster Council 1965–67; Chairman of the Tipperary County Board 1970–73; Chairman of the North Tipp Board 1957–66; Chairman of his club, Moneygall, from 1974–1984; Chairman of County Tipperary NACA in the fifties; a founder member of Féile na nGael in 1971.

Twice during his presidency he saw his native Tipperary defeated in the All-Ireland senior hurling final – in 1967 by Kilkenny, 1968 by Wexford.

His grandson Shane Ryan is at present excelling at senior hurling and senior football with Dublin.

Seamus O'Riain

1970 – PAT FANNING – WATERFORD

Pat Fanning

Pat Fanning, a Social Welfare Official, has been associated with the Mount Sion Club all his life – Secretary 1940–1955, Chairman 1955–1970 and 1978 – 1986, when he was honoured with life Presidency.

Pat has been the Waterford delegate to Congress since 1948. He was the County's delegate to the Munster Council in the forties and fifties. He was Chairman of the Waterford County Board from 1955 to 1963, 1969–1970 and 1975–1978.

Pat was Chairman of the Munster Council 1962–1965.

North Monastery deprived Pat and Mount Sion CBS of a Harty cup victory in 1936. He went on to win seven county senior hurling titles between 1938 and 1949 with Mount Sion, having earlier in 1934 won a county minor title. He played at all levels for his county and was a member of the All-Ireland panel of 1948 up to the Munster final. That same year Pat was the trainer of the Waterford minor hurling team that won All-Ireland honours.

He was the first Chairman of the GAA Policy Committee 1964–1970 and from 1975 to 1982 he was successively Chairman of the Development Committee and Communications Committee.

In the Centenary Year of 1984 he had the honour of chairing the Symposium Committee at UCC, as the GAA celebrated the centenary.

Born on August 25, 1918, Pat has witnessed many memorable games down the years. He has seen great men in action. Two occasions, in particular, will remain forever vivid in his memory. They call to mind the heroics and brilliance of that great hurling son of the Decies, John Keane, 'who played the game with verve and fire but always in true Gaelic spirit'.

'I recall 1937 at Clonmel. Few who saw Waterford's battle with unconquerable Limerick in 1937 will ever forget John Keane's display on the greatest ever forward, Mick Mackey of Ahane. The barely 20-year-old Waterford man took the honours in one of the best man-to-man tussles I have ever seen on a hurling field – the strapping figure in blue and white thwarting the great Mick

Mackey; the blonde, curly head bobbing, as Keane threw back attack after attack in one of the really great games of the Munster championship.

Then came the greatest display of courage and determination and perhaps his greatest personal triumph – his epic display at Dungarvan in 1943, when with a badly injured ankle he stood at centre back and almost alone broke the back of every Tipperary attack. Well I do remember cutting the boot from his swollen leg at the end of that excruciating hour. And I recall, too, the old wizened man of Tipperary who pushed his way through the crowd to where John lay, to shake, as he said "the hand of John Keane, the greatest man in Ireland."'

Pádraig Ó Fainín

1973 – DONAL KEENAN – ROSCOMMON

Donal, a medical doctor by profession, was a native of Elfin with whom he won a county title in 1937. He won an All-Ireland junior football medal in 1940 and was an outstanding member of a great Roscommon team of the 40s with whom he played until 1950 – winning Connaught titles in 1943, '44, '46, '47 and All-Ireland titles in 1943 and 1944.

The victorious 1944 team lined out as follows:

Owensie Hoare

Bill Jackson   J P O'Callaghan   Jack Casserly

Brendan Lynch   Bill Carlos   Phelim Murray

Eddie Boland   Liam Gilmartin

Frankie Kinlough   Jimmy Murray (Capt)   **Donal Keenan**

Hugh Gibbons   Jack McQuillan   John Joe Nerney

Donal also played for Connaught in the Railway Cup. He was the team's freetaker and was deadly accurate.

He won a Dublin county senior football medal with UCD whom he captained to victory in the early forties. In 1945, he won a Sigerson Cup title with the college under the captaincy of Sean Flanagan of Mayo. Some other great names on that team were Barney Cully, P J Duke of Cavan, Padraic Carney and Joe Gilvarry of Mayo, Jackie Culleton of Wexford and Frankie Kinlough of Roscommon.

He spent a term as Chairman of the Connaught council. Donal was County Board Chairman from 1957–1972 during which time he acted as coach and selector to Roscommon teams. In 1962, when Roscommon and Kerry met in the All-Ireland senior football final, it was a clash of doctors – trainer Donal Keenan v trainer Eamon O'Sullivan – with victory going to the Kingdom.

Donal Keenan died in the early nineties on a golf course in Kerry.

Donal Keenan

1976 – CON MURPHY – CORK

'Con Murphy's role as a player and referee, would earn him a place among the immortals of the Gaelic Athletic Association, but his amazing dedication and durability to the administrative side of the Association truly defies description . . .'
Tomas O'Mainnchin

'A man of amazing energy and commitment . . . He strove for perfection in all that he undertook and attained the highest levels of achievement as a player, referee, and an administrator.'
Christy Cooney

Con Murphy was born on October 28, 1922, in Toureen, Co Cork. From his days at primary school to date he has been involved in GAA affairs – proud of his club Valley Rovers and his divisional team Carraig. Club delegate to south-east Division 1938–1947 and from 1944 to 1950 was the South-east Division Representative on Cork County Board; from 1948 to 1956 was Chairman of South East Division Board.

Con Murphy

At North Mon CBS he won three Harty Cup hurling titles and was Captain in 1941 and 1942. He played inter-provincial colleges with Munster. For his county he played minor, junior and senior hurling as well as minor football.

Con was a member of a wonderful Cork hurling team of the 40s with whom he won five Munster titles, four All-Ireland medals and one National league.

He won his last All-Ireland with Cork in 1946. Many regard that team as one of the greatest ever to leave the Leeside. It lined out as follows:

Tom Mulcahy

Willie Murphy   **Con Murphy**   Din Joe Buckley

Paddy O'Donovan   Alan Lotty   Jim Young

Jack Lynch   Con Cottrell

Paddy Healy   Christy Ring (Captain)   Con Murphy

Mossie O'Riordan   Gerry O'Riordan   Joe Kelly.

Con was selected many times for Munster Railway Cup teams. Fond memories abide: clashes with Mick and John Mackey in epic Munster contests with Limerick; exchanges with Nicky Rackard in the Railway cup; participation in the classic All-Ireland final of 1947 against Kilkenny when Cork lost by a point.

Con refereed at all levels from an early age – chief among the games being seven Cork County Senior Hurling finals, National league 1947, Munster Final 1949, All-Ireland finals 1948 and 1950.

In the administration field his key posts include:

1947–1976	Member of the General Purposes Committee of Cork County Board
1950–1956	Represented Cork on the Central Council.
1951–1953	Vice-Chairman of Cork County Board – Chairman 1985–89
1954–1956	Treasurer of Cork County Board
1956–1976	Hon. Secretary of Cork County Board and delegate to Munster Council.
1987–onwards	Cork Representative on Munster Council
1964–onwards	Secretary Cork Athletic Grounds
1962–onwards	Chairman of Ciste na Banban Teo.

Con was a member of the RTE Authority 1979–1985. He was made a Freeman of the City of Cork on June 24, 1995.

During his Presidency, Con had an honour that came no other President's way. His native Cork won the senior hurling title in each of the three years of his presidency. So to Con fell the privilege of presenting the McCarthy Cup to Ray Cummins (1976), Martin Doherty (1977) and Charlie McCarthy (1978).

Con is a nephew of Sean McCarthy who was President of the Association from 1932–35.

1979 – PADDY McFLYNN – DOWN

Paddy MacFlynn

Paddy McFlynn, a teacher by profession, was born in Magherafelt, Co Derry on May 5, 1918. He was a founder member of the local O'Donovan Rossa Club and at the first meeting of the club on April 15, 1934, Paddy proposed the name O'Donovan Rossa.

Paddy was Derry Co.Secretary from 1939–1945. He played on the Derry minor football team in 1936. He won two county senior titles with O'Donovan Rossa in 1939 and 1941 and he played on the Derry Senior football team from 1939 to 1948 and during that time he represented Derry on the Ulster Council and on the Central Council.

In 1948 he moved to Ballynahinch and was involved at the local club as a player and official. He served for a time as Chairman of the East Down Divisional Board.

He took up a teaching appointment in the parish of Tullylish in 1958 where he served as Chairman of the local club for several terms.

Paddy was Treasurer of the County Board from 1955 to 1973 and during that time he was Chairman of the South Down Provisional Board 1961 to 1963.

Paddy represented Down on the Ulster Council 1949–1968 and he was the County's representative on the Central Council 1964–1978. He was Treasurer of the Ulster Council from 1947–1954 and was elected President of the Ulster Council for a three year term in 1961.

1982 – PADDY BUGGY – KILKENNY

Writing in the Centenary All-Ireland hurling match programme of 1984 Paddy had this to say:

> 'One of the problems of modern society is lack of discipline and it is vitally important that as an Association we impose a good disciplinary code which produces order, obedience and self-control . . . of course we expect players on a team to play to win but that objective should be achieved within the bounds of good sportsmanship and discipline.'

Paddy Buggy

Paddy Buggy was born on March 15, 1929 to William and Mary (née Dooley), both of Conahy, who played hurling and camogie respectively.

Paddy was educated at Slieverue and Ferrybank National schools and later at Mount Sion CBS. He worked initially with the Irish Press in Waterford before taking up a clerical position with Kilkenny County Council, where he remained until retirement in 1994. Hurling and the GAA have played a major role in Paddy's life.

He captained Mount Sion CBS at centre back in a Hackett Cup success in 1948. He won inter provincial colleges medals in 1947 and '48 with Munster and followed in 1954 with inter-provincial Railway Cup honours with Leinster – probably a unique achievement.

Other major successes include a county senior title in 1954 with Slieverue, All-Ireland senior hurling title 1957, five Leinster senior hurling titles, two Oireachtas titles, four Walsh Cup wins, Kilkenny senior football title with Glenmore 1954. Paddy made his debut at county senior hurling level in the National league against Galway in 1949 and retired in the spring of 1960.

The 1957 team that brought the All-Ireland title to the Noreside for the fourteenth time lined out as follows:

Ollie Walsh

Tom Walsh   Jim Walsh   John Maher

Paddy Buggy   Mickey Walsh   Johnny McGovern

Mick Brophy   John Sutton

Denis Heaslip   Mick Kenny   Mick Kelly (capt)

Dick Rockett   Billy Dwyer   Sean Clohessy

Paddy regards the fifties as one of the great hurling decades and points to the following attendances most of which have remained records to the present day:

> Leinster final 1950 Kilkenny v Wexford at Kilkenny 36,494;
> 1957 Kilkenny v Wexford at Croke Park 52,272;
> 1954 Railway Cup final 49,023 and 1956 Oireachtas final 37,171;

In 1955 he had the honour of captaining his native Kilkenny, but they fell to a great Wexford team in the Leinster final.

Paddy refereed for a 15 year period from 1960 to 1975; an Offaly county final, intermediate All-Ireland hurling finals 1964 and 1966, under-21 final 1971, club games all over Kilkenny, colleges games, national league and provincial games at all levels in Leinster.

He held many positions in his club Slieverue; was Leinster Council representative from 1961 to 1975, Vice-Chairman of the Leinster Council 1975 to '77, Chairman '78 to '80. Chairman Kilkenny County Board 1990 (resigned after one year on medical advice).

As County Selector Paddy had the following successes, National League titles 1961/62 and 1989/90 and All-Ireland titles 1967 and 1969. He was selector/manager of Leinster Railway Cup teams in Leinster's record breaking run of a successful five in a row, 1971–1975.

To Paddy, in his first year in office, fell the honour of delivering the graveside oration at the funeral of the legendary Mick Mackey of Limerick, who died on September 13, 1982.

To mark the centenary of the GAA, by the National University of Ireland, Paddy, as President of the Gaelic Athletic Association, was conferred with the Honorary degree of LL.D. on April 12, 1984 at the National University by T K Whitaker, Chancellor of the University.

He visited the British House of Parliament regarding the Crossmaglen Affair (the occupation of the local GAA grounds by British Army forces) and held discussions with Claire Shortt and Kevin McNamara while Prime Minister Thatcher's question time was in progress.

Accompanied by Liam Mulvihill he was received by the Australian Prime Minister, Bob Hawke, in the Australian Parliament, as Sporting Ambassador regarding the International Football Series.

Paddy recalls with fond memories some of the outstanding players he played against or marked: Vivian Cobb, Liam Maloney (Limerick), Matt Nugent, Jimmy Smyth, Pat Kirby (Clare), Jimmy Duggan, Tadhg Sweeney, John Killeen (Galway), Christy Ring, Willie John Daly, Pat Fitzgerald (Cork), Seamus Bannon, Paddy Kenny, Liam Devaney and Jimmy Doyle (Tipperary), Larry Guinan, Philly Grimes, Frankie Walsh (Waterford), Sean Og O'Callaghan, Bernard Boothman, Norman Allen (Dublin), Dominic Ahearne, Tim Russell, Padge Kehoe, Tim Flood, Ned Wheeler, Seamus Hearne, Harry O'Connor, Jimmy O'Brien, Ted Bolger (Wexford), Billy Dargan, Timmy Maher (Laois).

Paddy had quite a few encounters with, the maestro himself, Christy Ring. Following one of those in 1955 Paddy was nominated Sports Star of the Week. It was suggested in a publication that in one of those encounters Paddy hit Christy. 'Never happened' said Paddy, 'when you weigh a little over 10 stone, as I did, you have to concentrate at all times on playing the ball.'

1985 – Dr Michael Loftus – Mayo

Michael Loftus was born on August 9, 1929 in Kiltoom, Co Roscommon where his father, a Mayoman, was a Garda Sergeant.

When Michael was young the family returned to Co Mayo and in 1947 he won a County junior football title with Crossmolina – followed by a County senior title in 1949.

He played County minor for Mayo in 1947. They won the Connaught title and went on to play Tyrone in the All-Ireland final. The senior football final of that year was played in New York so the minor final took place before the junior football final. Michael recalls that they were ahead by 11 points at half time and lost in the end by 1 point

Dr Michael Loftus

to Tyrone. He once mused on how times have changed as he recalled whatever celebrations they had took place in an ice cream parlour.

Michael's other successes on the football field include, Sigerson Cup victories with UCG in 1948, '50 and '54, All-Ireland junior football titles with Mayo in 1950 and '57, when he had the honour of being Captain, and a National League title in the early 50's. He was also a sub on the All-Ireland winning Mayo senior team of 1951.

He became a referee somewhat by accident. When a referee for a local game failed to turn up Mick was handed the whistle. It led to him refereeing the All-Ireland minor football final of 1964 and the Senior finals of 1965 and 1968. He also refereed Connaught finals and one Ulster final. He had the honour of refereeing the World Cup game in New York – a two leg affair – in October 1968 between Down, the All-Ireland champions and New York – a game won by Down.

He also had the distinction of holding the following Chairmanships: Connaught Council 1979–82, Referees' Advisory Council, Centenary Committee. For the centenary celebrations of 1984 he was Chairman of the Centenary Committee.

Michael's experiences as a medical doctor and as County Coroner have led him to counsel unceasingly on the perils of excessive intake of alcohol.

1988 – John Dowling – Offaly

When May Carey married the late John Dowling she said:

> 'It was like home from home. I was going from one GAA house to another. My brothers Jim and Michael played hurling for Westmeath and my father Paddy served on the Leinster Council.'

John Dowling

John was introduced to Gaelic games at Scoil Bhríde in his native Tullamore, where he won Schools' championship medals in 1943 and 1945. Later he won County Offaly medals at various grades, including senior hurling and senior football, and he played junior hurling for his county. He was also a fine athlete and represented Offaly in both cross-country and track events. He was a founder member of Tullamore Harriers and its inaugural Chairman.

John, a post office official by profession, was a leading referee in both hurling and football. He had charge of the senior hurling finals of 1960, '62 and '68 (by coincidence, all between Wexford and Tipperary) and the senior football deciders of 1959 and 1960. He also refereed the 1959 junior football final, the 1968 intermediate hurling final, fifteen provincial finals, including the 1962 Ulster final, 'the day before we got married', and the National league hurling final in New York in 1968 as well as games at Wembley and New Eltham.

John's administration posts were many and included:

Secretary of Tullamore GAA Club 1953–1964;
Secretary of Offaly County Board 1965–1987;
Chairman of the Leinster Council 1981–1983;
Offaly's representative on the Central Council for 21 years, from 1959.

John served on various GAA committees and was a Railway Cup selector for Leinster in both hurling and football.

During his Presidency John played an active role in acquiring property from the Jesuit Order for the Croke Park Development programme.

This is an excerpt from a lovely letter I received from his wife May.

'When John retired as President he returned to Tullamore Club where he worked behind the scenes, including Bingo sessions. He was also involved in Church affairs – on the Parish Council and as Honorary Parish Administrator, and his final work was in cataloguing the records of our local cemetery, as all records had been lost when our Church burned down in the 1980's. As you can see, he was not one to sit idly by, but worked in a voluntary capacity right up to the end, which came quite unexpectedly.'

1991 – PETER QUINN – FERMANAGH

Peter was Fermanagh's first and Ulster's fifth President. He was a man vastly experienced in the business world and his flair in this field was of tremendous benefit to the Association. Quiet spoken and pragmatic, he played a key role in the development of the new Croke Park. Under the

Peter Quinn

Presidency of Sean McCague 2000–2003 he was appointed Chairman of the Strategic Review Committee. Peter had this to say:

> 'The GAA has huge strengths and assets but we are not using them as effectively as we should be. We are not well managed, it is as simple as that. In fact, we wouldn't survive if we were a business, so unless we change our management structure we will have serious difficulties.'

Peter, following his Presidency, remained closely involved with the Association and chaired the Amateur Status Committee and the Strategic Review Committee; he was also involved with the Croke Park Redevelopment Committee.

1994 – JACK BOOTHMAN – WICKLOW

Jack was the second Wicklow man to hold the prestigious post and the first from the veterinary profession. As far as Jack is concerned the Club is the very cornerstone and lifeblood of the GAA. He has a special affection for his own club Blessington with which he played football 'but no medals came my way'. In his time he held many positions in the club and is now its Honorary President. He spent terms as Chairman of West Wicklow Board and Vice-Chairman of the County Board. In the period 1987–1990 he was Chairman of the Leinster Council. He also spent a number of years as Wicklow delegate to the Leinster Council.

Jack Boothman

Jack, who was born on October 12, 1935, was a candidate in 1991 for the Presidency. However, it was Peter Quinn of Fermanagh who won the contest on that occasion.

Nominated in Wicklow by Baltinglass club and supported by his own club Blessington, Jack was again Wicklow's nominee in 1994. This time he held off the challenge of all rivals, including that of Galway's Joe McDonagh and Tipperary's Michael Maher who at one stage was a firm favourite.

Jack is immensely proud of having been elected to the prestigious office of President of the GAA. For him, no honour in the country could be higher.

As I talked with Jack I wondered what in particular stood out as the highlight of his Presidency.

'Everyday was a special day – a highlight. I loved visiting the clubs and the schools. Travelling the country now, fellows in their twenties come up to me and say "I know you – you came to our school".

I was at The Point in April 1994 at the Eurovision when Riverdance was first performed. It was such a world success afterwards that I now look back and feel I saw a piece of history.

It was great to be in the Presidency and witness the re-emergence of Clare, Offaly and Wexford in hurling. And of course to see Westmeath and Laois make the breakthrough in minor football and win All-Ireland titles will always be a special memory.'

Jack has tremendous praise for Liam Mulvihill – Director General at the helm – and the immense and outstanding contribution he has made to the growth and development of the Gaelic Athletic Association.

I reminded Jack that he was the first from the veterinary profession to hold the office and he responded by saying that he has told that fact to many people when they said to him that he was the first Church of Ireland President.

That made me call to mind others from the Church of Ireland who made a contribution to the GAA. In the early days of the Association Douglas Hyde, later to become President of Ireland, was one of its first patrons. J H Stewart of Tyrone was elected Vice-President of the GAA at a meeting in the Victoria Hotel, Cork, on December 27, 1884 and re-elected a year later on October 31, 1885 at the Annual Convention. In recent times Irene Barber produced a delightful publication titled *All About Hurling*, aimed at children. When I was stationed in Killorglin (1953–1955) I stayed in the digs of a local Church of Ireland businessman William S.Champ who proudly showed me a North Kerry hurling medal he won with Abbeydorney in his young days. This of course would have been exceptional, due in the main to the fact that the Church of Ireland population in parishes was relatively small. Jack told me that there was a player called James Kingston who won a minor All-Ireland football title with Cork in 1993, who was Church of Ireland, 'They took me from the hotel to meet him before he departed in the bus'. No better man than Jack to engage him in some friendly banter.

1997 – JOE McDONAGH – GALWAY

Joe McDonagh

Joe hails from the parish of Ballinderreen, South County Galway. He represented his native Galway at all levels in hurling – winning an under-21 title and a National league. He also won Oireachtas and Railway Cup medals and in 1976 was selected as an All Star. He was on the losing side in the All Ireland finals of 1975 and 1979. In 1980, illness cost him a place and an All Ireland medal in Galway's great victory over Limerick, after a lapse of 57 years.

After a number of disappointments, Joe won a Fitzgibbon Cup title in 1976/77 with UCG, on a team captained by Pat Fleury of Offaly and featuring such prominent players as Conor Hayes, Niall McInerney, Joe Connolly and Cyril Farrell of Galway, also Frank Holohan of Kilkenny.

His only county title was won in 1996 when, at the age of 43 and playing at fullback, he captained his native Ballinderreen to victory in the junior B final. His son Eoin who was to captain the Galway minor team the following year, played at centre half back that day to add to the occasion 'in what was a most memorable win'.

It is said that Joe became the first 'playing' President when he lined out the following year in a county junior championship game against Carnmore in Clarinbridge – a game that brought the curtain down on his playing career after 32 years involvement as a player with his club.

Joe has been as active in GAA affairs off the field as on – as the information below testifies:

GALWAY COUNTY BOARD.
1979–1983   Oifigeach na Gaeilge
1988–1996   Central Council Delegate
1992–1996   Secretary, County Galway Coaching and Games Develop-
            ment Committee
1981–1996   Secretary, Galway City Post-Primary Schools Hurling
            Committee
1991–1996   Chairman, Pearse Stadium Development Committee

CONNAUGHT COUNCIL
1994–1996   Vice-President
            Chairman Activities Committee

Chairman Connaught Coaching & Games Development
Committee
Chairman Connaught Scór Committee
Chairman Connaught Coiste na Gaeilge
1978–1994   Member of Connaught Colleges' Committee

NATIONAL COMMITTEES
1982–1985   Member of Coiste Cultúir CLG
1988–2001   Member of Central Council (Ard-Chomhairle) CLG
1994–2001   Member of Management Committee (Coiste Bainistí) CLG
1988–1991   Chairman National Hurling Work-Group
            Member of Coaching & Games Development Committee
1991   Member of Rules Drafting Committee
1991–1994   Chairman of National Coaching & Games Development
            Committee
1994–1997   Member of Coaching & Games Development Committee
            Chairman of National Youth Committee
2000–2002   Member of Strategic Review Committee
1996–1997   Member of Croke Park Museum Design Committee
1996–2000   Member of Croke Park Redevelopment Design Committee

Joe who was born in 1953 was originally a teacher by profession but is
now Chief Executive of Foras na Gaeilge – a body that promotes the Irish
language throughout the island of Ireland.

Joe Mc Donagh

2000 – SEAN McCAGUE – MONAGHAN

Sean McCague set off on Friday, April 16,
1999, for the Annual GAA Congress in
the Burlington Hotel, where he would
contest the election for the Presidency of
the GAA. He had thirty-three years of
service behind him at administrative and
managerial level and the blessing of his
ninety-one-year-old mother, Rose, who
said *'I hope you get the job if it's for your good'*.

There was rejoicing in Scotstown, his
native parish, Monaghan and Ulster,
when it became known on the Saturday
evening that, with 173 votes, Sean was
elected on the first count – Ulster's sixth
and Monaghan's first President.

Sean McCague

Sean's love of Gaelic football blossomed in his youth. There followed success at juvenile and minor level, but a back problem that necessitated a six month stay in Cappagh Orthopaedic Hospital in 1966, brought an end to his football ambitions on the GAA field.

By that time he had qualified as a national teacher via Colaiste Iosagain, Ballyvourney, County Cork and St Patrick's Training College, Drumcondra, Dublin. His thoughts now turned to the field of management and administration in the GAA world.

Sean became joint Secretary, with the late Francie McAtavie, of Monaghan County Board in 1970, having served as Secretary of his club since 1966.

In 1973 he became the Monaghan delegate to the Ulster Council and team Manager of the Scotstown Senior Football team that went on to capture the Monaghan title the following year.

Sean became Manager of the County Senior Football team in 1978. Under his guidance much was achieved in the decade that followed – an Ulster title in 1979 after a lapse of 41 years; two more Provincial crowns in 1985 and 1988; a National league in 1985; three Dr McKenna Cup triumphs; a draw with mighty Kerry in the All-Ireland semi-final of 1985 that left them to contemplate the might-have-beens after the replay; and a league final of 1986 that was lost by 1 point to Laois.

Sean's ascent in the GAA world continued. In 1985 he was chosen as Monaghan's delegate to the Central Council. After that he held the following positions:

Member of GAA Management Committee 1987–1990
Chairman of the Games Administration Committee
Assistant Manager to Eugene McGee in 1990 with the
team that played the Compromised Rules series in Australia
Chairman of Committee of Coaching and Games Development
Chairman of Policy and Planning Committee

Sean's range of talents were further evidenced in the 90s when he spent six years as an analyst on the BBC TV programme, *The Championship*.

It all added up to a background that equipped him well for the challenging task of President, where discipline on the field and disciplinary procedures were high on Sean's agenda.

2003 – Sean Kelly – Kerry

As President elect of the GAA Sean Kelly had this to say in an article in *The Irish Times* of October 24, 2002.

'The GAA has never been stronger . . . a National organisation which still has its roots in every local community.

An organisation which is based on tradition, yet has the vision to build one of the great stadiums of the world.

An organisation which spans the entire island and yet gives autonomy to clubs and counties to do their work.

An organisation totally committed to the amateur status, which gives everyone a special pride in their own place, yet insists on the most professional approach to the management of the game . . .

Amateurism and volunteerism is a core ethic of the Association and it is my view that this should continue so as to give all players equal status and to fulfil our commitments to our communities. . . .'

Sean hails from the parish of Kilcummin, near Killarney, and is a former Chairman of the Kerry County Board and the Munster Council. He played football with his local club and in 1982 started a hurling team in the parish. He was still togging out for his club at the age of 42 – a sure reflection of his enthusiasm for our games.

Sean progressed from East Kerry Board to the County Board where he served as Chairman for 11 years. He was elected to the post of President on the first attempt with 66 per cent of the vote. He knows and preaches that the club is the very lifeblood of the Association.

Sean Kelly

Chief among his objectives as President is the development of hurling in the weaker counties. Following his election he proceeded to appoint Nicky English, Ger Loughnane and Cyril Farrell to a special Work Group to that end. Sean has said that 'the hurley is as much a national symbol as the harp and the shamrock'.

Sean who was born in 1952 is a teacher by profession, at St Brendan's Killarney – his alma mater. In his opening speech at the Congress in Belfast he described himself as 'the first bearded President of the GAA since Maurice Davin'.

Sean Kelly

A Cork County final of the late forties, won by St Finbarrs

19
Secretary/Director
General

The post of Secretary – an honorary one – from the foundation of the GAA in 1884 to the end of that century was, as recorded by T F O'Sullivan in *The Story of the GAA*, held by the following: the date in each case being the date of election.

NOVEMBER 1, 1884 (FIRST MEETING)

Michael Cusack (Dublin), *John Wyse Power* (Naas), *John McKay* (Cork)
All three are profiled in the chapter, 'The Founding Fathers'.

OCTOBER 31, 1885 (FIRST ANNUAL CONVENTION)

The above were re-elected.

NOVEMBER 15, 1886 (SECOND ANNUAL CONVENTION)

John Boyle O'Reilly (Dublin), *John Wyse Power* (Naas) and *Timothy O'Riordan* (Cork).

NOVEMBER 9, 1887 (THE 'INFAMOUS' CONVENTION)

Timothy O'Riordan

John Boyle O'Reilly (Dublin) – he was employed in Clery's Drapery store and belonged to the Fenian tradition.

James Moore (Dundalk) – he spent a term as President of Louth County Committee.

Timothy O'Riordan (Cork) – he was a native of Tralee and a member of the reporting staff of the *Cork Herald* and *Cork Examiner*. He later joined the reporting staff of the Freeman's Journal. He died January 20, 1899.

JANUARY 4, 1888

William Prendergast (Clonmel)
Following the tempestuous Convention of November 1887 William Prendergast of Clonmel was appointed Hon Sec on January 4, 1888 at the Convention in Thurles to re-construct the Association.

He travelled to the US with the 'Invasion' team of 1888 and played on the hurling team. He came back to Ireland but later returned to the States where he joined the New York Police force. William played an active part in securing the Celtic Park Grounds for Gaelic Athletic fixtures.

At the January 1888 meeting Timothy O'Riordan of Cork was elected Hon Sec to the Central Council.

JANUARY 23, 1889 (BEING THE ANNUAL CONVENTION OF NOVEMBER 1888 – DELAYED DUE TO US 'INVASION'.

Patrick Roger Clery (Caherconlish, Co Limerick)

Patrick R Clery was born in Lagganstown, Thomastown, Co Tipperary and educated at Mungret College, Limerick. He later qualified as a teacher.

He was a close friend of Parnell and attended all the early GAA Conventions.

He was Secretary of the Limerick County Board for one year and also held a position on the Central Council.

He took up a teaching appointment in Caherline, Co Limerick and when he moved to Caherconlish he met and married Minnie Dooley.

Later in life he moved to Tipperary where he died in 1933 and is buried in Kilfeakle.

(I am indebted to Sean Murphy, Limerick GAA Historian, for this information).

Patrick Roger Cleary

Also at the meeting of January 23, 1889 S J Dunleavy of Clare was appointed Hon Sec to the Central Council.

NOVEMBER 6, 1889 (ANNUAL CONVENTION)

Patrick Roger Clery was re-elected.

NOVEMBER 27, 1890 (ANNUAL CONVENTION)

Maurice Moynihan (Tralee)

There followed on April 30, 1891 a meeting of the new Central Council at which Maurice Moynihan and Patrick Tobin (Dublin) were appointed Hon Secs.

At a convention held on July 22, 1891 it was agreed that 'a paid Secretary be appointed by the Central Council to summon meetings and to look after the work of the organisation'.

Maurice was a member of the John Mitchell's Club in Tralee and belonged to the Fenian tradition.

In October 1891 Maurice Moynihan left Kerry and resigned as Hon Sec of the Association. However, on his return he again immersed

Maurice Moynihan

himself in GAA affairs and was a leading figure in the Kingdom in promoting the ideals of the Association. Maurice was born in 1866 and died in 1918.

JANUARY 13, 1892 (BEING THE ANNUAL CONVENTION DUE TO HAVE TAKEN PLACE IN NOVEMBER 1891)

Patrick Tobin (Dublin)

Patrick Tobin

Patrick Tobin who was active with the Association from its establishment in Dublin was re-elected. He was a founder member of Brian Boru Club with which he hurled from 1888 to 1892 in the county championship.

He was Secretary of the Dublin County Committee from 1889 to 1891.

He held the position of Vice-President of the Association in 1895 and 1896.

A noted referee, he took charge of the All-Ireland hurling finals of 1889 and 1891, Dublin v Clare and Kerry v Wexford respectively.

APRIL 16, 1893 (BEING THE ANNUAL CONVENTION WHICH SHOULD HAVE BEEN HELD IN NOVEMBER 1892)

Patrick Tobin (Dublin) was re-elected.

APRIL 22, 1894 (ANNUAL CONVENTION)

David Walsh (Cork)

The following year, 1895, David Walsh was elected Treasurer.

APRIL 7, 1895 (ANNUAL CONVENTION)

R T (Dick) Blake, (Ladyrath, Navan)

MAY 10, 1896

Dick Blake was re-elected.

At the Annual Convention it was decided that the Secretary in future get 15 per cent of the gross receipts of the year as renumeration.

JULY 4, 1897

Dick Blake re-elected.

In a different social and political climate Dick Blake might well have emerged as an outstanding Secretary. He came from well-off farming stock and was liberal in his views.

During his time as Secretary, he devoted much energy to revitalising the Association. He would have opposed any form of ban, rather wishing to see players of other games eligible to play Gaelic games as well. He would also have aimed at keeping the Association politically neutral. His style, however, was rather authoritarian and as such, Dick built up a groundswell of opposition to himself.

A meeting of Central Council was summoned on January 16, 1898 to discuss the financial position of the Association.

A vote of no confidence in Dick Blake was carried by six votes to five, thus ending Dick Blake's term as Secretary.

Subsequent to his dismissal he issued a pamphlet giving a robust defence of his tenure:

'I protested against the meeting as an illegal one, sufficient signatures not having been obtained, and I demanded that the Auditors' report should be before the meeting before any discussion could have taken place . . . I maintained that the debts of the Association were due to no fault of mine . . . for which I was no more responsible than I was for the weather.'

Writing on this matter in *The GAA In Its Time*, Pádraig Puirséal had this to say.

'Some visible progress was made during his Secretaryship . . . hampered though he was by the debris of previous wrecks. He was the first to bring the finals to the Jones's Road venue and it was during his time that the cups presented by Dr Croke were put into competition. Mr Blake increased the revenue of the Central Council substantially during his term of office . . . a fine achievement for which he got little thanks. His removal from office was desired by a certain section and the intrigue which brought it about reflected no credit on its authors. It was so contrived that the Association as a whole knew little about it.'

Dick was a fine referee and had charge of the 1894 All-Ireland football final between Dublin and Cork.

MAY 22, 1898

Frank Brazil Dinneen

He was re-elected on July 16, 1899 and on September 9, 1900. He remained in the post until September 1901.

Frank is profiled in the chapter dealing with the purchase of Croke Park.

Office Holders of the Twentieth Century

1901–1929 LUKE O'TOOLE

Luke J. O'Toole

Luke O'Toole was born in 1873 in the picturesque setting of Ballycumber, where 'nature has scattered her charms with a liberal hand' near the village of Tinahely in Co Wicklow. However, at an early age he came to reside at 29 Mount Pleasant Square Ranelagh, in Dublin. In 1898 he became a member of the Hibernian GAA club.

It was as a member of the Dublin County Board delegation that Luke attended the annual convention of 1901 which was held on September 22, in Thurles.

In the election for the post of Secretary he defeated Michael Cusack by 19 votes to 17. Dick Blake's nomination – a former Secretary – was ruled out of order on the basis of not being a member of an affiliated club. Delegates attended the Convention from London, Dublin, Kerry, Kilkenny, Tipperary, Cork, Wexford, Limerick and Wicklow.

At the time, the post of Secretary was a part-time one. Luke also ran two Newsagent and Tobacconist shops at 56 Charlemont St and 44 Rathmines Rd. So to establish a base, and to bring a degree of order and method to the job of Secretary, Luke set up an office in a room in his private residence at 29 Mount Pleasant Square, Ranelagh. For three years, that is where the work of Secretary was carried out.

The challenge facing Luke was immense and in many ways quite awesome. For the GAA at the time was still a struggling outfit – scattered and disjointed and badly in need of co-ordination. As Pádraig Puirséal stated in *The GAA In Its Time*:

'He played a major part in building the GAA from the disjointed, debt-ridden and somewhat haphazard organisation it was when he took office, to the prosperous, efficiently-run national and nation-wide Association that he was still serving on the day he died.'

In assuming office, Luke set his sights on the following objectives as described in Pádraig O'Toole's absorbing book about his grandfather *The Glory and the Anguish*.

To procure an Association office, which was done when the GAA rented an office at 68 Upr O'Connell St in 1904.

The establishment of structured championships in hurling and football and the promotion of athletics

The purchase of a site to develop the Gaelic Athletic Association's own headquarters, incorporating its own playing pitch.

The publication of an official paper or organ by the Central Council to promote the Irish language, Irish Culture and Irish native pastimes.

In 1902, with a view to generating vitality and enthusiasm, Luke attended a number of county conventions. He also refereed games including the All-Ireland hurling final of 1902 between Cork and London which wasn't played until September 1904.

He also set about getting matches played on schedule and within the playing year. However, it took until 1909 before that was achieved.

After the purchase of Croke Park in 1913, the offices at 68 Upr O'Connell St were vacated and Luke moved to the new property at Jones's Road. From then on enhancing the property and facilities at Croke Park was always on Luke's agenda.

During his 28 years as Secretary he was called upon many times to steer the Association through difficult and challenging days – both financial and political.

Luke died unexpectedly at work on July 17, 1929.

In a tribute to him P J Devlin (Celt) wrote as follows:

'It would be strange and ungenerous if no tribute was paid in a survey of Gaelic Administration to the late Luke O'Toole. He has been connected with native games from his earliest years and in many capacities . . . when he succeeded the late Frank B Dinneen, the GAA was neither flourishing nor disciplined and few would have shouldered the burden and the duties entailed. Luke O'Toole did so cheerfully, confident in the destiny of the Association. The work grew heavier and more congenial as the years went by; for the intrinsic merits of the games and the worth of the movement were being appreciated at length and before he had laid down his task in 1929, Luke O'Toole had the pride and the heartease of seeing the Gaelic Athletic Association the most popular and non-political Association or organisation in Ireland . . . All the negotiations for Croke Park and much of the organisation of the first and second Tailteann games fell to his lot, and he had his full share of the anxieties of the years around the Treaty period . . . amongst other reforms effected during his term was the establishment of the Secretaryship as a permanent post . . . he had always given his allegiance and services to the attainment of the highest national ideals, and sentinelled Croke Park in dark and dangerous years.'

1929–1964 PÁDRAIG O'CAOIMH

Padraig O'Keefe.

'He gave this Association a place in the life of the country, no other body could aspire to. He engendered an amazing goodwill which is our most important asset. His attitude was the criterion of all our efforts. He was our most competent visionary, our most efficient businessman.'
(Alf Murray – GAA President 1964–1967)

Pádraig O'Caoimh (otherwise Paddy O'Keeffe) was initially a teacher by profession. He was an active officer of the Cork No 1 Brigade during the Black & Tan War (The War of Independence). He suffered a term of imprisonment and took the Republican side in the Civil War.

A Roscommon man by birth, he moved to Cork and at the age of 21 was appointed Secretary of the Cork County Board – then the biggest administration unit in the GAA. In this position he proved himself to be a gifted organiser and administrator – always noted for his high levels of efficiency.

He was a versatile hurler and footballer and won a reputation as a first class referee. Pádraig had charge of the All-Ireland hurling final of 1924 between Dublin and Galway and a few real needle affairs between Limerick and Tipperary in the mid-twenties which he handled with cool, tactful efficiency. Here is how Pádraig Puirséal recalled one of those games in an article in *The Irish Press* in May 1964.

'Pádraig O'Caoimh was a lithe, lively man in his late twenties when I first saw him on a sun-sweet day long ago in Dan Fraher's field in Dungarvan. . . . . The occasion was a "needle" hurling championship clash between Limerick and Tipperary and I, a small boy between my father's knees at the touchline, squatted wide-eyed with awe and admiration. Striding past me in the pre-match parade went Johnny Leahy and Bob McConkey, Martin Kennedy and Mickey Cross, Mick Darcy, Mick Fitzgibbon and other heroes of that Golden Age.

It was a day of Munster hurling at its fiercest and best, for though the clashes were keen and though men were bowled over like nine pins in the fray, there was no danger of the game getting out of control. The referee saw to that. Fast though the hurlers were, he was faster still. To my young eyes his bushy head of hair seemed to keep pace with the flying sliotar from one end of the field to the other and he never once had to let the players know who was boss. Well they knew that this tall, slim man in the Cork jersey, the neat togs and white running-shoes would take no nonsense.

I listened fascinated while a Limerick man told my father about the referee – 'under his whistle you can play as hard as you like, but you must play fair.'

The story is told that when Cork lined out for their first game in the National League in October 1925 they were short of players and called upon County Secretary Paddy O'Keeffe to man the goal. It seems that Laois led by eight goals to no score at half time. The Cork fullback Sean Og Murphy then suggested to Paddy O'Keeffe that he should try his luck at full forward adding that by then he must know how goals were scored.

When the question of finding a successor to Luke O'Toole arose, the GAA authorities set down a few markers. The candidates would have to be under 40 years of age and to sit exams in Irish, English, Mathematics and Book-keeping. They would be interviewed and then the appointment would finally be decided by a vote.

There were eleven applicants for the post. However, even in the early stages, it was felt that it would boil down to a contest between Pádraig O'Caoimh and Frank Burke.

Frank was a Kildare man, a Republican at heart, a scholar and an outstanding sportsman. He played football and hurling with the now defunct Dublin club, Collegians. He won All-Ireland hurling titles with Dublin in 1917 and 1920 and followed with football titles in 1921, '22 and '23.

Frank had a deep attachment to our native language and taught in Scoil Eanna.

In due course the original number of applicants was narrowed down to three.

The election, which took place on Saturday, September 3, 1929, was full of drama. Seamus Leahy, Tipperary GAA Historian, tells the story in a Tipperary GAA Yearbook:

'On the first count the voting was:

Pádraig O'Caoimh	*11–Cork*
Frank Burke	*10 –Dublin*
Hugh Corvin	*2–Belfast*

On the second count an extraordinary thing happened. Corvin's two votes transferred to Burke but another Ulster delegate – Eoin O'Duffy, Commissioner of the Garda Siochana and later to gain notoriety as leader of the "Blueshirts" – having voted for Burke on the first count, now switched to O'Caoimh. He had been, it is said, hard-pressed by Pádraig Pearse's sister to support the Headmaster of St Enda's and, feeling that he had satisfied honour by voting for him on the first count, he proceeded to vote thereafter for the man whom he considered best for the job.

Thus it was that the attendance of a proxy voter – O'Duffy was only there as a stand-in for an Ulster delegate who had been a candidate for the job and did not now wish to vote – decided the future of the GAA.'

Other records show 21 delegates voting as follows on the first count – Pádraig O'Caoimh 10; Frank Burke 9; Hugh Corvin 2; leading to a final count of Pádraig O'Caoimh 11 Frank Burke 10.

Pádraig O'Caoimh was an immensely successful General Secretary – the title today is Director General.

'I am particularly proud of the fact that I was the first person to get Paddy O'Keeffe to go forward as Secretary of the GAA. I realised that he had the three great qualities necessary for making a success of the position – and they are – tact, foresight and organising ability.'
(James Harrington – Former Chairman of Munster Council)

Like his predecessor, Pádraig too had to cope with challenging times – though these were different in nature. His guidance, leadership and total dedication to the task on hand during his 35 years in office, allied to remarkable skills in the field of organisation and administration, and supported by a keen intellect and high levels of mental and physical energy, saw him perceived by many as 'the architect of the modern GAA'.

Among the far-seeing things he undertook was the initiation of the practice of having the ownership of GAA grounds vested in Trustees. This ensured both control and continuity of these properties for the GAA. Pádraig also pioneered the promotion of Gaelic games in our schools and colleges

'He was a man of immense foresight. Those of us who were associated with him in the making of the new Croke Park were often terrified by his bold conceptions. But, always, his judgement proved sound.'
(Dr J J Stuart – President 1958–1961)

Pádraigh O'Caoimh in his Annual Reports at Congress usually had some special message for delegates regarding the mission of the GAA. On one such occasion he said, 'The GAA gave young Ireland a living cultural ideal and the force to expand and develop'.

Marcus de Búrca writing in the GAA Centenary Supplement of *The Irish Times* had this to say:

'The secret of O'Keeffe's success, the key to his outstanding work for the GAA over such a long period, some 45 years, if one includes his years as Cork County Secretary, lay in the rare combination of idealist and realist in one personality. No other major figure in the GAA before or since had this dual ability; none knew with such unerring intuition when to be one or the other.'

D'imigh Pádraig O'Caoimh ar shlí na fírinne i mí Bealtaine 1964 agus tá Páirc Ui Chaoimh i gCorcaigh, a h-osclaíodh go h-oifigiúl 6 Meitheamh 1976, ainmithe in onóir dó.

1964–1979 SEÁN Ó'SÍOCHÁIN

Seán Ó'Síocháin was born in Cill na Martra, near Macroom, Co Cork, in 1914. His early youth was enriched and influenced by the Gaelic traditions all around him – music, song, dances, games. And of course, there was the meitheal system at harvest time – the rural community supporting and co-operating with each other in a spirit of spontaneous neighbourliness. It left

Seán Ó Siocháin

a deep impression on Seán, moulded his character and stood to him in his adult life. He saw an extension of the meitheal in the volunteer work of countless thousands at club level, and further along the line, in the Gaelic Athletic Association.

This multi-talented personality, outgoing and gregarious, had a great speaking voice and in company he had a presence that radiated that indefinable trait, charisma.

He was always a great Ambassador for the GAA. He represented his native Cork as a delegate to Congress, on occasions, prior to and during the Second World War.

'My abiding memories of day-long sessions in Dublin's City Hall and, in later years, in the Aberdeen Hall of the Gresham Hotel, are of well-researched and convincingly-proposed motions from Cork; the serious earnestness of Ulster delegates; the lighter touches of the Kerry contingent and the ever-welcome interjections from the hardy annual 'characters', such as Paddy Leahy from Tipperary, whose clarion call was always whatever was 'for the good of the Association.'

At the age of 21, in 1935, Seán qualified as a national teacher. He remained in that profession until 1946 when the GAA decided to create a post of Assistant to the then General Secretary, Pádraig O'Caoimh.

Seán, one of six applicants, was successful and in 1964 following the death of Pádraig O'Caoimh he was appointed General Secretary of the GAA. He was ideally suited to, and equipped for, the job, having had the benefit and experience of functioning with the outstanding Pádraig O'Caoimh for eighteen years.

Seán had a fine singing voice which was heard by the public on three popular radio programmes: *Ireland is Singing* was popular in the late thirties, *Round the Fire* was famous through much of the forties – a programme this writer used to enjoy immensely in his youth as the family sat around the fireside and joined in the singing – *Ballad Makers' Saturday Nights* in the late fifties. Seán also sang overseas and did four concert tours of the U.S.

In his youth he played both hurling and football and represented his native Cork at minor, junior and senior football level. He was chosen for Munster in the 1936 Railway Cup football competition. During his teaching days in Dublin he played with Clanna Gael and had the honour of captaining the Dublin senior football team in the late thirties, only to lose to Kildare in the first round.

Writing in the GAA Centenary Supplement to *The Irish Times* in September 1984, Sean lamented the disappearance of individualistic style and also the decline in sweet ground striking in hurling.

'I regret the major transformation from the individualistic style, in both games, of 30, 40 years ago, to the more restrictive team-effort of the present day. Gone is much of the flair and the dash and the flashes of genius which elevated our great players into being supermen and legends in their own time, and we are the poorer because of it.

Today's genius has to conform to the team pattern, and his chances of being "honoured in song and story" are fading fast. Football has been the harder hit in this regard, principally because of the new cult of retaining possession and the consequent pulling and dragging which stems from it. Gaelic football, with quicker delivery on the one hand, and a more legally effective manner of dispossessing on the other, could be almost as spectacular and as exciting as hurling at its best.

My wish for hurling is that our players, generally, will move away from the constant lifting of the ball into the hand and concentrate on the speedier ball-control and first-time striking with the hurley, both in the air and on the ground.'

Seán Ó Síocháin

In 1979, at the age of 65, it was time to resign and Seán's innings as General Secretary came to a close. But his work for the Association, which was always a labour of love, continued. From 1979 until 1982 Seán was Ceann Árus Director and in that capacity he was instrumental in raising one million pounds for the new headquarters at Croke Park.

When Seán died in February 1997, Gaeldom mourned the departure of a name and personality that will always be synonymous with the Gaelic Athletic Association.

1979 – To Date Liam Mulvihill

To the vast bulk of GAA followers Liam Mulvihill was an unknown when he was chosen to succeed Seán Ó'Síocháin at the helm of the Gaelic Athletic Association in 1979. This was in stark contrast to the appointment of Seán Ó'Síocháin in 1964. At that time Seán's name was a household word in GAA circles. He had, after all, been Assistant to Pádraig O'Caoimh

Liam Mulvihill

since 1946. Even though Liam was generally unknown, he had, nevertheless, a deep and firm footing in the world of the GAA.

Liam came of farming stock in South County Longford where he was born in 1946. From his primary school days he was immersed in Gaelic games – influenced and motivated by his teacher Tom Casey.

At St Mel's College in Longford Liam excelled at football – with a preference for half back play – and won Leinster, Junior and Senior titles with the College. The Senior success of 1963 was converted into an All-Ireland Colleges title with a semi-final win over St Colman's (Newry) and a final victory over St Brendan's (Killarney).

Liam represented Longford at all grades of football. However, when he became a Longford selector, a rule in the county barred him from being chosen as a player. He was very loyal to his native parish of Kenagh and shared in their many successes until he retired from club activity in 1984.

In 1969, at the age of 23, Liam was elected Vice-Chairman of the Longford County Board. A year later he was the County Chairman. He had to relinquish this post in 1971 when he became the Longford delegate to the Central Council – a position he still held at the time of his appointment as Director General in 1979.

Liam is due to retire in 2006. What panorama will unfold as he gazes and reflects on the remarkable progress of the Association under his leadership?

Croke Park has been transformed. Gone is every structure that existed in 1979 – the Cusack Stand, officially opened in August 1938 – the 'new' Hogan Stand, officially opened in June 1959 – the Nally Stand, build in 1952 – and, of course, Hill 16 as we knew it.

The GAA now has a stadium of design and facilities to rival any stadium in the world – a monument to the tremendous progress made by the GAA since its foundation in 1884. 'Incredibly ambitious', but Liam believes it ' . . . will have far greater significance for the Association than might initially have been realised'.

One of Liam's ambitions was 'to modernise the Organisation, enhance its image and effectively sell its games'.

High on his agenda was the question of competition structures and the promotion of hurling. In this regard we are at present witnessing an evolving process. The picture emerging is most encouraging.

> 'I saw hurling in particular as requiring examination. I didn't want a situation where the few dominated the many. I was acutely aware that success spread around – the variety and glamour that new faces bring – is the very lifeblood of the Association and the oxygen on which it thrives.'

When Liam retires in 2006 he will be able to look back with pride on the achievements of 27 years in office. And if he should choose to read what Thomas F O'Sullivan wrote about the Association 100 years earlier in 1906, he will note, with interest, the following:

> 'The Annual Convention of the Association, which should have been held in November 1905, did not take place until January 28, 1906 in the Confraternity Hall, Thurles. Fourteen counties were represented; all the Munster counties, none from Connaught, Tyrone and Fermanagh from Ulster, Dublin, Louth, Wexford, Wicklow, Kildare and Laois from Leinster.
>
> Steps were taken to conclude the hurling and football championships – the finals of which were almost two years in arrears – in the year to which they were attached.
>
> The total receipts of the Central, Leinster, Munster and Ulster Councils amounted to over £2,901 and when all expenses had been defrayed there was a credit balance of £673.'

1949, Wexford Park. The Mayor of Wexford, James Sinnott gets a '98 senior football Tournament game under way between Wexford and Wicklow. Going highest for the ball is Jimmy Goodison of Wexford. Other Wexford players from right to left are Des O'Neill, Willie 'Spider' Kelly and Tim O'Leary. The Wicklow team lost their jerseys on the way to the game and togged out in the jerseys of St. Peter's College. (Courtesy Liam Lahiff, Wexford.)

20
Spreading the
Gospel in the Media

In the early days of the GAA, the games were popularised by word of mouth at a time when the Association had 'swept the country like a prairie fire'. The deeds of heroes and glamour of our games were kept alive in ballad and story. The result of some games was not known until supporters returned home. In some cases it would be days before many people found out the score in a game.

Phil O'Neill ("Sliabh Ruadh")
Courtesy Philips, Waterford

The late Tom Ryall, Kilkenny GAA Historian, told me the story of a woman who a few days after the All-Ireland final of 1895 (played March 15, 1896 at Jones's Road), told her son to go across the fields to Coogan's house and find out who had won. He returned with the news that Michael had got Kilkenny's only score – a goal, and that Tipperary had scored 6:8. How times have changed.

Down the decades the media in all its forms began to play a major role in the promotion and spreading of our games. Telecommunication played its part. In 1912 Kilkenny faced Cork in the All-Ireland final. Around 5 p.m. on the Sunday evening of the game, a large and anxious crowd gathered outside the post office in Kilkenny. Then a telegram arrived. The good news was received with exultation and spread rapidly to the surrounding districts, Kilkenny 2:1 Cork 1:3.

The Irish Press was to the fore in the promotion and popularising of our games. Seamus O'Riain, President of the GAA 1967–1970 recalls it:

'*The Irish Press* was launched in September 1931 carrying full pages of bright accounts of hurling and football games written by expert reporters, illustrated by banner headlines and head-and-shoulders photographs of individual players. This was a godsend to us young people and we became busy with scissors, cutting out, and pasting into scrap books, our favourites and storing them away as prized possessions. Other daily newspapers had to accept and follow the new trend in reporting in order to attract their readers. The players were no longer merely names but now their faces were familiar to us and we recognised them as individuals.'

It is believed that the first broadcast, anywhere in the world, of field games took place in Ireland in 1926. P S O'Hegarty, a Corkman, who loved hurling was Secretary of the Department of Posts and Telegraphs. He approached P D Mehigan ("Carbery"), having already established that it was technically possible, to do a broadcast of the All-Ireland senior hurling semi-final between Kilkenny and Galway at Croke Park on August 29, 1926. "Carbery" agreed and a new era had dawned for the GAA and its games. Those with radios – and they were few indeed – saw the game through 'Carbery's' eyes and voice and learned as the final whistle blew that Kilkenny had won by 6:2 to 5:1

Understandably, there was concern among some that such broadcasts would badly affect attendances – that the games would suffer – that finances would suffer. Others with vision and a wider perspective saw matters differently.

William P Clifford of Limerick, the President of the Association, was enthusiastic:

Paddy Mehigan, "Carbery"

> 'These broadcasts of yours P.D. are worth a thousand pounds a year to the GAA as publicity.' And so it proved to be. The attendance graph went upwards.

Over 90,000 people saw the three hurling games of the 1931 final between Cork and Kilkenny. Limerick and Kilkenny proceeded to break All-Ireland hurling final official attendances:

1933 – 45,176
1935 – 46,591
1936 – 51,235

In football the trend was the same:

1935 – Cavan v Kildare – 50,380
1936 – Mayo v Laois – 50,168
1937 – Kerry v Cavan – 52,325; Replay 51,234
1938 – Kerry v Galway – 68,950; Replay – 47581

1947, New York, Micheál O Hehir, John Joe O'Reilly (Cavan Captain), Bill O'Brien — aide to Bill O'Dywer, Mayor of New York and Mitchel Cogley

Despite wartime conditions Roscommon and Kerry attracted 79,245 people in 1944.

According to Seamus O'Riain:

'A new dimension in sports communication was added when radio began broadcasting the games over the air. Groups gathered eagerly around the available radio sets enchanted by the word-pictures woven by Micheál O'Hehir in describing every puck and kick of the ball in the ebb and flow of a game. Listeners felt as if they were present at the game, sharing in its excitements and tensions through the unique power of the broadcaster's voice.

The influence of broadcasts was seen clearly in the remarkable increase in public support for GAA games, swelling the attendances especially at the major games. They also had a part in creating an atmosphere of support for publications dealing with affairs of the Association.'

Following requests from Irish Missionaries in Africa, arrangements were made to relay the commentary of the 1953 All-Ireland football final between Kerry and Armagh to that continent, following arrangements with Radio Brazzaville in French equatorial Africa, the late Micheál O'Hehir, Prince of broadcasters, in his book *My Life and Times* tells us that:

'the response to Radio Eireann was overwhelming and hundreds of letters and telegrams poured into the station . . . from as far away as Queensland in Australia, Italy and Sweden, . . . all parts of Africa . . . even heard on a ship in Hong Kong harbour . . .'.

These broadcasts together with some Railway Cup games on St Patrick's Day continued until 1961. I can still hear the voice of Micheál O'Hehir sending personal messages to Missionaries in faraway Africa – the dark continent, in parts, the white man's grave – light years away from the shores of Ireland. Those messages touched the hearts of listeners and brought tears to the eyes.

The author and his wife Mary with Micheál O Hehir

Then came television and it brought with it the same doubts as regards attendances as radio had done not too many years earlier. The worries were all without foundation of course. Croke Park's development programme had increased its seating capacity and major games became all ticket affairs. And tickets became like gold dust.

Strange as it may seem the first GAA match to be televised was a hurling game at Gaelic Park, New York in 1951. I had the pleasure and honour of meeting and corresponding with a man who was present at that historic event. I refer to the late Fr Sean Reid, Order of Carmelites, a native of Ballyhale, Co Kilkenny. He died on September 14, 2003, aged 93 – a scholar, poet and theologian, who spent 70 years in the US and never lost his love for the land of his birth and its native games:

'I re-organised the Kilkenny hurling club of New York and put a team back in play and in order to have 15 players had to line out after being some fifteen years out of action. I was President or Chairman of the club for twenty five years and its delegate to the Central body of the New York GAA for the same time. Then in 1961 I was elected its President and again the next year. When asked to run for a third term I declined and was succeeded by the late John O'Donnell, who was then the lessee of Gaelic Park.'

Here is how Fr Sean recalled the televised game in Gaelic Park:

'I was assigned to act as an aide to the announcer, (or whatever he was called), who had never seen a hurling match and had no idea what it was like. The camera was set up on the sidewalk outside the park looking into the field and during the first half I was up there helping him, explaining what a foul was, a sideline puck, how many points equalled a goal, etc. When the halftime whistle blew he asked me to go in as a player, as I was already togged out in my black and amber. The teams were my own Kilkenny and I believe Galway. And he added that the camera would follow me. I went in as a sub and I don't think the ball ever came near me, or if it did, my attempts to play it were, to say the least, feeble.'

As already stated Fr Sean was a poet. From his many poems I have chosen the one below It produces in verse a concise history of Ireland from early times, culminating in an expression of patriotism from the heart of an exile. Father Sean called it Irish History –

I would have called it My Native Land.

Irish History

First to reach Ireland
About 6000 B.C.
Visitors from Scotland
Just a small company
Ice Age long ended
Climate had improved
Ireland a dense forest
From present far removed.

Those few explorers
Perished in Noah's Flood
For a while thereafter
Nothing there but mud
Then came Partholonians
Supposedly from Spain
A plague destroyed them
Or maybe 'twas the rain.

Next to come the Firbolgs
Said to be from Greece
And to be uncultured
Short was their lease
Soon to be defeated
By Tuatha de Danann
"Tribe of goddess Danu"
Realm by magicians ran.

At the time of Solomon
Celts to Ireland came
Led by Milesius
From whence the name
Of the Milesians
Who won out and stayed
Inisfail their Ireland
Rare talents displayed.

De Danann defeated
Were sent underground
To become the Fairies
To hold Ireland spellbound
Ireland then peaceful

Until Vikings or Danes
Robbing Monasteries
Bloody their campaigns.

Danes finally defeated
By King Brian Boru
No more incursions
One more overdue
It came from England
Are in Ireland still
Maintaining a foothold
But only until

Comes the inevitable
They must evacuate
With De Danann magic
Ireland will repatriate
Her displaced children
To all will guarantee
Freedom of religion
Leprechaun and Banshee.

Abbreviated history
Of Eire its Irish name
Known to all as Ireland
And it finally became
The Isle of destiny
Celtic Inisfail
Once more and forever
The land of the Gael.

Fr. Sean knew well the influence and power of the media when he participated in the 1951 T.V. broadcast of the hurling game in New York.

Within his lifetime he had seen the changes from the day when a woman in Co.Kilkenny got the All Ireland hurling final result a few days after the game, to the days when the telegram brought the news following the final whistle, later still to the radio broadcasts and finally the advent of television that gave us, not only, instant action but immediate replays of deeds of valour and on occasions acts of folly.

The media, in all its forms, press, radio and TV have played a special role in promoting and popularising our national games, while at the same time enriching the lives of many, many people – sa bhaile and i gcéin.

Paddy D Mehigan "Carbery"

The old-style throw-in as Mick Mackey anxiously awaiting
the break in a Limerick v Cork encounter

21
A Trip Down Memory Lane –
Childhood Memories

FADA SIAR MO SMAOINTE, BREIS AGUS CAOGA BLIAIN.

Some moments remain etched in the memory. Time neither dims nor erases them and the distant memories remain much more vivid than memories of recent times.

1945

My earliest recollections of a GAA Championship affair centre around the

Jack Lynch

All-Ireland Football final of 1945, Cork v Cavan. People were talking about whether or not Jack Lynch of Cork would add a football medal to his four in a row hurling ones of 1941–1944. There was I deciding before dinner time on a lovely sunny Sunday to have a bet of sixpence on Cork (about 4 cent, a lot of money then) with my father who hailed from the Longford/ Cavan border and collecting my winnings that afternoon.

Years later when I met Jack Lynch I told him of that bet and he said, 'Your judgement was sound'.

Tom O'Reilly, Cavan

1945 CORK FOOTBALLERS

Mol O'Driscoll

Eamonn Young

Caleb Crone

Tadgh Crowley

Mick Tubridy

1946

The first hurling match I listened to on the radio was the Munster Championship clash between Tipperary and Limerick in 1946. Tipp were reigning All-Ireland champions and had beaten Limerick in the Munster final of 1945 by 4:3 to 2:6. Within two minutes or so of Micheál O'Hehir saying, 'the whistle, the throw-in and the game is on' Tipp had the sliotar in the Limerick net twice. Disaster loomed for my native county. By half-time, however, scores were level and when the full time whistle blew Limerick had won by 3:5 to 2:2. It was Mick Mackey's second last full hour in the green and white of Limerick.

J Sayers, full back for Laoighis

The hurling final of '46 was between Cork and Kilkenny. What I remember of that game is the dramatic solo run of Christy Ring from around midfield shortly before half-time, as he opened up the Kilkenny defence and from close range gave Jim Donegan in the Kilkenny goal no chance of saving. The second half solo runs of Jim Langton along the wing for Kilkenny as described by Micheál O'Hehir also remain vivid in my mind but they were not enough to save the day for the Noresiders.

The football final of '46 was full of drama. Kerry reached the final with a 3 point win over a dashing Antrim outfit with names alien to the Southern ear – Armstrong, O'Hara, Watterson, McCorry and Gibson. It was exciting stuff. Bill Casey of Kerry and Harry O'Neill of Antrim got their marching orders in the second half. In those days you were merely told that a player from each side had been sent off. However, by listening carefully you quickly deduced who was gone.

ANTRIM   *Members of the Antrim Team of that era*

M McMahon

J Morgan

Harry O'Neill

Ray Beirne

B McAteer

J McCallin

W Feeney

G Watterson

Pat O'Hara

S McAleavey

Peter O'Hara

Sean Gallagher

Jimmy Roe

Roscommon got to the final with a rather fortunate 2 point win over Laois in a highly exciting game that attracted over 51,000 spectators.

Those semi-finals were played on August 18 and 25 respectively. By that time, however, there were grave concerns for the harvest. From mid-year there had been downpours of rain making it the wettest year in living memory. The country was facing an emergency. Rationing was still in being. Post-war Europe was still in a state of devastation with many parts close to starvation. The Government issued a call for volunteers from all walks of life to help save the harvest. As a consequence, the football final was postponed until October 6, 1946. For Kerry it meant that Bill Casey's suspension was up and he would line out at centre back.

Paddy Burke

With about five minutes left to play I felt sure that Roscommon were about to add a third title to their wins of '43 and '44 and plant the seal of greatness on their football teams of the forties. The score was Roscommon 1:7 Kerry 4 points. Then, based on the trend of play up to then, the seemingly impossible happened. First, Paddy Burke – 'lovely dark haired Paddy Burke' – scored a goal. And if my memory is right a sideline kick to Kerry resulted in Tom "Gega" O'Connor sending the equaliser to the net.

Work on the beet harvest caused the replay to be postponed until October 27. It was a closely fought affair. Scores were level as the closing minutes ticked

Gus Cremins

away. Gus Cremins, who had been Kerry's captain in the drawn game, was dropped. Now he came on as a sub. He fielded a Roscommon clearance around mid-field, side-stepped Eddie Boland, and sent over a mighty point – something that he had practised every evening in training. A goal followed and Kerry were All-Ireland football champions for the sixteenth time.

Eddie Boland

ROSCOMMON

A selection of Roscommon's footballers.

Jack McQuillan

Mick Culhane

Bill Carlos

Donal Keenan, a Roscommon forward.

John Casserly

G. Nolan

Bill Jackson

Frankie Kinlough

Jimmy Murray, Roscommon's Captain

1947

Willie Fahy, Galway

1947 brings to mind much drama. The football final was played at the Polo Grounds, New York. Cavan, who had defeated Roscommon in the semi-final, faced Kerry who had accounted for Meath at the same stage. Micheál O'Hehir painted a vivid picture of the game as it unfolded and we listened spell-bound as we sat around the range in the kitchen. I still have those line-outs off by heart, so here goes:

Jim Brophy, Galway

CAVAN

Val Gannon

Willie Doonan

Brian O'Reilly

Paddy Smith

John Wilson*
(capt.)

John Joe O'Reilly

Simon Deignan

P J Duke*

Phil Brady

* no image available

Tony Tighe

Mick Higgins

Columba McDyer

Joe Stafford

Peter Donoghue

T P O'Reilly

KERRY

Dan O'Keeffe

Dinny Lyne (capt.)

Joe Keohane

Paddy Bawn
Brosnan*

Jackie Lyne

Bill Casey

Eddie Walsh

Eddie Dowling*   Eddie O'Connor*

Gerald O'Sullivan*

Dan Kavanagh

Batt Garvey

Tom 'Gega'
O'Connor*

Frankie O'Keeffe   Paddy Kennedy

The official programme of the match showed Gerald O'Sullivan at right half-forward for Kerry. Other records show his brother Eddie occupying the position.

It seemed like a miracle in 1947 that a game being played in New York could be broadcast across the Atlantic to listeners in Ireland. The quality of reception wasn't great, but that didn't take anything from our sense of awe.

In the early stages it began to look like a cake-walk for Kerry. Not only did they go eight points up but they also had two goals disallowed.

It's the closing five minutes I remember best. Cavan were a point up. Micheál O'Hehir had realised some minutes earlier that the radio lines were booked five minutes short – the result of protracted preliminaries at the Polo Grounds. Micheál kept appealing for five minutes more. We kept wondering would we get the final score at all. Would Kerry stage a traditional rally and carry the day? They didn't. Micheál O'Hehir got his five minutes. Cavan tacked on three points. It ended 2:11 to 2:7 – great excitement, time for a cup of tea.

Cork and Limerick, Kilkenny and Galway and finally Cork and Kilkenny produced the greatest thrills of the 1947 hurling campaign. In the Munster final Limerick dominated and when the final whistle blew were most unfortunate to be on the wrong side of a 2:6 to 2:3 scoreline.

Galway, who had beaten the cream of Munster in the Railway Cup final on St Patrick's Day, were equally unfortunate at Birr in the All-Ireland semi-final. They matched the best that Kilkenny could produce and were a point ahead when the referee blew the whistle and Galway supporters rushed onto the pitch to hail their heroes. But it wasn't the final whistle. There was more 'lost' time to play. The game resumed and in the seconds remaining Kilkenny added two points to snatch a one point victory. Galway were left to ponder the might-have-beens.

Terence Leahy

Cork and Kilkenny produced an epic final:

Unlike the previous year, Ring is contained and is scoreless from play. Kilkenny are two points clear at half-time. Entering the closing stages – there is a lot of time added on – Kilkenny has never been headed. Then Mossie O'Riordan goals for Cork and it looks like a winner as they go ahead for the first time by one point. Play continues. Kilkenny adds three points. Now they have gone two points clear. Cork strike again for a goal via the flying Joe Kelly. Cork one point up. More time to play. A free to Kilkenny. Terry Leahy stands over the sliotar. Micheál O'Hehir says he wouldn't be in Terry's shoes for all the tea in China. Leahy equalises. Surely a draw now. But with seconds remaining Terry Leahy, who got half of Kikenny's scores, gathers a short Cork clearance, swerves away from Alan Lotty and sends over the winning point – Kilkenny 0–14 Cork 2–7.

Later that year – November 9 to be precise – Limerick and Kilkenny met in the National League hurling final. Kilkenny were in search of a double. Only part of the game was broadcast. It was tea time when Micheál O'Hehir came on radio to announce that the game had ended in an exciting and thrilling draw, Limerick 4:5 Kilkenny 2:11

Dick Stokes of Limerick, who had been pursuing his medical career in England, travelled back to Dublin by boat for the game. Years later he recalled it for me:

Joe Kelly

'The ship was tossing a bit and I said to a steward – "What's it going to be like?" "Ah, just a bit of a swell," he said.'

Well, as Dick said to me:

Paddy Collopy

'If that was just a bit of a swell I'd hate to have been there in a storm. I was as sick as a dog when I landed. I got a few hours sleep and lined out at centre forward. I was as a weak as a thraneen. After a while I switched to full forward and wasn't long there when I pulled on a ball that finished in the net.'

The replay took place on March 8 the following year. It was another thriller. Paddy Collopy in the Limerick goal was superb and brought off two 'impossible' saves from close range. 'Goalkeeper Collopy's Wonderful Saves' was a heading on the sports page of a Monday morning newspaper. At wing back Seán Herbert was an inspiration and at centre forward Dick Stokes gave an exhibition. This time he flew home for the game.

When I met Mick Mackey we talked about that game and the victory over a great Kilkenny team. He told me that his brother John wasn't going to travel at all that day. It was his last year in the Limerick jersey. In the end he did travel and came on as a sub.

The Limerick team which defeated Tipperary in the 1947 Munster Senior Hurling Championship. **Front Row**, (*left to right*): Jackie Power, Seán Herbert, Peter Cregan, Owen O'Riordan, Johnsie O'Donoghue, Paddy Fitzgerarld (Askeaton), Paddy Fitzgerald (St. Patricks), Jerry Pigott. **Back Row**: Michael Herbert, Michael Ryan, John Mackey, Thomas O'Brien, Jim Sadlier, Derry McCarthy, Toddy O'Brien, Timmy Ryan.

It was just as well. He scored two goals. 'They wouldn't have won without him,' said Mick to me.

1948

The first shock of 1948 came when Laois defeated reigning All-Ireland champions Kilkenny in the Leinster Championship. Another surprise awaited hurling fans in Munster. In the provincial final Waterford defeated Cork, the kingpins of Munster hurling, by one point. Waterford had gradually lost a lead of eight points in the final quarter of the game. Cork had whittled it down to one point when Ring gained possession about 40 yards out. His shot was barely wide of the upright. Jim Ware's puck out ended the game.

In the final against Dublin, Waterford had a convincing win and brought the McCarthy Cup to the Decies for the first time. Jim Ware was captain with John Keane as the centre forward. Veterans of the 1938 final (lost to Dublin) Mick Hickey and Christy Moylan were recalled.

In football 1948 beckoned the end of an era for Kerry. They lost the All-Ireland semi-final when they were outclassed by a rising Mayo team on the score 13 points to 3. Many great names were consigned to football history.

In the final, Mayo faced Cavan – reigning All-Ireland champions. It was an amazing game played in gale wind conditions. Cavan had the wind in the first half. In the twelve minutes before half-time they swept in on the Mayo goal to score three goals. Incredibly, Mayo were scoreless. Cavan led by 3:2 to nil at half-time.

The second half belonged almost entirely to Mayo. But they did concede a vital goal to Cavan. And with about five minutes remaining the scoreline stood Cavan 4:4 Mayo 4:4.

It was all excitement now. And Mayo had the wind. A Cavan attack brought a free and a point from sharp shooter Peter Donohoe. Then on the call of time Mayo won a fourteen yards free. A draw looked a certainty. Padraig Carney took the kick. Cavan centre forward, Mick Higgins, was back defending. He blocked the kick (it was argued afterwards that he had charged before the kick was taken and was therefore not back the required distance from the ball) following which the ball was sent wide. The kick out brought the final whistle.

P Carney

1949

Tipperary had suffered three years of first round defeats, 1946, '47 and '48, at the hands of Limerick. In 1949 the Tipperary mentors set about rectifying matters. Among the steps they took was a visit to Dublin to talk with Tipperary born Jimmy Kennedy. Jimmy was based in Dublin and had played with his adopted county in the 1948 All-Ireland final. Negotiations with Jimmy went on for hours. He didn't want to leave Dublin. But, doggedly, the mentors persisted and eventually wore Jimmy down. He declared for Tipperary. This was lucky for Tipp, as we shall see.

At the Gaelic Grounds in Limerick in 1949 Cork and Tipperary played a hurling marathon. It took two draws and extra time to decide the issue in Tipp's favour. It was hard physical bruising stuff that prompted letters of criticism to the papers afterwards.

Jimmy Kennedy

In the next game Tipperary had a victory over Clare. Limerick had dethroned All-Ireland champions Waterford so the way was now clear for a Limerick/Tipperary Munster final.

It was a repeat of the 1945 Munster final. And the result was the same – a three point win for Tipp. Limerick fans were left to ponder a disallowed goal and wonder why as good a goal by stout-hearted Jackie Power as he had ever engineered in a great career – wasn't allowed.

Mutt Ryan's display in '45 caused the Munster final of that year to be called the Mutt Ryan final. 1949 was definitely the Jimmy Kennedy final. The final score was Tipperary 1:16 Limerick 2:10. Jimmy Kennedy contributed something like ten or eleven of those points – all but one from frees – frees taken from all angles and distances. The man was a marksman supreme. In the four games of the Munster championship Jimmy scored two goals and 27 points.

For the second year in a row – this time in the Leinster final – Laois disposed of Kilkenny. They then beat Galway in the All-Ireland semi-final, to reach their first All-Ireland final since 1915. There the dream ended. At half-time in the final

J Kearney

the contest was close. Unfortunately, Laois's earlier championship form completely deserted them in the second half. They lost heavily – 3:11 to 3 points. Tipperary took their fourteenth title – thanks without a doubt in the world to sharp shooting Jimmy Kennedy.

In football Cavan were in search of a first ever three in a row. Kerry fell in '47, Mayo in '48. Only Meath now stood between them and a little bit of history. Meath had been improving since '47. They recalled Jim Kearney to midfield, veteran of the 1939 lost final against Kerry. Cavan had the bulk of the Polo Grounds team of '47 still intact. It was the first meeting of the counties in an All-Ireland final. Cavan's dream was not to be and Meath won the close contest. They took "Sam" to the Royal County for the first time.

MEATH

Some of the players on that famous Meath team.

P Meegan

K McConnell

K Smyth

C Hand

P O'Brien

M McDonnell

Seamus Heery

C Kelly

P Connell

1950

1950 saw me witness for the first time the hurling skills of Dick Stokes. It was the Munster championship meeting of Limerick and Tipperary at the Gaelic Grounds Limerick. Dick had played inter-provincial hurling with Munster Colleges in the late '30s and in 1940 he'd won an All-Ireland title with Limerick.

He won Fitzgibbon and Sigerson Cup titles with UCD and County Dublin hurling and football titles with the same club. He was also a regular on Munster Railway Cup teams in the early forties.

In 1950 he won a Munster junior football title with his native county. He was a versatile performer and could play on any line in the field.

Now, as the autumn of his career beckoned, I was watching him in the fullback line – full of hurling craft, great positional sense, uncanny anticipation, crisp, clean striking and above all the complete sportsman.

Limerick had missed a few points, some from frees, before Dick stood over a free that must have been all of 90 yards out and with a beautifully controlled movement of lift, swing and strike, he sent the sliotar soaring over the bar for a great point.

Tipperary won and went on to contest the All-Ireland final with Kilkenny and win a game that Kilkenny lost by going for goals when points were there for the taking.

1951

I was in Thurles on a sunny Sunday afternoon to witness Tipperary and Limerick in action. Limerick broke away from the throw-in. Their midfielder Mick Ryan gained possession. He soloed goalwards and from about 21 yards sent in a shot that bounced in front of Tony Reddan in the Tipperary goal and finished up in the back of the net.

Sean Flanagan

That day I saw Pat Stakelum of Tipperary at his majestic best. In the centre half-back position he commanded the field and dominated the game. His hurling was a joy to watch. A sportswriter reporting on the game said he had not seen such a performance from a centre back since the days of Paddy Clohessy of Limerick and Jim Regan of Cork.

Great things were happening in Leinster. Wexford, unlucky to lose the 1950 Leinster final to Kilkenny by one goal, defeated

Laois to capture the Leinster crown for the first time since 1918.

We had a unique and glamorous pairing when Tipperary and Wexford faced each other to contest the All-Ireland final. Wexford's hour hadn't yet come but their arrival on the scene beckoned a new dawn and a new era. In the two decades to follow they would illuminate the hurling scene with great performances, add to hurling as a spectacle and leave a lasting impression where sportsmanship was concerned.

In football, Mayo made it four in a row in Connaught and under the captaincy of corner back Sean Flanagan, two in a row in All-Ireland titles with a fine victory over Meath.

MAYO PLAYERS

J. Munnelly

S. Wynne

H. Dixon

J. Staunton

J. Gilvarry

P. Irwin

M. Flanagan

P. Solan

Eamonn Mongey

Two of Mayo's team after a spot of practice, John Forde (1948 Captain) on the left and club-mate Peter Quinn. Photo Battle Ballina.

Tom Acton, a Mayo corner forward. Photo: Battle Ballina.

1952

The year I saw Croke Park for the first time. It was Sunday, September 7 – All-Ireland hurling final day – Dublin and Tipperary in the minor game, Dublin and Cork at senior level.

I had begun my working life in Dun Laoghaire in July so the trip to Croke Park was a short one. For the majority of enthusiasts it was a case of first come first served. The all-ticket occasion was still a long way off. However, it wasn't one of those days when the gates were closed and thousands couldn't gain admission, as was the case for the football final of '49 between Meath and Cavan, when, with almost 80,000 people crammed in like sardines, upwards of 10,000 were turned away. The 1952 hurling attendance was about 65,000.

I was positioned behind the Canal goal – standing room in those days. The first half of the minor game was superb with Tipperary a point to the good at half-time. In contrast the second half made no sense at all. Tipperary piled on score after score, goals and points, to walk away with the game.

People wondered how Des Ferguson would fare on Christy Ring. Des had a fine first-half and his every clearance from the right halfback position was roundly cheered. Dublin didn't deserve to be a goal behind at half-time. They had played very well but Dave Creedon in the Cork goal was in splendid form. For the first ten minutes of the second half the pattern was the same. Then Dublin seemed to fade, or perhaps it was a case of Cork discovering the form that had halted Tipperary when they'd set their sights on a fourth in a row All-Ireland title. It was also the form that stymied Galway who had come within two points of defeating the Cork side in the All-Ireland semi-final in Limerick.

Cork added 1:9 to their half-time score of 1:5. Dublin could only muster two points to bring their final score to 7 points. I would, in the years ahead, see many more-enduring finals. But being a first it left landmark memories.

The memories of those early years in no way diminished or overshadowed the games of subsequent decades that I witnessed. The sense of occasion, the excitement, the high level of sportsmanship and the mingling of good-humoured supporters continued year after year.

Could the thrills of this year's Munster hurling final between Waterford and Cork be surpassed; or the subsequent All-Ireland semi-final between Kilkenny and Waterford; or the two great drawn games of the 2003 hurling campaign between Limerick and Waterford and Cork and Wexford?

Childhood memories of a new generation!

GREAT LOUTH FOOTBALL NAMES OF MY YOUTH

Tom Conlon

Jack Bell

Jim McDonnell

Stephen White

Sean Boyle

Paddy Markey

An all Ardee halfback line

Mr. P. McNamee, President of the G.A.A., starts the memorable final at Croke Park yesterday

Mr P McNamee, President of the GAA, starts the memorable final at Croke Park.
Kilkenny v Cork 1939.

22
Ladies Football

Caitriona Ambrose
(Limerick) and Evelyn
Kehoe (Wexford), 2004
(Courtesy Paddy Delaney,
New Ross)

Have you seen the teams parading
with the pipers on before?
Have felt the hot blood coursing
through your veins?
Have you chafed and grown impatient
for the coming treat in store?
As you listened to the piper's
stirring strains.
  (Frank Doran)

Salute the fastest growing sport in Ireland – ladies football. Around the turn of the last century the organisation had a membership of 25,000. In the short interval since, that figure has rocketed to almost 100,000. Attendances are up too. On All-Ireland final day the crowd has continued to grow and grow. So let's trace the game's origin and growth.

Seventy years after the foundation of Cumann Camogaíochta na nGael, the Ladies Gaelic Football Association (Cumann Peile Gael na mBán) was established following a meeting at Hayes's Hotel, Thurles in 1974. It was a modest beginning. Only four counties were represented at the meeting –

Offaly, Kerry, Galway and Tipperary. Those four counties, together with Laois, Roscommon, Cork and Waterford took part in the first All-Ireland championship in 1974.

The final was held at Durrow. Tipperary defeated Offaly on the score 2:3 to 2:2. Their captain, Kitty Ryan, proudly took possession of the Brendan Martin cup and returned in triumph to Tipperary. The occasion got good press coverage from *The Evening Press* and *The Irish Press*.

In the first eight years, five counties shared the senior titles – Tipperary (3) Offaly (2) Kerry (1) Cavan (1) and Roscommon (1). Then Kerry took over and dominated. They won nine titles in a row, 1982–1990 inclusive.

After that, Waterford, Monaghan and Mayo reigned supreme, capturing five, two and four titles respectively, between 1991 and 2003 inclusive.

Luckless Laois were the losers on seven occasions dating back to 1985 before eventually beating a great Mayo team in 2001 to take a well-earned and well-deserved All-Ireland crown.

In 1981 the first All-Star selection was chosen. The four provinces and seven counties were represented. The team lined out as follows:

Martina McGuire
(Cavan)

Ann Maher   Eileen O' Connor   Bridget Sheridan
(Tipp)   (Kerry)   (Cavan)

Bernadette Stankard   Rose Dunican   Bernie Dunne
(Galway)   (Offaly)   (Offaly)

Mary Twomey   Jean Dunne
(Kerry)   (Offaly)

Bridget Reynolds   Eliz O'Brien   Mary J Curran
(Offaly)   (Roscommon)   (Kerry)

Lilian Gory   Deirdre Quinn   Patricia O'Brien
(Tipp)   (Leitrim)   (Cavan)

Then came the day of the great breakthrough for ladies football. It was June 1986. Waterford faced Wexford in the junior final. The venue was Croke Park. It was the first time a ladies football game was played in the great stadium. On that historic occasion, Waterford had a resounding victory, 4:13 to nil. The game was a curtain-raiser to the senior final in which Kerry defeated Wexford on the score 1:10 to 8 points.

The structure of the Association is a replica of the GAA – clubs, county boards, Central Council, and Congress which meets annually. The President is elected for a three year term – a post held at present by Geraldine Giles of Westmeath. The current Chief Executive is Helen O'Rourke.

Cumann Peile Gael na mBán like its sister organisation Cumann Camogaíochta na nGael, is independent of the GAA. However, both have the support and blessing of the Gaelic Athletic Association.

As the game gradually spread, it began to capture the public imagination. Nowadays, it rivals men's Gaelic football as a spectacle. And in the art of shooting points from play the ladies have tended to overshadow their male counterparts.

A few of the rules differ from those of men's Gaelic football:

All deliberate bodily contact is forbidden and that includes use of the shoulder.
Outfield players may pick the ball off the ground from a standing position. If on the ground the player may play the ball away but may not take possession of it.

As well as a senior All-Ireland championship there are many more All-Ireland competitions that include – Junior, U18, U16, U14, Senior club, Inter-Provincial, Post-Primary Senior and Post-Primary School Junior.

The most recent TG4/O'Neill's Ladies All-Star Team was chosen in 2003 as follows:

Action from Limerick v Wexford game 2004 (Courtesy Paddy Delaney, New Ross)

Andrea O'Donoughe
(Kerry)

Nuala O'Se
(Mayo)

Helena Lohan
(Mayo)

Maria Kavanagh
(Dublin)

Annalisa Crotty
(Waterford)

Martina Farrell
(Dublin)

Emer Flaherty
(Galway)

Angie McNally
(Dublin)

Mary O'Donnell
(Waterford)

Lisa Cohill
(Galway)

Christina Heffernan
(Mayo)

Michelle McGing
(Mayo)

Mary O'Rourke
(Waterford)

Geraldine O'Shea
(Kerry)

Kasey O'Driscoll
(Kerry)

As Con Houlihan commented earlier:

'And I haven't forgotten a quiet revolution that is taking place under our eyes. Camogie has come of age; now it is played with teams of fifteen and on a full pitch. And Ladies Football is rapidly becoming a salient part of our culture – the best is yet to be.'

A practice stint gets under way at O'Loughlin's Gaels ground, Kilkenny.

A Distinguished Group: Munster Final, Thurles 1928. **The above group includes**: Most Rev Dr Harty, Archbishop of Cashel, Patron of the GAA (*seated in centre*), Mr Sean Ryan, solicitor, President of the Association; Ref J.J. Meagher, C C, President, Tipperary County Board; Rev Dr Doyle, C C, Kilkenny; Rev M Maher, P P, Killenaule; Rev T O'Connor, C C, Thurles; Rev M J Lee, Diocesan Inspector, Thurles; General Eoin O'Duffy, Major Fitzmaurice (famous Atlantic flyer); Chief Supt Hannigan, Thurles; Mr W Myles, Editor, Tipperary Star; Mr Con Browne, GAA, Limerick; Mr Dan Morrissey, Dungarvan, etc., etc.

23
Neglected Heroes

The football and hurling world of the GAA is strewn with neglected heroes. Understandable, in a way, when you consider that we are dealing with a span of 120 years. I was reminded, in different ways, in recent times of just a few of the GAA's neglected players.

THE PURCELLS OF TIPPERARY

Sister Stephanie Purcell wrote me a series of letters between January 1999 and February 2001 and recalled old times.

> 'Phil Purcell was my only brother and eldest of the family. He was born on November 13, 1902 and died February 2, 1961. He lived for the camán and our house was the meeting place of many of the "lads". They played and replayed games and the younger people of us hardly knew anything, any world, existed outside the clash of the ash! A different world, a different culture – God bless you for helping to keep it alive.'

Phil Purcell was a brilliant Tipperary defender in the 1926–36 era. He played eight times for Munster and won five Railway Cup titles. He won All-Ireland honours in 1930 and in the administrative field spent a term as Tipperary County Secretary. He was a fine referee and had charge of the classic 1947 hurling final between Cork and Kilkenny.

> 'Fr Phil, a first cousin, will be home for a holiday this year. He was a sub on the 1937 All-Ireland team. He feels a bit like Oisín in dhiaidh na Féinne; so many he knew have gone heavenwards. He was the elder brother of Tom who did great hurling in a short spell, got a fatal disease and died at 28 years.'

Tom, too, was a first class defender with Tipperary. Standing hip to hip with the maestro Christy Ring in Munster championship clashes in the forties, he wouldn't give an inch and would emerge with reputation enhanced.

JOE BAILEY – WEXFORD

Joe was born in 1918 and in his early youth learned the skills of good full-back line play in his native New Ross. It is a reflection of Joe Bailey's ability as a hurler that when Wexford hurling was at a relatively low ebb Joe, together with the legendary Nick Rackard, caught the eye of the Leinster Railway Cup selectors. For five years in the early forties Joe lined out at corner back for Leinster. But he never won a Railway Cup medal. Each year defeat was Leinster's lot – often by the narrowest of margins.

In 1943 they met Munster in the final. They came tantalisingly close – a one point defeat on the scoreline, 4:3 to 3:5.

This is the Munster forward line, in a team captained by Jack Lynch, that Joe and his colleagues faced on St Patrick's Day 1943.

Christy Ring	Jackie Power	Tommy Doyle.
(Cork)	(Limerick)	(Tipp)
Johnny Quirke	Willie O'Donnell	Mick Mackey
(Cork)	(Tipp)	(Limerick)

In the course of the game John Mackey of Limerick replaced Willie O'Donnell. Great men all.

In the last quarter of the game Leinster went six points clear and seemed set for victory. But then, goals by Johnny Quirke and Jackie Power levelled matters before Christy Ring sent over the winning point to deny Leinster, and Joe Bailey, a Railway Cup victory.

Joe played at fullback for his native Wexford from 1939 to 1949, when he retired at the age of 31. There was still a lot of hurling left in Joe when he decided to call it a day and it probably cost him a Leinster medal in 1951.

During Joe's days in the purple and gold jersey he saw the signs of progress that would lead to the great successes of the fifties. On June 18, 1944 at Barrett's Park, New Ross, Wexford for the first time since 1908 defeated Kilkenny by 6:4 to 4:6 in a Leinster semi-final. The game was

Wexford Senior Hurling Team, 1945. Joe Bailey, Front row: 2nd from left.

refereed by Dr J J Stuart, who was later to become President of the GAA.

In a National League game at Wexford Park in 1945 Wexford again defeated the Noresiders by 3:6 to 3:4. The good days for Wexford were slowly approaching.

Off the field Joe was one of nature's gentlemen. On the playing pitch he was a close, teak-tough, hard-hitting, uncompromising defender. There was no drawing back. With Joe it was give and take and get on with the game. On one occasion following a game against Kilkenny he had to get 19 stitches in his head.

In his playing days Joe came shoulder to shoulder with many of the greats – among them, John Mackey and Mick Mackey of Limerick, Paddy Larkin and Jimmy Langton of Kilkenny, Jim Young of Cork and Mutt Ryan of Tipperary.

Joe won four county senior titles with New Ross in 1939, '43, '44 and '45. Those were the war years. Players cycled to the venues and often togged out by the side of the ditch.

I spoke recently with Joe's widow Mary – a lovely lady who will be 80 this year. She recalled those hurling days, as she used to travel to all the matches. During the war if the team was travelling by car it was necessary to get a permit. Mary used travel with them – illegally of course – and so to hide her they would cover her with a rug behind the front seats.

She recalled too, carefree occasions when they cycled return journeys with friends to Dublin and Ballybunion – 'we were young, we were young'. In Ballybunion they stayed at Bob Stack's of Kerry football fame and struck up a lifelong friendship. When Joe died on November 8, 1990, aged 72, Bob's widow Bridget, aged 89, travelled from Ballybunion to attend Joe's funeral.

MICK KENEFICK – CORK

Mick Kenefick played at centre forward for the Cork minor hurling team that defeated Galway by 3:11 to 1:1 in the 1941 final. He won a senior title the following year when the Leesiders, captained by Jack Lynch, made it two in a row.

In 1943, Mick, playing at left half-forward, had the honour of leading his county to their fourteenth All-Ireland senior title following victories over Kerry, Waterford and Antrim. Hurling of course was in the blood and in the genes. His father Dan, was on the 1912 team that lost to Kilkenny by one point, 2:1 to 1:3. 'Sliabh Ruadh' described the closing moments of the Munster final against Limerick as follows:

> 'One of the toughest and most terrible tussles ever waged for a
> Munster crown . . . stubbornly fought from start to finish with a

Cork v Antrim, 1943. Mick Kennefick (captain), Sean Condon,
Billy Murphy, Jim Young, Jack Lynch, Con Murphy, etc.

slight advantage in favour of Limerick. Leading by a point coming on to time, Limerick fought like demons. Then Byrne of Sarsfields pulled at a wing ball, up to Kenefick, the latter crossed to Kennedy of Carrigtwohill and the Limerick citadel fell.'

Cork 2:2 Limerick 1:3

Mick's sister, Eileen Sexton, wrote to me in January 2003 and here is an excerpt from her letter:

'I am going to GAA games, both codes, for years. I am eighty-one years. My first remembrance of a championship game was in Cork city in 1928, I think, or 1929. My first All-Ireland was 1937 in Killarney, Tipperary v Kilkenny, next in 1939 Cork v Kilkenny. I have not gone last year or this year. I was not feeling too good... Ours was a real hurling house. My three brothers played with the Barrs in Cork. My father played with a team called St Mary's who are now gone. We often in the Summer here in Cork would see four matches every Sunday and walk to all . . . I love the games on TG4 . . .

Now my reason for writing to you is as follows. My brother was Captain of Cork in 1943. He wasn't a long time player with Cork. He was injured in the first round in 1944 against Tipperary – a broken wrist that took a year to heal – and played no more . . . my brother was as far as I know the youngest captain of any All-Ireland winning team. Now if that record still stands it is unique and deserves a mention. . . .'

*Cork's youngest captain, 19-year-old Mick Kennefick,
chaired off the field after leading his team to victory
in the 1943 final against Antrim.*

Mick Kenefick was 19 in July 1943. Contemporaries have described him as being tall, athletic and versatile – a player who would have blossomed into a first-class centre back but for injury. Mick taught in St Colman's Community College in Midleton. Despite a short hurling career he was never forgotten by the people of Cork. He was a folk hero. At matches all over the county, whenever he appeared, people would be whispering and pointing him out to their children.

He died in 1982.

WILLIE GOODISON – WEXFORD

Willie Goodison

Willie Goodison was born in 1924 and was one of a family of 16 children. His love for Gaelic games came from his father, James 'Dinger' – himself a fine exponent of both hurling and football with the St John's Volunteers Club at the turn of the last century.

As a minor footballer, Willie showed tremendous promise and by 1943 he was part of the county senior panel. Thus began an illustrious career at senior level that lasted for over a decade.

Willie was one of the all time great centre half-backs of Gaelic football. He was a tower of strength in that position. Certain qualities set him apart – great fielding, timing his jump, a wonderful pair of safe hands, an ability to cover on the

(Left to right): Tony Tighe, P.J. Burke, Jim Cody, Peter
Donohoe, Willie Goodison, Jack Culleton, Joe Stafford.

wings, and finally a side-step coupled with a dummy that baffled many an
opponent. And he could point a 50 too – a rare feat – in the days of the old
style leather football. At the height of his career some sportswriters were
comparing him to the magnificent Jack Higgins of Kildare who played in
the 20s and 30s.

Willie played his club football with Volunteers – a team with which he
won six county senior titles. He also hurled, but Volunteers abandoned
hurling in 1945 – they were breaking too many hurleys and replacing them
was costing too much.

He was honoured many times by the Leinster Railway Cup selectors but
unfortunately no medals came his way. He was first chosen in 1946 and was
captain. A semi-final win over Ulster by just one goal paved the way for a
final meeting with Munster, with a team powered by Cork and Kerrymen. It
was close – 2 points in it at the final whistle, Munster 3:5 Leinster 1:9. And
in the years that followed it continued to be a case of 'so near and yet so far'.

For Willie 1945 was a year of partial success on the one hand and bitter
disappointment on the other. Wexford hadn't won a Provincial senior title
since 1925. The Leinster campaign of 1945 got under way at Dr Cullen Park,
Carlow, against Kildare. An outstanding display by the half-back line of Jack
Culleton, Willie Goodison and John Morris set the foundations for victory.

Laois fell at the next hurdle where Willie had the better of matters with that
classical Laois man, Tommy Murphy. The final was played at O'Moore Park,
Portlaoise, against Offaly. Wexford won by 1:9 to 1:4. They now had a team
that was improving with every game – blending and combining well,
physically strong and fit – capable of matching the best in the land. Only
Cavan now stood between them and a final day in September in Croke Park.

It is generally believed that a well-intentioned but unsuitable training
programme caused Wexford's downfall in the semi-final. The team were

sent to Rosslare for a fortnight's collective training – away from home and away from family. It was an unfamiliar environment for a team with an average age 22. It wasn't a success. But that is hindsight.

Cavan won by 1:4 to 5 points. It was little consolation to Willie Goodison that he had played the game of his life.

During Willie's era in the purple and gold of Wexford, the county produced quite a few first class dual players: Nicky, Bobby and Billy Rackard – Nicky was the most famous of the three in this capacity – Paddy Kehoe, Des O'Neill, Billy Keilthy, Wilkie Thorpe, Padge Kehoe and Bobby Donovan.

In 1950 Willie was chosen on an Ireland selection that played the combined Universities. He was also an excellent referee and was called upon to take charge of county finals in the neighbouring counties of Carlow, Wicklow and Laois. His greatest moment came when he was honoured with the whistle for the 1955 All-Ireland football final between Kerry and Dublin.

Willie's brother Jimmy represented the Model County at senior level from 1939 to 1948. He too was a fine footballer. He was also very much in demand as a referee.

The following amusing story is told by Jimmy – against himself. He refereed a county final in Carlow. On his own admission he had a 'stinker'. Willie, who had also taken to refereeing was appointed to do the Carlow County final the following year. At the last minute he found he could not carry out his duties and asked Jimmy to fill in for him.

'Do you want me to be lynched?' retorted Jimmy. 'With one of the teams from last year's championship again in that year's final.'

But Willie was persistent.

'I will do it,' said Jimmy, 'on condition that you say nothing about withdrawing, also give me your Ireland jersey and stockings to wear.'

Togged out in those and a peak cap pulled down over his eyes he got away with it.

In fact, Jimmy convinced the crowd so well that after the match one old fellow came up and said, 'Willie, would you mind signing your autograph for my friends?'

'Certainly,' replied Jimmy, as he penned the name of Willie on the book.

As the old man was walking away he shouted back to Jimmy, 'Oh, by the way, Willie, did that brother of yours ever get his eyes tested for glasses?'

(My sincere thanks to Liam Lahiff of Wexford, who supplied much of the detail for this article.)

DERRY MCCARTHY – LIMERICK

Derry McCarthy hails from Dromcollogher on the Limerick/Cork border. Many take the view that he was the best hurling forward ever to emerge from West Limerick. Unfortunately, at crucial stages, the Limerick selectors, or at least some of them, seemed blind to his talents and followers of the Limerick team believe that Derry's omission cost Limerick dearly on occasions.

Derry could score goals. He knew the art of full forward play – the whip on the ground ball – the creating of space – the drop puck.

He won county junior titles with his native parish in 1949, 1959 and 1963. His career in the senior jersey of Limerick began in 1946 when the Shannon-siders defeated reigning All-Ireland champions

Jimmy Smyth

Tipperary in the first round of the Munster championship. Here is how Tommy Doyle remembers that game –

'John Mackey took all the hard knocks without a murmur . . . and if he couldn't get the goals himself he kept our backs busy while Jackie Power or Derry McCarthy added salt to our wounds.'

The following year, 1947, Limerick and Tipperary met again on a June Sunday in Cork Athletic Grounds. Another day of agony for Tipperary and Tommy Doyle:

"We were out-generaled, out-manoeuvred and out-hurled by a rampant Limerick team . . . Power, Mackey and McCarthy forming the full line, had four goals between them in the hour."

1948 brought more of the same for Tipperary:

'John Mackey, Jackie Power and Derry McCarthy were Limerick's match-winning trio.'

Limerick defeated All-Ireland champions Waterford in the Munster semi-final of 1949. Now, for another joust with Tipperary – with the Munster title the prize for the winners. Inexplicably, Derry McCarthy found himself on the reserves' bench. Limerick lost by 1:16 to 2:10 to Tipperary with particular help from Jimmy Kennedy. Many Limerick supporters were convinced that their match winning forward had watched the game from the sideline.

The Munster Railway Cup selectors, however, held Derry in much higher regard. He was chosen at full

Derry McCarthy

P Kenny

forward for each of the years 1951–1954 – flanked by the most illustrious of company, Paddy Kenny of Tipperary and Christy Ring of Cork from 1951–1953, when the title was won and Jimmy Smyth of Clare and Christy Ring of Cork in 1954. He could hold his own in top class company. I saw him in action and marvelled at his skills and in particular his ability with the drop puck.

Billy Rackard recalled for me an incident in the 1953 Railway Cup final in which Derry McCarthy played a key role. Leinster hadn't won the title since 1941.

'We were almost there after all those years – Leinster two points up in the dying minutes of the game – when a certain Christy Ring came thundering towards the Leinster goal, having rounded my brother Bobby, who was now literally glued to Ring's right elbow. The marking was close, and Christy without question was running into a cul-de-sac. From my right fullback position hugging Seamus Bannon I observed the following sequence of events. Ring knew he had nowhere to go – that is if we all sat tight in the fullback line – but lo and behold the fabulous old Diamond (Hayden), obsessed with the prospect of finally upending his arch-rival of many years, could not resist the temptation of such a golden opportunity. He just took off like a wounded rhino to clobber you-know-who.

Ring, the Maestro that he was, saw the chance, actually tempted him, then palmed the ball past the unfortunate Diamond and faded away. Meanwhile Derry McCarthy, a Limerick man and a master of the drop shot, made no mistake with a ball that was unstoppable, lifting the mist clear of the rigging.'

In 1952 Derry was chosen at full forward on the Rest of Ireland team. In later years he won the 'Hall of Fame' award and Dinny Lanigan Trophy at the Limerick GAA Supporters Club gathering.

MICHAEL "GAH" AHERN & PADDY "BALTY" AHERN – CORK

'An rud a beirtear sa cnámh, is deacair scarúint leis sa bhfuil'

Hurling skills continue to travel in the genes and flow in the blood. Deirdre Ahern played in the Mini-Sevens at half-time during the 2003 All-Ireland Hurling final between Cork and Kilkenny. Let's trace her lineage:

Deirdre Ahern with the Liam McCarthy Cup and a replica presented to her great-grandfather, Michael "Gah" Ahern.

Michael "Gah" Ahern is her great-grandfather, married to Carrie Coughlan, daughter of Patrick "Parson".

Paddy "Balty" Ahern, Eudi Coughlan and John Coughlan are her great grand-uncles.

Patrick "Parson" Coughlan (father of Eudi and John) is her great great-grandfather and his brothers Dan, Tom, Denis and John are great grand-uncles.

Kathleen Coughlan of camogie fame is a great grand-aunt.

All are steeped in hurling fame and glory with All-Ireland titles aplenty – 27 senior and one junior between them all.

Deirdre's more recent forebears matched the enthusiasm of earlier generations without scaling the same heights. Her grandfather, Paddy Ahern, starred with North Mon during his school days and later played senior with Blackrock. Her father, Michael, captained the Under-16 team at St Finbarr's, Farranferris, in his school days.

Deirdre Ahern's early ancestors on the Ahern side were sea-faring people, ships' stewards, maritime fire-officers, merchant navy. (The only relation who wasn't a seaman was "Gah's" maternal grandfather who was a master tailor).

On the Coughlan side her early ancestors were salmon fishermen who earned their money on the sea, waited for the tides and lived their lives

Michael "Gah" Ahern

following the rhythm of the sea. They had their own fleet of boats and for generations they lived this simple and hard life.

The common bond between the two families was love of the sea, loyalty to Blackrock and a passion for hurling.

Let's now return to "Gah" and "Balty".

The love of their lives was playing the game of hurling. This they did rain, hail or snow – no matter what was going on in the community around them.

They both belonged to a golden era in Cork hurling that stretched from 1919 to 1931. Both were giants in the company of giants – Jim Regan, Sean Óg Murphy, Tom Barry, Dinny Barry-Murphy, Jim Hurley and Eudi Coughlan, to name but some.

"Gah" was born in 1904. As a hurler he was a pure stylist, a ball player, full of subtlety and guile, all flicks and tricks. He relied completely on his wrist-work and stick-work. He could hit equally well from either side – it didn't really matter to him – 'a master of the ash' said "Carbery".

According to Jack Lynch, "Gah" had a 'hold' on the crowd because he created in them an expectation of goals. Jack added:

'he had a cheeky bold little face which was very appealing and

Michael "Gah" Ahern

that the crowd would be shouting at "Balty" to go and bail him out if anyone was horsing into "Gah".'

Cork trainer, Jim "Tough" Barry thought the world of "Gah" as a player and "Gah" knew it. Jim's belief in "Gah" was unshakeable for he knew that "Gah" was a prolific scorer and had the talent to convert half chances.

"Gah's" career coincided with the infancy of radio broadcasting when very few people owned a radio. In Cork, supporters who couldn't get to a game would assemble outside Brabant's Radio Shop in the Grand Parade to listen to the broadcast.

On one such occasion Cork were trying to come from behind but despite plenty of possession the sliotar went everywhere but between the posts. During a lull in play an elderly supporter pushed his way to the front and, not realising that the commentator couldn't hear him, shouted into the loud speaker, 'please sir, tell them to pass it to "Gah".'

Paddy "Balty" Ahern

"Gah" was one of the greatest forwards of all time. In the 1928 All-Ireland final against Galway in a 60 minute final he scored 5:4 – a record that still stands. No one knew better than "Gah" where the goal posts were. He would whip on the sliotar, watch the net shake, the green flag wave and the crowd go wild in admiration and celebration. And he did it regularly.

He was nominated for the right half-forward position on the Millennium team – but the position went to Christy Ring.

"Gah" died young – it all happened suddenly in the end, on December 30, 1946, aged 42. His funeral was one of the biggest ever seen in Cork.

Frank Doran of Clonakilty honoured "Gah" in the following poem aptly titled, *The Late "Gah" Ahern.*

The Late "Gah" Ahern

He sparkled in the Gaelic sky
A scintillating star,
His camán craft and artistry
Won fame on fields afar.
A forward fleet, of genius high,
A raider without par.

Sleep on, great Gael,
Brave "rocky" sleep,
Both calm and deep,
God's peace be thine.
While camáns clash
And rings the ash,
Thy name shall fail
To fade – 'twill shine –
Great deeds entwine,
And everlasting keep.

"Balty" was the older of the two brothers, born in 1900, he lived to be 71. Both "Balty" and "Gah" were wonderful personalities – light-hearted, full of fun and always enjoyed a good song.

"Balty" had an incredible physique and phenomenal strength. On the field he was forceful, fearless and uncompromising. He was a left-handed player – a ciotóg. From the time he made the team in 1919 until 1931 he was a permanent fixture. If he was fit, he was on.

He was the heartbeat, the engine, the driving force of the brilliant Cork team of the 1926/1931 era. He played at centre forward but also at full forward when the occasion demanded.

Between 1919 and the signing of the Anglo-Irish Truce, the GAA came a very poor second to the 'National struggle' for many in Cork hurling circles. And that included "Balty". He played his part in the movement. However, following the signing of the Treaty he played no part whatsoever in the tensions of the Civil War period.

Michael Ahern, "Gah's" grandson, said that 'like Jim Hurley there was something happened to them between 1919 and 1922 that left them unfazed by everything that came after it'.

"Balty" became the first man in either hurling or football to win senior All-Ireland medals spanning three decades on the field of play. He was the first Corkman to win five All-Ireland senior hurling medals and one of the first teenagers to win an All-Ireland.

A friend inserted the following in the 'In Memoriam' Columns of *The Evening Echo* on Monday October 23, 2000:

Ahern: Paddy "Balty" Oct. 23. 1900–Oct.2. 1971. In proud and everlasting memory on the Centenary of his birth, hurler supreme with Blackrock and Cork, humorist, friend and gentleman.

The following is a summary of the hurling successes of "Gah" and "Balty" Ahern.

SENIOR ALL-IRELANDS	COUNTY CHAMPIONSHIPS
1919 B	**1920** B
1926 G + B	**1924** B
1928 G +B	**1925** G+B
1929 G + B	**1927** G+B
1931 G + B	**1929** G+B
	1930 G+B
JUNIOR ALL-IRELANDS	**1931** G+B
1925 G	
	RAILWAY CUP TEAMS
NATIONAL LEAGUES	**1927** B+G
1926 G +B	**1928** B
1930 G+B	**1929** G
	1931 G
MUNSTER CHAMPIONSHIPS	**1932** G
1919 B	**1933** G
1920 B	
1926 G+B	TAILTEANN GAMES
1927 G+B	**1932** G
1928 G+B	
1929 G+B	
1931 G+B	

(My thanks for the research work done by Michael Ahern – father of Deirdre and grandson of "Gah" – which was a major contribution to this article.)

SEAN BRENNAN – KILKENNY

Mention the name Kilkenny in sporting circles and people immediately think of hurling and hurling men. And well they might, for the county has produced many household names in this particular field.

So, instead, let us now call to mind an outstanding son of Kilkenny who excelled at football. I refer to Sean Brennan, still hail and hearty and self-employed delivering beer – son of Joe and Mary (née Dormer) – one of a family of ten children – born in 1927.

The football pedigree was good. His father Joe and Uncle Tom were both on the Kilkenny football panel of 1922 – beaten by Dublin in the Leinster final on November 5 of that year – the last time Kilkenny took part in a Leinster senior football final.

Sean started his football career at Moneenroe NS under the guidance of his teacher, Mr McCann. Sean gave evidence of his potential in 1945 when he played in the Kilkenny senior and minor football finals on the same day – winning the senior game with a North Kilkenny selection and losing the minor game with Moneenroe.

Sean has been described as 'the complete footballer' with height, strength and ability and a great dash about his play which made him capable of playing at halfback, midfield, half forward or full forward.

In 1946 Sean joined the Army and was attached to the Corps of Engineers in the Curragh. There he made an immediate impact on the football scene. He played in six Kildare senior football finals between 1947 and 1952. He won four – his first with the army in 1948. He left the army in 1950 and after a short while working in Guinness's Brewery he returned to County Kildare. There he joined the Sarsfields club with whom he won three in a row 1950/51/52, a club record that still stands in Kildare.

Sean played at county level with Kildare in 1947 and his talent was soon spotted by the Leinster Railway Cup selectors. He played many times for the province and won Railway Cup medals in 1952, playing at centre half-back, and in 1953 at midfield – the only Kilkenny man to win two Railway Cup football medals. Later in 1953 Sean emigrated to New York where he played with Clare, Kerry and Cork at different times.

He was a regular on the New York football team which in those years played the National League winners in the St Brendan Cup – alternatively in the Polo Grounds and Croke Park. The trip home was always special. One of those games was at Croke Park in 1958 against Dublin. Sean was full forward. Paddy Flaherty, the Dublin goalkeeper was 'buried' in the net. The finger was pointed at Sean. He always protested his innocence saying that the credit belonged to Mick Furlong of Offaly. Sean's last trip as a player was in 1960.

In 1962 he founded a Kilkenny football team that won the New York championship that year and dominated the football scene for a number of years in that city.

Then came a very special trip home. In 1997 he was invited to be a Guest of Honour when the Gaels of his native parish assembled to celebrate the fortieth anniversary of the club's 'five in a row' county senior football title successes of 1957–1961. The club played under the name The Railyard.

A great night of celebration that went on into the early hours of the morning was had by all at the Newpark Hotel in Kilkenny – an assembly that included all the players of that era – some of whom returned from overseas for the occasion.

And when it was all over, Sean returned with his wife Gertrude to his home in Yonkers where his grown up family of six all live close at hand.

JOHNNY CULLOTY – KERRY

A recent trip to the Kingdom recalled to mind that great dual player, Johnny Culloty of Killarney.

Almost half a century had elapsed since we played on opposite sides in a county minor hurling championship game between Killarney and Killorglin at the J.P.O'Sullivan Memorial Park in Killorglin.

That was 1954 – a year when Johnny played minor and junior hurling and football with his native Kerry. He was a fine hurler, both as a goalkeeper and outfield player. In 1961 he was full forward on the Kerry junior hurling team that defeated Meath in the Home Final and London in the final. To this hurling victory he added four National League Division Two medals.

However, it is as a footballer that Johnny really shone. And, as in hurling, he did that both in goal and outfield. Seán Óg O'Ceallacháin picked Johnny in goal in his football team of the 1950–1980 era.

Johnny was right corner forward in 1955 when Kerry had a surprise win over a much vaunted Dublin 15. And if my memory serves me right he caused havoc in the Cavan defence in the semi-final replay of that year. Injury the following year kept Johnny sidelined for some time. He made a comeback in 1959 and was in goal when Kerry outplayed Galway in the All-Ireland final under the captaincy of Mick O'Connell from Valencia Island.

Kerry were back in Croke Park again the following year. Johnny was in goal. Down, making their first All-Ireland appearance, provided the opposition. Great men make mistakes and it happened to the highly talented Johnny in this game about 10 minutes into the second half when scores were level. As I watched from the Hogan Stand I saw a high ball float into the Kerry square and come down just under the crossbar at the Railway end. Johnny, unimpeded, seemed to have everything under control as he reached to catch. Somehow the ball slipped from his grasp and into the net. From then on Down were in the ascendancy and Kerry lost by 2:10 to 8 points.

Johnny put that disappointment behind him two years later when Roscommon were defeated in the All-Ireland final. A goal by Garry McMahon shortly after the throw-in pointed the way to victory. Johnny collected his third All-Ireland medal. Then injury struck again and he was out of the game for almost a year.

1964 and 1965 were dark years for Kerry football. Twice in a row they lost to Galway in the All-Ireland final. Never before had a team succeeded in doing that to Kerry. Defeat wasn't Johnny's fault. No goals were conceded in either final by either team – 1964, 15 points to 10; 1965, 12 points to 9.

A two point defeat by Down in 1968 made it three losses in a row by Kerry at Croke Park. However, they got back on the winning trail again in 1969. Johnny was captain. Offaly provided the opposition. It was a great day for the Kingdom. On the score 10 points to 7 Kerry became the All-Ireland champions for the twenty-first time – leading the role of honour and four titles ahead of their nearest rivals, Dublin. The glory didn't end there as Kerry won again the following year at the expense of Meath.

Johnny played in nine All-Ireland senior football finals. He tasted victory on five occasions. He won twelve Munster senior football titles. He also won five National League medals and was captain when Kerry took the title in 1969. He played in three Railway Cup finals but without success.

Johnny will always rank as one of the greats of Gaelic games.

Munster Final, 1926 – Cork v Tipperary. Tipp Levels Up! Thurles,
September 19, 1926. (Courtesy of Tipperary Star.)

24

Ulster Makes Its Mark

A wilder in his day
They said
Could toe to hand
The hard-fought ball
Then tacking through
A reef of rolling shoulders
Drop-kick hammer leather home
To a spume of wild applause.
(Christy Keanneally)

Success and glory in senior competition were slow in coming Ulster's way.

Antrim were the first team from the province to contest a senior final. In 1911, with a Shauns club selection, they lost to Cork in the football final by 6:6 to 1:2. They were back again the following year, represented by a Mitchel selection, and in a much closer contest lost to Louth by 1:7 to 1:2. Both of these finals were 17-aside contests.

The years sped by and in 1928 Cavan failed by one point, 2:6 to 2:5, to a great Kildare team captained by Bill "Squires" Gannon – the first player to be presented with the Sam Maguire trophy.

In 1930 Monaghan produced a surprise result in the All-Ireland semi-final, when they accounted for Kildare on the score 1:6 to 1:4. The final proved to be a game too far. They lost heavily to a star-studded Kerry team – one of the greatest of all time, a four-in-a-row team with names like John Joe Sheehy as captain, Johnny Riordan, Joe Barrett, Johnny Walsh, Paul Russell, Con Brosnan, Bob Stack and John Joe Landers – by 3:11 to 2pts.

At last a great day dawned for the province. It was September 24, 1933. Cavan, captained by Jim Smith, put Ulster football on the map. Having defeated four-in-a-row All-Ireland title holders Kerry by 1:5 to 5 points in the All-Ireland semi-final, they faced Connaught champions Galway in the final. History was made. Cavan, on the scoreline 2:5 to 1:4, took the Sam Maguire northwards. It was Ulster's first senior title and fueled hopes of better days to come. Two years later they repeated the success when they defeated Kildare in the final.

In the forties the strength of football in the province of Ulster began to manifest itself in the Railway Cup competition. They won titles in 1942, '43, '47 and '50. Great names appeared on those teams. Let's recall some of them:

Barney Cully, Tom O'Reilly, T P O'Reilly, Simon Deignan, John Joe O'Reilly, Mick Higgins, Paddy Smith, P J Duke, Tony Tighe, Phil Brady, Victor Sherlock, Peter Donohoe (all Cavan), Jim

McCullagh, Alf Murray, Sean Quinn and Bill McCorry (all Armagh), Vincent Duffy (Monaghan), Hughie Gallagher and Columba McDyer (Donegal), Kevin Armstrong, George Watterson, Harry O'Neill, Sean Gallagher, Sean Gibson and Brian McAteer (All Antrim).

Ulster Railway Cup Team 1943 (Winners).

By 1952 Cavan had captured a fifth title. They were, however, still the only Ulster County with a senior football crown.

Then came the sixties and things began to change. Down made history when Kevin Mussen (1960), Paddy Doherty (1961) and Joe Lennon (1968) took the Sam Maguire trophy across the border. They gave to Gaelic football many more legendary names – among them, Leo Murphy, Dan McCartan, Jim McCartan, Sean O'Neill, Pat Rice, Brian Morgan, Colm McAlarney, George Lavery, Jarlath Carey and Tony Hadden.

Kevin Mussen

Those famous victories, at the expense of Kerry, Offaly and Kerry respectively, brought the Ulster All-Ireland total to eight titles. However, it left

The Down Team of 1960

seven Ulster counties still without the ultimate reward, despite much valiant effort and a high standard of performance from many of them.

But it's a long road that has no turning. In 1991 the tide really turned for Ulster and a run of wonderful successes ensued. In a thirteen year span the province won six football crowns – four in a row from 1991 to 1994 when Ulster counties reigned supreme.

Anthony Molloy

Down led the way in 1991. Captained by Paddy O'Rourke they accounted for Kerry in the All-Ireland semi-final and in a nail-biting finish held on to defeat Meath in the final – two points to spare, 1:16 to 1:14. They repeated the success in 1994 under the captaincy of D J Kane.

Armagh Players of the 1953 era

G. O'Neill

Eamon McMahon

Sean Quinn

Bill McCorry

Pat O'Neill

M. O'Hanlon

G. McStay

E. Morgan

Tyrone fell in the Ulster final, Cork in the semi-final and in the final itself Down had to call on all their football and fighting qualities to defeat Dublin by 1:12 to 13 points. It was the county's fifth senior football title. It gave them parity with the men of Breffni.

The remaining four victories represented breakthroughs for the first time – each causing outpourings of indescribable joy and elation.

Donegal in 1992 were appearing in their first All-Ireland final. Captained by Anthony Molloy they defeated Dublin by 18 points to 14 points.

In 1993 Derry under the captaincy of Henry Downey defeated Cork by 1:14 to 2:8. It was the county's second All-Ireland appearance. They had lost to Dublin in 1958; a day when Jim McKeever and Sean O'Connell were majestic; a day when even the introduction of veteran Rody Gribben in the second half was not sufficient to save the day.

I witnessed the semi-final of 1958 – Derry v Kerry. It was a wet, miserable August day. Rain fell throughout the game. The quality of the football suffered. Derry advanced with one point to spare – 2:6 to 2:5. They would meet Dublin in the final, the first meeting of the counties in a championship game since they had clashed in the All-Ireland hurling semi-final of 1902.

Armagh's moment of glory came in 2002. They were captained by their centre half-back Kieran McGeeney. Their opponents Kerry were favourites but when the final whistle blew the honours belonged to Armagh. It was their third time in the final, having lost to Kerry in 1953 and Dublin in 1977. The '53 final was one of the great games of football. Stationed in Killorglin I listened to Micheál O'Hehir's broadcast on radio. At the throw-in the crowd in Croke Park had swelled to 90,000. Some of those had travelled on the 'Ghost train' from Kerry – leaving the Kingdom shortly after midnight on Saturday and puffing its way to the capital. Armagh led by a point at the break. It was anyone's game. With time ticking away Armagh got a penalty that would have restored their lead. Micheál O'Hehir conveyed the tension and the urgency. From the boot of Bill McCorry the ball flashed wide of the post. The Kingdom prevailed.

For Tyrone the long wait ended in 2003. It was their third final appearance. They lost to Kerry in 1986 and to Dublin in 1995. History was made when they faced Armagh, reigning All-Ireland champions, in the 2003 final. It was the first time that teams from the same province contested a football final. It was a proud day for Tyrone when their long serving captain Peter Canavan held the Sam Maguire cup aloft to a scene of highly delighted red and white supporters.

It was 'Sam's' first trip to Tyrone – its eighth to the six counties – its fourteenth to Ulster. Now, Antrim, Monaghan and Fermanagh await their day.

Unfortunately, within six months of a wonderful victory, tragedy struck Tyrone. Cormac McAnallen, their full back and newly appointed captain, died suddenly in the early hours of March 2. The GAA world was stunned. In a short lifetime he had achieved much on Gaelic fields, winning All-Ireland titles at minor, under-21 and senior level. He was only 24.

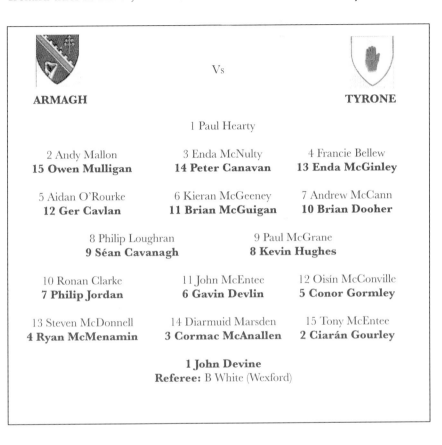

ARMAGH   Vs   **TYRONE**

1 Paul Hearty

2 Andy Mallon   3 Enda McNulty   4 Francie Bellew
15 Owen Mulligan   **14 Peter Canavan**   **13 Enda McGinley**

5 Aidan O'Rourke   6 Kieran McGeeney   7 Andrew McCann
12 Ger Cavlan   **11 Brian McGuigan**   **10 Brian Dooher**

8 Philip Loughran   9 Paul McGrane
9 Séan Cavanagh   **8 Kevin Hughes**

10 Ronan Clarke   11 John McEntee   12 Oisín McConville
7 Philip Jordan   **6 Gavin Devlin**   **5 Conor Gormley**

13 Steven McDonnell   14 Diarmuid Marsden   15 Tony McEntee
4 Ryan McMenamin   **3 Cormac McAnallen**   **2 Ciarán Gourley**

1 John Devine
Referee: B White (Wexford)

Griffith, De Valera, Laurance O'Neill (Lord Mayor) and Michael Collins at
Croke Park.

25
The Camogie Centenary

This year, AD 2004, is the Centenary of the Founding of Cumann Camogaiochta na nGael, originally titled An Cumann Camo-guidheachta. The name of the game was invented by a well-known Gaelic scholar of those days, Tadhg O'Donoghue. The driving force behind its foundation were the lady members of the Keating branch of the Gaelic League and in particular Maire Ní Chinneide BA who later became Mrs John Fitzgerald.

T F O'Sullivan in his book *The Story of the GAA* records that:

'The rules were drawn up by the committee of the Keating Camoguidheacht Club (established 1903) with the assistance of some members of the Keating Hurling Club.

The weight of the hurley was recommended not to exceed 32 ozs.

The weight of the ball was to be from 4–5 ozs and the circumference 7–9 inches.

The size of the ground was fixed at, from 60–100 yards long and from 45–60 yards wide.

A team was not to consist of more than twelve players.

Intentionally stopping the ball with the skirt was a foul.'

The Keating Canogie Team, founded by the members of the Keating branch of the Gaelic League in Dublin in 1903. Keatings won the first ever public camogie match when they beat Cuchulainns in July 1904 at the Meath Aricultural Grounds in Navan, by a goal to nil.

The game was, of course, strictly non-physical contact.

In 1904 the following officers were appointed to the Keating Club:

President – Maire Ní Chinneide
Vice President – Margaret Curtain
Secretary – Nora Roche
Treasurer – Anastasia Rafferty
Captain – Cait O'Donoghue (sister of Tadhg)
Vice-Captain – Mary O'Sullivan.

The second Camoguidheacht Club to be established was in Newry in May 1903 with the following officers:

President – M Lavery
Treasurer – K Grant
Secretary – R McAnulty
Captain – L Lavery
Vice-Captain – M O'Callaghan

Committee: M Derham, A Courtney, L McAnulty, K Burns, J McCorry, M Fealy, and M McGrath.

The first inter-club camoguidheacht match was played in the Co Meath Agricultural Grounds at Navan, on Sunday, July 17, 1904. It was between the Keatings and the Cuchullains who were the second club to be formed in Dublin. Final score Keatings 1 goal Cuchullains nil.

In 1904 a club was formed amongst the students of The Dominican Convent, Muckross Park, Donnybrook, Dublin – the first educational establishment to take up the game.

In 1906 games involving the following clubs were played – Dundrum Volunteers, Cuchullains, Lucan, Ard Craobhs, Rathmines, Keatings, Crokes (all of Dublin), Newry, Dundalk Emers, and Castleblaney.

The spread of the game was slow. However, by 1912 'Slieve Ruadh' was able to report 'steady progress' and listed the affiliated clubs as follows:

Dublin 11
London 2
Wexford 5
Meath 2
Louth 2

The appeal of the game in the early days appears to have been confined to the East Coast.

The first inter-county game is believed to have taken place in 1912 at Jones's Road, where Dublin defeated Louth.

The game continued to spread and by 1932 sufficient progress had been made to enable an All-Ireland senior camogie championship to take place. On July 30, 1933, the final was contested by Dublin and Galway at the Sportsfield, Galway. Victory went to the Metropolitans on the score 3:2 to 2 points. The Dublin captain Maura Gill became the first camogie player to be presented with the O'Duffy Cup – named after Sean O'Duffy, an engineer from Co Mayo and a member of the Crokes GAA club, who had shown a keen interest in promoting camogie from as far back as 1911.

The rules and, indeed, the attire changed over the years. The long flowing dresses of the early days were replaced by the gymslip and in 1974 Kilkenny broke with tradition and set the tone with a new outfit consisting of a jersey and skirt.

The duration of the match was another area subject to change. The All-Ireland finals of 1932 and '33 were of forty minutes duration. That was changed to fifty minutes in 1934. A further review in 1988 saw the introduction of a sixty minute game.

The 1942 final, Dublin 4:1 v Cork 2:2 was the first to be broadcast and in 1956 the Gael Linn Senior inter-provincial competition began. Leinster won the title with a 7:1 to 3:1 victory over Ulster.

Una O'Connor

Máiréad McAtamney Magill won the Camogie Player of the Year Award in 1979.

To mark the Diamond Jubilee of the Camogie Association in 1964 the All-Ireland club championship was inaugurated. Celtic of Dublin won the title. They defeated Deirdre of Antrim by 5:2 to 1 goal. Celtic had in their line-out Una O'Connor, one of the all time greats of the camogie world.

A decision to run the senior championship on an open draw basis was taken in 1973. Cork and Antrim met in the final; Cork won on the score 2:5 to 3:1

The final of 1998 between Cork and Galway which was won by the Rebel County on the score 2:13 to 15 points was the first final to be televised. Since then we have seen some cracking All-Ireland camogie finals on television. Bord na Gaeilge has been sponsoring the All-Ireland senior championship since 1995.

Major developments took place in 1999. Team size was increased to fifteen and players lined out like their hurling counterparts and the game was played on a full size GAA pitch.

In a wonderful final Tipperary and Kilkenny served up an absorbing contest. The Premier County made camogie history by winning their first ever senior All-Ireland title. It was a game to remember and a score to remember too, Tipperary 12 points Kilkenny 1:8.

Seven counties have won the O'Duffy Cup: Dublin (26) Cork (20) Kilkenny (12) Antrim (6) Tipperary (4) Wexford (3) and Galway (1). Since the championship began in 1932 there have been five draws. From the time the All-Ireland club championship was initiated in 1964 success has been well spread among the clubs of the aforementioned counties (excluding Antrim) but including Limerick

Just as in hurling and football, camogie, down the decades, has had its quota of heroines and superstars. I have met some of them and profiled them in my previous books *Hurling Giants, Legends of the Ash* and *Captains of the Ash*.

Angela, Shem, and Ann Downey (Courtesy of Jim Connolly Photography)

They read like a team of all time greats. So let's name them in team format – worthy ambassadors for the game of camogie in its centenary year –

Eithne Leech
(Dublin)

Liz Neary   Margaret O'Leary Lacey   Marie Costine
(Kilkenny)   (Wexford)   (Cork)

Marian McCarthy   Bridget Doyle   Elsie Walsh
(Cork)   (Wexford)   (Wexford)

Orla Ní Shíocháin   Mairéad McAtamney
(Dublin)   (Antrim)

Mary O'Leary   Angela Downey   Kathleen Mills
(Cork)   (Kilkenny)   (Dublin)

Ann Downey   Sophie Brack   Una O'Connor.
(Kilkenny)   (Dublin)   (Dublin)

Sophie Brack died in recent years. She played with Dublin in the forties and the fifties; won eight successive All-Ireland titles in the era 1948–1955 incl; and captained her county to victory on six occasions.

Kathleen Mills went to her eternal reward in August 1996 at the age of 73. Kathleen played camogie with Dublin from 1941–1961 incl. She won fifteen All-Ireland medals. She leads the field and has set a record that may never be equalled. Her closest rivals are Una O'Connor with thirteen titles and the Downey twins, Angela and Ann, with twelve each.

Orla Ní Shíocháin, daughter of the late Seán Ó'Síocháin, former General Secretary of the GAA, wife of Jack Ryan and mother of Naoise, Shane and Feargal, died on December 22, 2003 following a brave and courageous fight against a protracted illness.

Orla played camogie with Dublin from 1964 to 1982. During that time she won three All-Ireland titles and eight county titles.

Solas na bhFlaitheas don triúr acu.

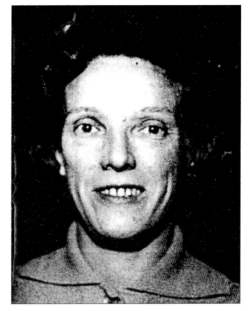

Kathleen Mills

Orla Ni Shíocháin

Another Great Fifteen:

Pegg Hogg
(Cork)

Vera Mackey   Alice Hussey   Jackie McAtamney
(Limerick)   (Dublin)   (Antrim)

Ann Holden   Biddy O'Sullivan   Bridie Martin
(Kilkenny)   (Kilkenny)   (Kilkenny)

Teresa Maher   Helena O'Neill
(Galway)   (Kilkenny)

Linda Mellerick   Sue Cashman   Sandie Fitzgibbon
(Cork)   (Antrim)   (Cork)

Mary Geaney   Deirdre Lane   Pat Moloney
(Cork)   (Tipp)   (Cork)

BANLAOCHRA NA CAMOGAÍOCHTA 2003

Cumann Camogaíochta na nGael, together with generous sponsorship from the Lynch Hotels Group, announced the top 15 Camogie players of 2003 – titled *The Lynchpins Team of 2003* – at Croke Park on November 25, 2003:

Jovita Delaney
(Tipp)

Rose Collins   Una O'Dwyer   Stephanie Dunlea
(Limerick)   (Tipp)   (Cork)

Mary O'Connor   Ciara Gaynor   Therese Brophy
(Cork)   (Tipp)   (Tipp)

Vera Sheehan   Jane Adams
(Limerick)   (Antrim)

Emer Dillon   Claire Grogan   Eileen O'Brien
(Cork)   (Tipp)   (Limerick)

Eimear McDonnell   Deirdre Hughes   Fiona O'Driscoll
(Tipp)   (Tipp)   (Cork)

On Saturday, February 28, 2004, a Gala Centenary Banquet was held at City West Hotel in Dublin to honour the camogie players chosen on the Centenary Team. In reality it represented sixty-three years of camogie as those chosen covered the period 1941 to date and the senior championship only began in 1932.

Two of those chosen were imithe ar shlí na fírinne – Kathleen Mills and Sophie Brack.

The oldest surviving member is goal keeper Eileen Duffy O'Mahoney who played for Dublin from 1949 to 1957 when she captained the team. In that time she won eight All-Ireland medals. At the banquet Eileen recalled how their club Celtic had a pitch at Coolock and that they themselves used cut the grass.

Modern day players chosen on the team were Angela Downey, Linda Mellerick and Sandie Fitzgibbon.

Angela Downey

Deirdre Hughes, the Tipperary full forward, was the only current day player chosen.

Six of the players chosen have featured in my books *Hurling Giants* and *Legends of the Ash*.

This is the team of the Centenary 1904–2004.

Eileen Duffy O'Mahoney
(Dublin)

Liz Neary   Marie Costine O'Donovan   Mary Sinnott Dinan
(Kilkenny)   (Cork)   (Wexford)

Sandie Fitzgibbon   Bridie Martin McGarry   Margeret O'Leary Lacey
(Cork)   (Kilkenny)   (Wexford)

Mairéad McAtamney Magill   Kathleen Mills Hill
(Antrim)   (Dublin)

Linda Mellerick   Pat Moloney Lenihan   Una O'Connor
(Cork)   (Cork)   (Dublin)

Sophie Brack   Deirdre Hughes   Angela Downey Browne
(Dublin)   (Tipp)   (Kilkenny)

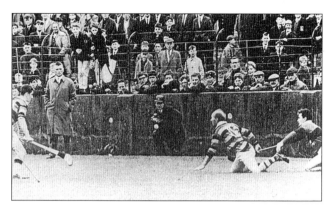

Christy Ring in action during his last championship v UCC,
25 June, 1967. (Aged 47 – 2nd from right)

26
The Structure of the GAA

THE CLUB

The club is the very cornerstone of the Gaelic Athletic Association. That has been the case since its foundation in 1884. The club provides the roots from which the lifeblood of the Association is generated. It is the oxygen of the Association's very being.

Each club is an independent entity – an unincorporated body, managing its own finances and preparing its teams for the championship.

Its members may prepare and submit motions for consideration at Congress.

Teams are affiliated to the County Board and clubs are represented by delegates at District and County Board level.

Club and committee meetings take place as the necessity arises. All clubs are expected to hold an Annual General Meeting (AGM).

COUNTY BOARDS

Each County Board is an independent entity – an unincorporated body. It may operate a variety of committees to meet various needs.

Among its tasks are the running of the county championships and the organisation of county teams for the inter-county competition.

It also deals with matters of discipline within the county.

DIVISIONAL BOARDS

Divisional Boards are a sub-division of the County Boards. They ease the workload at County Board level by dealing with games in their district/division.

PROVINCIAL COUNCILS

These have formed part of the GAA structure since the dawn of the last century. The Provincial Councils organise the provincial championships for clubs and county and also inter-provincial games. Every county in the province is represented by delegates at the Provincial Council.

Within the province they deal with disciplinary and organisational matters, other than disciplinary matters relating to the senior championships which are looked after by the Games Administration Committee (GAC).

The financial accounts of each provincial council, when audited, are submitted to the Central Council.

THE CENTRAL COUNCIL

This is a key body and powerful entity within the organisation. In general Central Council would meet about four times a year.

It consists of:

Chairmen of the Provincial Councils
Two Trustees
The President
The President elect for one year or immediate Past-President (one year)
The Director General (without voting rights)
A delegate from each County
The Chairman of the Council of Britain
The London delegate

A delegate from each of the following:

Britain
All-Ireland Secondary Schools Council
The Vocational Schools
The Primary Schools
The Universities
Irish Handball Council
The North American Board
New York
The Players Committee
Higher Education Council

THE MANAGEMENT COMMITTEE

The Management committee could be described as a mini-Central Council dealing with routine matters that would not require a convening of a Central Council meeting.
   This consists of:

The President
The Chairman of each of the four Provincial Councils
The Director General (without voting rights)
The President elect for one year or immediate Past President (one year)
Two Trustees
One Central Council member from each province

CONGRESS

Congress is held annually at Easter time. It is the counterpart of the AGM of a Limited Company attended by shareholders. Various motions, which may emanate from as far down as club level in the organisation, are aired and dealt with.

Every three years Congress elects a President elect who acts in that capacity for one year, before taking on the role of President for a three year term. Congress is attended by the President, the President elect, the Director General, delegates from each county in proportion to the number of clubs in the county and delegates from overseas, as well as Central Council.

The Director General presents his report which is wide ranging in content.

The proceedings of Congress are dealt with on the basis of an agreed standing orders programme being observed.

THE PRESIDENT

The President is elected by Congress for a three year term, having already completed a one year term as President elect. He may propose, advocate and initiate various activities – all of which should be in accordance with the aims and aspirations of the Association.

The President participates at Congress, Central Council and the Management committee. He may also have an involvement in other committees

The role of a President is also ambassadorial. He attends functions, launches books, performs formal openings of clubhouses and pitches. The President is the public image of the Association.

COMMITTEES

Within the GAA structure a whole variety of committees operate, for example, Motions, Bye-laws, Strategic Review, Games Administration (GAC), Referees, Finance, Coaching, Insurance, Public Relations and Marketing.

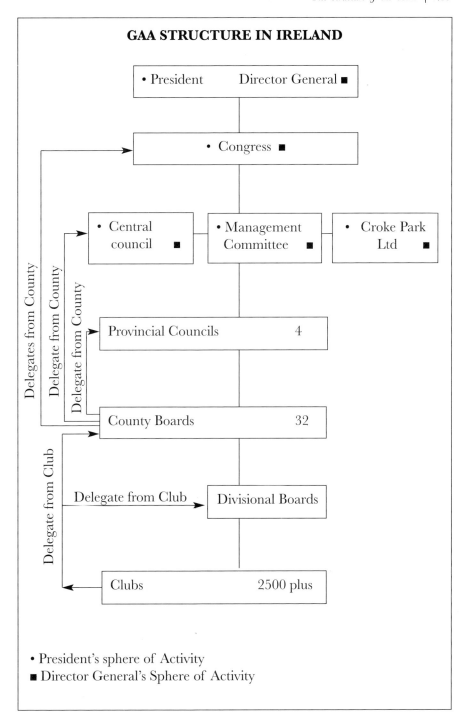

GAA STRUCTURE IN IRELAND

- President   Director General ■

- Congress ■

- Central council ■   • Management Committee ■   • Croke Park Ltd ■

Provincial Councils   4

County Boards   32

Delegate from Club   Divisional Boards

Clubs   2500 plus

Delegates from County

Delegate from County

Delegate from County

Delegate from Club

- President's sphere of Activity
- ■ Director General's Sphere of Activity

Michael Cusack Tells the Story of his Life

Colmans Abbey, Newry.
I left Newry in the summer
of 1871. After one month
with my brother in
Co. Monaghan, I taught
at the French College, Blackrock.
In Jan. 1874 I went to
St. John's College, Kilkenny.
Three months later I turned
up in Dublin, got married,
went to teach at
Lyons ... Co. ...
back to Dublin and
stayed here. The rest of
proceedings is well known.
That is briefly the story
of my life. My brother's is
an equally simple story.
Michael Cusack

[PAGE FOUR]

Cad..., ... Day 1896.

My dear John Botello:
I was born in the parish of
Carron Burren, Co. Clare,
on or about the 41st
anniversary of the murder
of Robert Emmett, ...
ball it the 20th of
September 1847.
My mother died on
Friday the 18th of May 1884.
Her remains were laid
in the Flannery plot
under the Kissane shadow
of the round tower of
Drumcliffe

[PAGE ONE]

27
Team Selections

Team selections fascinate. Any selection, irrespective of the era involved, will bear a subjective view. And, of course, every selection is sure to generate debate, criticism, argument and counter suggestions. One thing, however, is certain. Those chosen will have made an indelible impression, under a range of headings, on the selector(s).

When one considers that an All-Star selection representing just one year rarely satisfies everyone, how could a selection from a decade or a quarter century or an all time great, be expected to satisfy.

The danger, of course, with a selection covering a wide span of time is that, while it honours fifteen great players, it may be perceived by some as dishonouring, by omission, many outstanding performers.

In the mid-fifties P D Mehigan "Carbery" was asked by the editor of *The Gaelic Sportsman* to select 'the best men of my time' for the special Christmas number. "Carbery" had witnessed over fifty All-Ireland finals in hurling and in football. He felt he had established a little record of his own but conceded that Jim Clarke of Ballybunion would beat him in football finals, as he had seen them all since 1887.

"Carbery" was born on St Patrick's day 1884 in Ardfield, Co Cork. He played on the London team of 1902 that was beaten by Cork in the All-Ireland Final. He also played on the Cork team of 1905 that lost to Kilkenny in the final of that year. He retired from the Civil Service in 1934 and took up journalism full time.

Having chosen his teams he realised that it was fifteen hundred great men he could have chosen in hurling and football – not just fifteen.

HURLING FIFTEEN

John "Skinny" O'Meara
(Tipperary)

Dan Coughlan   Sean Óg Hanley.   Mick Derivan
(Cork)   (Limerick)   (Galway)

Pat Stakelum   James Kelleher   Dick Grace
(Tipperary)   (Cork)   (Kilkenny)

Lory Meagher   Jim Hurley
(Kilkenny)   (Cork)

Eugene Coughlan   Mick Mackey   Tom Semple
(Cork)   (Limerick)   (Tipperary)

Mattie Power   Martin Kennedy   Christy Ring.
(Kilkenny)   (Tipperary)   (Cork)

The only hurlers still playing when "Carbery" picked his team were Pat Stakelum and Christy Ring. Of his team "Carbery" had this to say:

Christy Ring and Nick Rackard

'I had little difficulty in naming John O'Meara of Toomevara in North Tipperary, as the greatest goalie I ever saw between the posts. Memories of the great games played by Dr Tommy Daly of Clare, Andy Fitzgerald of Cork and Paddy (Fox) Maher of Kilkenny crowded in on me; but the tall, cool, imperturable figure of "Skinny" Meara stands out for uncanny anticipation and superb skill. They told me in North Tipperary that he trained stopping swallows in an open barn door.

A Great Hurler

The late Sean Og Hanley, the famous Kilfinane hurler.

Sean Og Hanley

Dan Coughlan of Blackrock, Cork, was the longest hitter I ever saw, and he was a delightful hurler to watch. For a huge man he was fast on his feet and I've seen him drive a ball from end to end of Turner's Cross pitch in 1904 – 120 yards with a following wind. He was one of five great brothers, Dan, Pat, Jerh., Denis and Tom. Their father, and his five sons, were on Blackrock's winning team in one Cork championship.

Sean Óg Hanley of Kilfinane, Co Limerick, was the greatest hurler of his day – 6 ft. 1.1/2 inches, powerfully built; his name lives on with Limerick and London-Irish – phenomenal length of drive.

Mick Derivan of Galway, at left full-back, was one of the finest natural hurlers I ever saw. His ground drives off either hand and his accuracy overhead, were models of supreme caman artistry.

Of all the present-day hurlers, I consider Pat Stakelum of Tipperary the master artist; he's been outstanding in every important game he ever played and he has held this pride of place over all his fellows for half a dozen years.

James Kelleher of Dungourney, Co Cork, was perhaps the greatest Roman of them all. Someone asked me, a few years ago, when the great captain died, why I put him on a pedestal above all hurlers, and I answered: I saw him play in 26 major matches and he never left the field without being the outstanding hurler of the hour. Kelleher had brains, skill, stamina and ash-craft in abundance. Dick Grace of Kilkenny was another master-hurler. One of a great three – Jack, Pierce and Dick – the youngest was

Mick Mackey and Jimmy Doyle

perhaps the best. A great, fearless leader of men he hit long balls from all angles and was at his best when the game was hottest.

I had a score of strong characters for mid-field – Bob Mockler of Dublin and Tipperary, Mick Gill of Dublin and Galway, and many more. But I could not get away from the power and dominance of Jim Hurley of Cork and Lory Meagher of Kilkenny, who were on opposite sides in the immortal 1931 series. Both were master hurlers and left their mark on the hurling history of the period.

Eugene Couglan, the Cork captain of vintage 1931, stands head and shoulders above all right-wingers, and that is saying a lot – nephew to Dan above.

And the 40 yards mark on my hurling team, surely and without question, belongs to that "playboy of the southern world" – Munster's pride and Limerick's glory – the one and only Mick Mackey! For a combination of skill and power, of brains and brawn, the Castleconnell man, son of the great Tyler Mackey brought joy and thrills galore to thousands.

At the other wing I can find no peer for the great Tom Semple of Thurles, Co Tipperary. A deer of a man and a glorious striker of the ball, captained great teams.

As a right corner man, I boldly select that scoring genius Matthew Power of Kilkenny City. I've seen him beat a good team in eight minutes of a second half. Sprinter's pace, abundant ball control.

From 1922 to 1935 Martin Kennedy reigned supreme at full forward in the Tipperary and Munster jersey. A master of ground

GAA President, Mr Paddy Buggy, making a presentation to 88-year-old Larry Stanley, captain of the 1919 All-Ireland winning Kildare side, at Croke Park. September 1984.

play and first time striking he found the net with great consistency. For nine successive years from inception of the Railway Cup in 1927 he lined out for Munster. By the mid-50s Christy Ring had long laid claims to being a "must" for any all-time great hurling team. Indeed, he could be handed any jersey from the No 8 at midfield to the No 15 at left full forward.'

FOOTBALL FIFTEEN

Dan O'Keeffe
(Kerry)

Maurice McCarthy   Joe Barrett   Pat Prendergast
(Kerry)   (Kerry)   (Mayo)

John Joe O'Reilly.   Jack Higgins   Jos Rafferty
(Cavan)   (Kildare)   (Kildare)

Con Brosnan   Jack Carvin
(Kerry)   (Louth)

Cocker Daly   Paddy Moclair   Larry Stanley
(Dublin)   (Mayo)   (Kildare)

Bill Mackessy   Dick Fitzgerald   John Joe Sheehy.
(Cork)   (Kerry)   (Kerry)

Dick Fitzgerald

JIM MCLOUGHLIN

In the centenary year Jim McLoughlin of Ballinlough Road in Cork selected his best fifteen for the Gaelic Sport magazine. Jim who was born in 1898 was an avid hurling enthusiast all his life and was a founder member of the Civil Service Club in Dublin. Here is his selection:

Paddy Scanlon
(Limerick)

John Doyle
(Tipperary)

Sean Og Murphy
(Cork)

John Joe Doyle
(Clare)

Jackie Power
(Limerick)

Paddy Clohessy
(Limerick)

Paddy Phelan
(Kilkenny)

Lory Meagher
(Kilkenny)

Jim Hurley
(Cork)

Mick Mackey
(Limerick)

Jack Lynch
(Cork)

Christy Ring
(Cork)

Charlie McCarthy
(Cork)

Martin Kennedy
(Tipperary)

Jimmy Barry-Murphy
(Cork)

Sean Og Murphy

Paddy Scanlan

John Doyle of Tipperary

Jackie Power   Lory Meagher   Paddy Phelan

I, myself, first became interested in Gaelic games in the mid-forties. I have decided to pick a football team – a random selection – from my youthful memories. Here is my selection:

Dan O'Keeffe
(Kerry)

"Weeshie" Murphy   Eddie Boyle   Jim McCullagh
(Cork)   (Louth)   (Armagh)

Brendan Lynch   Willie Goodison   Vincent Duffy
(Roscommon)   (Wexford)   (Monaghan)

Tommy Murphy   Paddy Kennedy
(Laois)   (Kerry)

Phelim Murray   Mick Higgins   Kevin Armstrong
(Roscommon)   (Cavan)   (Antrim)

Sean Gibson   Tommy Langan   Peter McDermott
(Antrim)   (Mayo)   (Meath)

Pádraig Puirséal was born in Mooncoin Co Kilkenny in 1914. In 1937 he graduated from UCD with a First Class Honours MA in English Literature.

He wrote a number of very successful novels but abandoned this field in 1950 to pursue a career in sports journalism – founded *The Gaelic Sportsman* in 1950 and joined *The Irish Press* in 1953 where he remained until his death in 1979.

Pádraig watched his first senior hurling final in 1926. His hurling team, covering the period 1930–1970, is based on players in their respective

Brendan Lynch

Kevin Armstrong

Paddy Kennedy

Tommy Murphy

Dan O'Keeffe

"Weeshie" Murphy

Sean Gibson

Peter McDermott

Phelim Murray

Eddie Boyle

Mick Higgins

Tom Langan

Jim McCullagh

Jim McCullagh

positions who provided him with the most pleasure, excitement, entertainment and satisfaction, as published in *Our Games* (1979).

Tommy Daly
(Clare)

Bobby Rackard
(Wexford)

Nick O'Donnell
(Wexford)

John Doyle
(Tipp)

John Keane
(Waterford)

Mick Roche
(Tipp)

Paddy Phelan
(Kilkenny)

Lory Meagher
(Kilkenny)

Jack Lynch
(Cork)

Josie Gallagher
(Galway)

Mick Mackey
(Limerick)

Christy Ring
(Cork)

Jimmy Doyle
(Tipperary)

Nicky Rackard
(Wexford)

Eddie Keher
(Kilkenny)

Pádraig's football team covers the period 1930–1960 and was published in *The Gaelic Weekly* in 1961.

Tom Bourke
(Mayo)

Jerome O'Shea
(Kerry)

Joe Barrett
(Kerry)

Sean Flanagan
(Mayo)

Sean Murphy
(Kerry)

Jack Higgins
(Kildare)

John Joe O'Reilly.
(Cavan)

Padraig Kennedy
(Kerry)

Tommy Murphy
(Laois)

Phelim Murray
(Roscommon)

Sean Purcell
(Galway)

Paul Doyle
(Kildare)

Paddy Moclair.
(Mayo)

Paddy McDonnell
(Dublin)

Kevin Heffernan
(Dublin)

Kevin Heffernan
of St. Vincent's,
Marino.

Paddy Moclair

Jack Lynch was Taoiseach of his country and a star hurler and footballer with his native Cork with which he won six successive All-Ireland medals 1941–1946 – five in hurling and one in football in 1945. His team covers, roughly, the era 1930 to 1960 and encompasses his own playing days of 1935 to 1951.

Paddy Scanlon
(Limerick)

Paddy Larkin   Nick O'Donnell   Willie Murphy
(Kilkenny)   (Wexford)   (Cork)

Tommy Doyle   John Keane   Bobby Rackard
(Tipperary)   (Waterford)   (Wexford)

Eudi Coughlan   Timmy Ryan
(Cork)   (Limerick)

Christy Ring   Mick Mackey   Jimmy Langton
(Cork)   (Limerick)   (Kilkenny)

Eddie Keher   Nicky Rackard   Josie Gallagher
(Kilkenny)   (Wexford)   (Galway)

Tommy Doyle playcd with his native Tipperary from 1937–1953 and won five All-Ireland titles. His illustrious career is recounted in *A Lifetime in Hurling* as told to Raymond Smith. Tommy choose 'My Best Fifteen' from the twenty-five years ending 1950 or thereabouts. It reads as follows:

Tony Reddan
(Tipp)

Johnny Leahy (capt)   Sean Óg Murphy   John Joe Doyle
(Tipp)   (Cork)   (Clare)

John Keane   Paddy Clohessy   Paddy Phelan
(Waterford)   (Limerick)   (Kilkenny)

Jim Hurley   Lory Meagher
(Cork)   (Kilkenny)

Christy Ring   Mick Mackey   Phil Cahill
(Cork)   (Limerick)   (Tipp)

Eudi Coughlan   Martin Kennedy   Mattie Power
(Cork)   (Tipp)   (Kilkenny)

Tony Reddan

Eudie Coughlan

Paddy Cohessy

Christy Ring

Martin Kennedy

Raymond was born in Killaloe, Co Clare but came to live in Thurles when he was about 13 years old. In 1966 Raymond Smith published *Decades of Glory*. In his book he selected two hurling teams. The first team covered the period from 1920 to 1935:

Tommy Daly
(Clare)

"Marie" O'Connell   Sean Óg Murphy   John Joe Doyle
(Cork)   (Cork)   (Clare)

"Builder" Walsh   Jim Regan   Paddy Phelan
(Kilkenny)   (Cork)   (Kilkenny)

Mick Gill   Lory Meagher
(Galway)   (Kilkenny)

Phil Cahil   Mick King   Eudi Coughlan
(Tipp)   (Galway)   (Cork)

"Gah" Aherne   Martin Kennedy   Mattie Power
(Cork)   (Tipp)   (Kilkenny)

Mick King

His second team covered from 1935–1965:

Tony Reddan
(Tipp)

Bobby Rackard	Nick O'Donnell	John Doyle
(Wexford)	(Wexford)	(Tipp)

Jimmy Finn	John Keane	Tommy Doyle
(Tipp)	(Waterford)	(Tipp)

Jack Lynch   Timmy Ryan
(Cork)   (Limerick)

Christy Ring	Mick Mackey	Jimmy Doyle
(Cork)	(Limerick)	(Tipp)

Jackie Power	Nicky Rackard	Tim Flood
(Limerick)	(Wexford)	(Wexford)

Seán Óg O'Ceallacháin, known to all GAA fans as Seán Óg, is well positioned to select hurling and football teams. For he was in his day player, referee, commentator and sports writer. He played hurling and football with Dublin. He played hurling with Leinster and encountered on the pitch many of his chosen players.

In selecting his football team Seán Óg made one very wise decision – 'to give only one position to a county on a line'. It made a very difficult task a little easier.

Sean O'Neill, Dan McCartan

FOOTBALL TEAM 1950–1980

Johnny Culloty
(Kerry)

Enda Colleran   Paddy O'Brien   Sean Flanagan
(Galway)   (Meath)   (Mayo)

Sean Murphy   Kevin Moran   Joe Lennon
(Kerry)   (Dublin)   (Down)

Jack O'Shea   Brian Mullins
(Kerry)   (Dublin)

Matt Connor   Sean Purcell   Pat Spillane
(Offaly)   (Galway)   (Kerry)

Mikey Sheehy   Sean O'Neill   Kevin Heffernan
(Kerry)   (Down)   (Dublin)

HURLING TEAM 1940–1980

Noel Skehan
(Kilkenny)

Bobby Rackard   Pat Hartigan   Tony O'Shaughnessy
(Wexford)   (Limerick)   (Cork)

Jimmy Finn   Ger Henderson   Seamus Cleere
(Tipp)   (Kilkenny)   (Kilkenny)

Harry Grey   Joe Salmon
(Laois/Dublin)   (Galway)

Christy Ring   Mick Mackey   Jimmy Langton
(Cork)   (Limerick)   (Kilkenny)

Jimmy Doyle   Nicky Rackard   Eddie Keher
(Tipp)   (Wexford)   (Kilkenny)

Joe Salmon

Michael Monagle

I asked my friend Michael Monagle to pick fifteen footballers that he saw in action – men whose style of football he admired – men who caused him to enthuse and rejoice.

Michael is a native of the Inishowen Peninsula but he has spent many years in Kilkenny where he has been actively involved with the O'Loughlin Gaels Club.

Many a time he has recalled for me the pilgrimages of bygone days to Croke Park. When he was on temporary duty in the National Bank in Listowel in 1958 he set off for Croke Park to watch Kerry and Derry battle it out in a semi-final for the right to play Dublin in the final. In 1962 Castleisland was the starting point and he was part of a carload that travelled to watch Kerry and Roscommon in action – and Kerry took their twentieth senior crown. By 1963 he had become the proud owner of a ten year old Morris and this time Killorglin was the starting point – a round trip of 410 miles that started on Saturday afternoon and ended in the early hours of Monday morning. In the interim Dublin defeated Galway by two points – a Galway team, that the following year would embark on a great run of three in a row All-Ireland successes.

Michael concluded his selection on Wednesday, April 7, 2004 and made special comment on his decision to select en bloc the Galway fullback line that had made a major contribution to Galway's All Ireland victories of 1964, '65 and '66. Little did we know then that by news time at 1 p.m. on the following day we would be hearing 'gur ghlaoig Dia ar Enda Colleran gan choinne agus go raibh sé anois i gcomhluadar Dé'.

Enda was one of the immortals of Gaelic football. He played at right half-back on the Galway team that won the All-Ireland minor football title in 1960. He occupied the same position when he captained the senior team to National League success in 1965.

When Galway won three in a row senior football titles, 1964, '65 and '66 they had the same goalkeeper, Johnny Geraghty, and fullback line, Enda Colleran, Noel Tierney, and Bosco McDermott on each occasion. For the fourth year in a row that defensive formation won major honours when Connaught won the Railway Cup title in 1967.

Enda was captain for the All-Ireland wins of '65 and '66 and the Railway Cup victory of '67. In later times he was selected on the Centenary team of 1984 and the Millennium team of 2000. Enda also spent some time as a very erudite analyst on *The Sunday Game*.

Enda Colleran

This is Michael's team:

Paddy Cullen
(Dublin)

Enda Colleran
(Galway)

Noel Tierney
(Galway)

Bosco McDermott
(Galway)

Tony Davis
(Cork)

Dan McCartan
(Down)

Joe Lennon
(Down)

Anthony Molloy
(Donegal)

Jim McKeever
(Derry)

Sean O'Neill
(Down)

Mairtin McHugh
(Donegal)

David Hickey
(Dublin)

Colm O'Rourke
(Meath)

Tony Boyle
(Donegal)

Peter Canavan
(Tyrone)

The presentation to Enda of the Sam Maguire trophy in successive years is a rare honour. A trawl through the records unearthed the following players who had the same rare moment:

Jim McKeever

Martin McHugh

Paddy Cullan

Joe Lennon

Jimmy Murray (Roscommon)   1943/44
John Joe O'Reilly (Cavan)   1947/48
Sean Flanagan (Mayo)   1950/51
Tony Hanahoe (Dublin)   1976/77

Joe Barrett of Kerry took "Sam" twice – but not in successive years – 1929 and 1932.

Joe Barrett, Most Rev. Dr. Cullen, Bishop of Kildare,
Jack Higgins

The first football captain to be presented with "Sam" was Bill "Squires" Gannon of Kildare in 1928.

Prior to that the following players captained their counties to All-Ireland football success on more than one occasion.

John Kennedy (Dublin) 1891/92/94
Matt Rea (Dublin) 1898/99
Jack Grace (Dublin) of that famed Tullaroan family 1906/07
Dick Fitzgerald (Kerry) 1913/14
Sean Kennedy (Wexford) 1915/16/17 – this 3 in a row success of
    the New Ross man is unique in Gaelic games.
John Joe Sheehy (Kerry) 1926 and 1930

This is Michael's hurling selection – players for whom he has a special grá:

Davy Fitzgerald
(Clare)

Sylvie Linnane	Noel Hickey	Brian Corcoran
(Galway)	(Kilkenny)	(Cork)

Brian Whelehan	Billy Rackard	J J Delaney
(Offaly)	(Wexford)	(Kilkenny)

Phil Grimes	Andy Comerford
(Waterford)	(Kilkenny)

Henry Shefflin	Joe Cooney	Jimmy Doyle
(Kilkenny)	(Galway)	(Tipp)

D J Carey	Martin Comerford	Eamon Cregan
(Kilkenny)	(Kilkenny)	(Limerick)

LIAM GRIFFIN

Liam Griffin, who guided Wexford hurlers to a memorable All-Ireland success in 1996, is at present a hurling columnist with *The Sunday Tribune*.

Liam played hurling and football at all grades with his native Wexford. When he went to Shannon to study hotel management he played hurling with Clare. However, a promising hurling career came to an early end when Liam went to Switzerland to pursue his career.

Liam has selected a hurling and football team consisting of players he enjoyed watching and whose skills he particularly admired – 'I agonised over quite a few positions'.

In the hurling selection he omitted players chosen on the Centenary and Millennium teams and also those of the 1996 All-Ireland winning Wexford team.

The hurling selection:

Pat Nolan
(Oylegate, Wexford)

Jimmy Brohan   Brian Lohan   Tom McGarry
(Cork)   (Clare)   (Limerick)

Seannie McMahon   Billy Rackard   Jimmy Cullinane
(Clare)   (Wexford)   (Clare)

Ned Wheeler   Phil Grimes
(Wexford)   (Waterford)

Sean Clohessy   Padge Kehoe   Frankie Walsh
(Kilkenny)   (Wexford)   (Waterford)

Oliver "Hopper" McGrath   Nicky English   D J Carey.
(Wexford)   (Tipp)   (Kilkenny)

The football selection:

Johnny Geraghty
(Galway)

Sean Turner   Noel Tierney   Enda Colleran
(Wexford)   (Galway)   (Galway)

"Red" Collier   Kevin Moran   Martin O'Connell
(Meath)   (Dublin)   (Meath)

Jack O'Shea   Mick O'Connell
(Kerry)   (Kerry)

Eamon O'Donoghue   Mattie McDonagh   Pat Spillane
(Kerry)   (Galway)   (Kerry)

Mikey Sheehy   Jimmy Keaveney   Sean O'Neill
(Kerry)   (Dublin)   (Down)

Now finally, my own hurling fifteen.

It consists of players that I saw in action over the years; players that I found it a pleasure to watch; players with a wide range of hurling skills; each a master of his craft; each a true sportsman.

Needless to say it is only one of many I could have chosen. As Dick Stokes once said to me 'there were so many'. And Jim Young of Cork summed it up well when he said 'the greats: Mackey (Mick), Ring (Christy), Lynch (Jack), King (Mick), Kennedy (Martin), and more than likely the others were just as good'.

Ollie Walsh
(Kilkenny)

Jimmy Brohan   Pat Hartigan   Willie O'Connor
(Cork)   (Limerick)   (Kilkenny)

Pat Stakelum   Billy Rackard   Phil Grimes
(Tipp)   (Wexford)   (Waterford)

John Fenton   Johnny Dooley
(Cork)   (Offaly)

Joe Cooney   Tom Cheasty   D.J. Carey
(Galway)   (Waterford)   (Kilkenny)

Oliver "Hopper" McGrath   Tony Doran   Eamon Cregan
(Wexford)   (Wexford)   (Limerick)

Tom Cheasty

Willie O'Connor

Oliver McGrath

Tony Doran

TITLE TABLE OF ALL-IRELAND VICTORIES

COUNTY	SH	JH	MH	IH	U21H	SHB	NL	SF	JF	MF	U21F	SFB	NL	TOTAL
Clare	3	2	1	-	-	-	3	-	-	1	-	1	-	11
Cork	28	11	18	4	11	-	14	6	12	10	9	-	5	128
Kerry	1	2	-	-	-	3	-	32	13	11	9	-	16	87
Limerick	7	4	3	1	4	-	11	2	-	-	-	-	-	32
Tipp	25	9	16	5	8	-	18	4	3	1	-	1	-	90
Waterford	2	2	2	-	1	-	1	-	1	-	-	-	-	9
LEINSTER														
Carlow	-	-	-	1	-	1	-	-	-	-	-	1	-	3
Dublin	6	3	4	-	-	-	2	22	5	-	1	-	8	51
Kildare	-	2	-	1	-	3	-	4	-	-	1	-	-	11
Kilkenny	28	9	18	1	8	-	11	-	-	-	-	-	-	75
Laois	1	-	-	-	-	2	-	-	1	3	-	1	2	10
Longford	-	-	-	-	-	-	-	-	1	-	-	-	1	2
Louth	-	2	-	-	-	-	-	3	4	2	-	1	-	12
Meath	-	5	-	-	-	1	-	7	5	3	1	-	7	29
Offaly	4	2	3	-	-	-	1	3	-	1	1	-	1	16
Westmeath	-	1	-	-	-	3	-	-	1	1	1	-	-	7
Wexford	6	2	3	2	1	-	4	5	1	-	-	-	-	24
Wicklow	-	2	-	-	-	-	-	-	2	-	-	1	-	5
ULSTER														
Antrim	-	1	-	-	-	3	-	-	-	-	1	1	-	6
Armagh	-	3	-	-	-	-	-	1	1	1	-	-	-	6
Cavan	-	-	-	-	-	-	-	5	1	2	-	-	1	9
Derry	-	2	-	-	-	1	-	1	-	4	2	-	5	15
Donegal	-	-	-	-	-	-	-	1	-	-	2	-	-	3
Down	-	1	-	-	-	-	-	5	1	3	1	-	4	15
Fermanagh	-	-	-	-	-	-	-	1	-	-	2	-	3	
Monaghan	-	1	-	-	-	-	-	-	1	-	-	1	1	4
Tyrone	-	-	-	-	-	-	-	1	1	5	-	-	2	9
CONNAUGHT														
Galway	4	2	5	2	7	-	7	9	4	5	2	-	4	51
Leitrim	-	-	-	-	-	-	-	-	-	-	-	1	-	1
Mayo	-	3	-	-	-	-	-	3	5	6	3	-	11	31
Roscommon	-	3	-	-	-	1	-	2	2	3	2	-	1	14
Sligo	-	-	-	-	-	-	-	-	1	-	-	-	-	1